No Ordinary Pilot

ONE YOUNG MAN'S EXTRAORDINARY
EXPLOITS IN WORLD WAR II

No Ordinary Pilot

SUZANNE CAMPBELL-JONES

FOREWORD BY
WING COMMANDER
CHRIS HOYLE

OSPREY
PUBLISHING

OSPREY
Bloomsbury Publishing Plc

PO Box 883, Oxford, OX1 9PL, UK
1385 Broadway, 5th Floor, New York, NY 10018, USA
E-mail: info@ospreypublishing.com

www.ospreypublishing.com

OSPREY is a trademark of Osprey Publishing Ltd

First published in Great Britain in 2018

ISBN: HB: 978-1-4728-2827-9
eBook: 978-1-4728-2828-6
ePDF: 978-1-4728-2826-2
XML: 978-1-4728-2829-3

18 19 20 21 22   10 9 8 7 6 5 4 3 2 1

Index by Marie Lorimer

Typeset by Deanta Global Publishing Services, Chennai, India
Printed and bound in Great Britain by CPI Group (UK) Ltd, Croydon, CR0 4YY

Front cover: Hurricane aircraft © John Dibbs
Back cover: All images © Suzanne Campbell-Jones

Osprey Publishing supports the Woodland Trust, the UK's leading woodland conservation
charity. Between 2014 and 2018 our donations are being spent on their Centenary
Woods project in the UK.

To find out more about our authors and books visit www.ospreypublishing.com.
Here you will find extracts, author interviews, details of forthcoming events
and the option to sign up for our newsletter.

Contents

Foreword

As circumstance would have it, I write this foreword whilst deployed on combat operations with the RAF in 1(Fighter) Squadron. It was not lost on me that the current cohort of 1(F) Squadron fighter pilots are again engaged in the application of airpower in close support of ground units – amazingly, flying Typhoons, as Bob Allen did in June and July 1944, just before his path took a catastrophic and shocking turn.

Every fighter pilot is hugely influenced by, and maintains a special bond with, their first frontline squadron – Bob's experience on 1(F) Squadron is certainly no different. His time with the Squadron would provide him with the best preparation he could have hoped for to help him through the incredible, life-or-death challenges he would come to face.

A great deal has been written about the exceptional achievements of RAF fighter pilots in World War II. Indeed, there is even a significant volume of work dedicated to the exploits of No. 1 Squadron. However, not only are the gripping tales of courage and skill in this wonderful account worthy of a place alongside the best and most famous biographies, it brilliantly sheds light on the broader challenges of attempting to lead a normal life in the midst of extraordinary happenings. It provides a fascinating insight into a young family attempting to survive and grow in the way that any newlyweds would hope to do – showing how love can blossom even in the darkest of times, in absence and in despair.

Foreword

As the Commanding Officer of an RAF frontline squadron, I pray that no person under my command should experience even a fraction of the extreme situations that Bob Allen did. Several generations later, it is hard to fathom the scale of destruction and misery that global conflict inflicted, nor the harsh realities for the countless families and individuals caught in the grip of war as they tried to play their part, or attempted simply to survive.

I have no doubt that you will find Bob's story as inspiring, gripping and moving as I have. He was a man who displayed courage, strength and compassion in adversity and a man who was loved and respected. Through her father's story, Suzanne Campbell-Jones has masterfully shown that in wartime there is no such thing as an ordinary pilot – a statement which certainly applies to Group Captain Bob Allen.

Wing Commander Chris Hoyle
OC 1(Fighter) Squadron

Prologue

We were in Paris. A spring day in 1970. My father, Bob Allen, looked up at the glass roof of the Gare de l'Est and surprised us. 'The last time I was here I was trying to escape.' We were full of questions but he would not elaborate. We had always known that he was a fighter pilot in World War II, decorated, a man who loved flying, who had been a prisoner – but his wartime experiences remained wrapped in silence.

Decades later, long after he had retired from a distinguished career in the RAF, one of his great-grandchildren was writing a school project on the war. He allowed her to open his black tin trunk. It was full of memorabilia, including his official flying logbook, right in the middle of which was the line 'KILLED WHILST ON OPERATIONS'.[1] Now, even the great-grandchildren joined in the questioning, prompting him to reveal that for family and historical reasons he had left us a memoir of his experiences between 1940 and 1945. He hoped it would give us some sense of those times when life itself was not too great a price to pay for justice and freedom. My mother, Alice Allen, had transcribed it for him and at around the same time decided to write her own account of life on the home front, bringing up baby – me – on her own. He presented us with copies of his memoir. He would not talk about it. The trunk was closed.

When we read Bob's memoir we realised that he had changed all the names and places. He had invented new ones for them. Why? It may have been an ingrained adherence to wartime secrecy codes or to protect the memories of his fellow officers. However, he also changed his own name and wrote the whole account in the third person, so maybe it had the effect of distancing himself from the action. He recorded events as he saw them without emotion or any attempt to overdramatise or be heroic. He did, though, make a conscious effort to be scrupulously accurate and detailed. Despite this, without real names, times and places I found it hard to follow as an historical account. There were too many unanswered questions.

It was only after I inherited the black tin trunk that I began to decode the memoir, starting with the logbook, letters and papers. Research in museums and libraries and official documents[2] corroborated Bob's story. More than that, since as facts were released from their camouflage they revealed the wider context, political and military, that he could not have known at the time.

Bob was 19 when he left his reserved occupation as a chemist in a cement factory to join up. Within six months he was in 1 Squadron, flying a Hurricane in his first dogfight over the English Channel. He married his childhood sweetheart, Alice. Then he was sent abroad. Destination secret.

For almost two years he lived in West Africa. He earned a DFC (Distinguished Flying Cross) for his determined efforts flying dangerous unarmed photo-reconnaissance missions. His contribution to the protection of southern Atlantic shipping lines forms part of a largely untold story connected to the conflict in the Middle East.

Christmas 1942 found Bob back at home, meeting for the first time his one-year-old daughter and experiencing the conditions of austerity that had overtaken wartime Britain. He retrained as a fighter-bomber pilot flying Typhoons and was one of the first over the Normandy beaches on D-Day. On 25 July 1944, Bob was shot down. He leaves a vivid description of escaping from his burning plane and landing among German soldiers.

He spent the rest of the war as a POW. He was held in solitary confinement, interrogated by the Gestapo and imprisoned in the infamous Stalag Luft III until the 'long march' in the bitter winter of 1945. In the final weeks of the war, after the Russians had liberated their camp, he and a colleague escaped. They reached the American allies at Torgau on the Elbe just days before the war in Europe was over.

No Ordinary Pilot is the story of Group Captain Robert Neil Greig Allen, CBE, DFC (1920–2008) who went to war and came home with extraordinary memories that he kept to himself for more than 50 years. Its sources are threefold: Bob's matter-of-fact account of adventures in unlikely foreign places; Alice's more emotive account of life at home; and my own more academic research, which included visiting locations. It is the story of one man's war in a global conflict. In wartime there is no such person as an ordinary pilot.

1

Head in the air

TWO TALL LADS, PALE faced, slipped their shoulders beneath the coffin. Men from the undertakers understood, gave them a chance to feel the weight of their Grandad Bob. Their great-grandfather. They carried history with them as they left the high-vaulted church accompanied by a solo voice singing 'We'll Meet Again'. The wartime hero was accorded proper respect, his hat and his medals on view. He had been barely older than a boy when he left home one summer day in 1940.

The Spitfire straightened out. Bob Allen: 19 years old. Aim: to be a fighter pilot. Facing off the Hun. The German enemy. 'Flying level is difficult for a beginner. You'll soon get the hang of it.' Bob was flying solo. Not yet totally confident. Hands tense. Glancing down at a river below, he saw that he was wandering. Straighten up. Stand tall. Shine shoes. Buttons bright. It had been a tough few weeks. Now freedom. Careful. Try more speed. That's it. Check instruments. Head for the clouds. Swing higher, higher. Pull back. The horizon disappeared and reappeared behind his head. The air began to scream. No, that would be later, later. Another time. Another country.

There was no one in the house. Still the clock in the hall chimed the quarters, halves and hours. He gave the front door an extra tug. Just to make sure it was shut tight. A rainbow of coloured glass set in the fanlight sparkled in the early morning sun. A few strides and he was at the front gate, narrow, painted dark green, attached by big bolts to a low pebble-dash wall. The latch made a definite click-clack as it shut. Click. Clack. An echo further down the street of identikit houses as another worker left home.

The street where Bob grew up is in the Medway towns, a collection of three random urbanisations, tight by the River Medway in North East Kent. Rochester has an ancient castle and a cathedral. Chatham is famous for its naval dockyards, crucial in the early 19th-century wars against France. Gillingham was built after the railway age. It expanded rapidly after World War I, with ribbons of terraced housing. Three up. Two down. An outside lav. A garden front and back. The back letting on to a narrow lane. There was an apple tree, currant bushes and fat hens named Queenie and Lil.

Robert Neil Greig Allen, Bob, was born in 1920 in Scotland in a castle. It still exists as a burned-out ruin marooned in an adventure theme park. There are family graves but none for Fanny, his mother. Bob kept her photo, a pretty young girl, on his desk all his life. A local archivist helped him find her name in the parish ledgers. She died of fever shortly after he was born. Fanny Greig was an assistant housekeeper at Loudoun Castle in Ayrshire when such establishments had a large staff. She married Arthur Allen in 1918, just after the end of the first great war. He was a warrant officer in the Medical Branch of the Royal Navy. After her death, unable to look after the child himself, he took his baby son to his brother and sister-in-law in Yorkshire. They loved their small charge. Three years later, while working at the Royal Naval Hospital at Gillingham in Kent, Arthur Allen met and married Gladys Claggett, a large, capable woman who managed the Personnel Department at Shorts Brothers, the local aircraft manufacturer in Chatham. Gladys welcomed her stepson and doted on him, always calling him by the diminutive Robbie. He called her Mother.

2

No cars in the street in 1940. Some windows still have blackout blinds shutting out the sun. Anticipating the terror of night raids. How quiet it is. No one else in the Gillingham house. Bob's stepmother was in South Africa. Stranded by the conflagration of war. She had been en route for Hong Kong where Arthur was stationed at the naval base. There is a photo of Bob and his father. Bob looking a shy young man in blazer and slacks, his father in tropical whites representative of a time when the British Empire encircled the world. When the British Navy patrolled the seas and sailors in sway-flared trousers and tight jackets swaggered through foreign ports. Girls swooned before a uniform. Bob's father would be dead before his son wore a uniform. Dying of a heart condition. Buried in Hong Kong in a military cemetery on the Peak. Both natural parents dead. Stepmother Gladys awaiting a ship home from South Africa. Bob 19. Home alone.

Bob was a scholarship boy. Good at sports. At Gillingham Boys Grammar, founded in 1925, the boys were taught well. They had a full curriculum to get them through Matriculation. They played rugby, tennis and hockey. They believed in Scout's honour, chivalric codes and held clearly defined ideas on right and wrong. They attended services in the Church of England, regarded Catholics with a degree of suspicion and French Catholics as definitely suspect. German Protestant culture was familiar, German politics barely touched them, while German was the second language of choice, especially for scientists.

In a later era, Bob would have had three or four years of higher education at university. Then, war or no war, university was an option for very few. Bob, like many of those interested in scientific or technical subjects, opted for external examination, studying at night school after a ten-hour working day. He cycled the 7 miles to the cement works. Cycling on history. Roman history. On Watling Street, a straight deliberate march along the North Kent coast towards clays rich with calcium carbonate, silicates and aluminates. The Romans were the first to exploit the rich alluvial clays of Kent and Essex. Around 200 years ago these were the raw materials used to fortify the British coastline against Britain's traditional enemy, the French. A series of bastioned fortifications, the Great Lines, were reinforced, in Napoleonic times, to defend the Chatham dockyards. Then came the discovery that a correct mixture of chalk and clay could produce a hydraulic cement. It proved invaluable in the construction industry. By 1938, the Cement Works at Gillingham had become the premier supplier of modern building products. Patent after patent was developed in the laboratories where Bob worked. Cement would be useful in another war. The signs were all there, though few in Britain were ready to admit the possibility. News from across the English Channel was alarming. Barcelona and Guernica had been bombed. There were reports of bombing from far-away China. If there was to be war it seemed it would come from the air.

It was a hard winter, the winter of 1939. Bitter winds swept across Europe from Russia, following the shadow tracks of Panzer divisions and heavy bombers. Britain had had time to prepare. Gas masks were issued, trenches dug, barrage balloons launched, shelters built and children evacuated. The first Jewish refugees arrived from Germany. By the spring of 1939, with the invasion of Czechoslovakia, British opinion was beginning to change, along with the realisation that just 20 years of peace had been broken. It hardened swiftly. 'War came slowly and smoothly and there was no shouting, no demonstrating, not even much talking, and no flags.'[1] Just before dawn on 3 September, the news of Germany's invasion of Poland broke. Within hours, young men were joining up. By 11am, the time the Prime Minister announced that 'Britain is at war with Germany', there were long lines of men ready to put on a uniform to fight for their country. Some older men carried memories of the 1914–18 war, accounts etched in mud and trauma and bitter sacrifice. 'We seemed to be going to war as a duty … going in solidly to kill or be killed because we felt it was the only wise counsel to take.'[2] Bob Allen was 19 years old, studying for his chemistry degree and working at the cement works.

The first skirmishes of this new European war were at sea, around the north of Scotland at Scapa Flow and in faraway Montevideo, where there were reports of the Battle of the River Plate. The German pocket battleship *Graf Spee* was trapped by three plucky British cruisers. Cinemas and theatres reopened. Newsreels carried stories of derring-do. The black-and-white pictures were accompanied by stirring music. At Christmas, the blackout rules were relaxed. For a few months people once again moved about visiting friends and relatives. Then petrol rationing began. The news from Europe was bad. The cement works in Gillingham were never busier; preparations, inventions and productions were in high demand. The chemists were too valuable to be spared for the military. They were declared a 'reserved occupation', excusing them military service. Joining up was not an option for Bob. His work was considered too important to the war effort, although many of his friends and family were already in uniform.

There are photos of Bob and friends on a yacht – the smiling faces of confident young men sailing down the Medway and out into the English Channel; a group of friends playing tennis in the grounds of a big house overlooking the Downs. Within a few months, every one of those fit young men had joined the navy or the army. None of them survived the war. Bob had other ideas. Almost on impulse one Saturday morning in the spring of 1940, without discussing it with anyone, he walked into the local recruiting office and asked to join the Royal Air Force Volunteer Reserve (RAFVR) as aircrew, preferably a pilot. Several of his friends had joined the RAFVR before the war and were now in front-line squadrons.

Just like that. He left a cold, quiet house to begin the big adventure. It would be a frustrating few months before his life would change forever. The first hurdle was passing the 'selection board'. He was called to RAF Uxbridge and tested physically and academically. He was, they noted, 5ft 10in., fair hair, dark eyes; his only distinguishing feature was that he was missing the end of his middle finger on his left hand. Physically fit. Academically able. He stood a reasonable chance of selection.

Other eager young men have described the process of joining up as almost one of elimination. The physical examination involved walking before a line of medics who checked hearing, eyesight, heart, lungs, genitals and possible 'risky' infectious diseases. The academic papers were nothing that a boy who had passed School Certificate couldn't manage. There was no real programme in place for testing aptitude. It was said later, 'If a candidate had been to the right school, was tall, smart and in possession of rugby boots and a Bible, he was officer material. If he rode horses as well, he was pilot material.'[3] Unfortunately, this interview-style selection resulted in 50 per cent failing to stay the course. By 1942, proper psychological tests and a system of grading had been developed and the proportion of young men sent back into civvy street, swapping their military caps for a bowler hat, decreased. Bob was accepted as a trainee pilot. As an aircraftsman second class, he was entitled to wear a metal badge with the initials RAFVR on his civilian jacket. This marked him as a successful volunteer but he had to wait to begin active service. While he was waiting, the Battle of Britain began.

In April 1940, just before Bob started wearing the RAFVR badge on the lapel of his suit, Germany occupied Denmark and Norway. Within weeks the bellicose and brilliant Winston Churchill took over from Chamberlain the appeaser. Churchill was just in time to see Holland and Belgium attacked in a blitzkrieg of dive-bombing and heavy artillery. On 20 May, the German Army reached the English Channel. Quite suddenly, the war was but a breath away from Britain's shores. British troops had to be rescued from French beaches. Over the course of two days, fleets of ships brought 338,000 men home during the evacuation of Dunkirk.[4] The first casualties of war were to be seen on streets and stations, in pubs and bars. What would happen next?

The government prepared for invasion. Emergency powers were announced for securing the safety of the public, the defence of the realm and the maintenance of public order. Leaflets stating what to do 'If the Invader Comes' were distributed throughout the land. Barbed wire snaked along the beaches. There were lots of new comrades in arms – Poles, Belgians, Czechs, Dutch, Free French and not forgetting the 'Colonial boys' from South Africa, the African colonies and Australia and New Zealand. By the end of June, 1.5 million men had volunteered for the Home Guard. These were the momentous events that occurred during the months Bob was waiting. By the time his call came and Bob put on his uniform and left for ground training in Wales, the War Cabinet was preparing the next stage.

Bob missed the Battle of Britain. During Britain's finest hour he was being marched to and fro. Being told to shine his buckles. Learning how not to answer back, however unfair the situation. Sleeping in a bunk in a hut with 20 others. Following orders. Saluting. Later – many, many years later – he took a parade himself. His men were marching with absolute precision. He was wearing a sword and medals and lots of gold braid. His salute was as precise as the men's. He smiled as he talked to each man in turn. He was an admired leader. But then, back in 1940, he was scarcely more than a boy.

Once in uniform, Bob wore a white flash on his cap to mark him as potential aircrew. The RAF was quite unlike the other military services. Having been formed at the very end of World War I, it was only 20 years old. Military historian John Terraine noted that the RAF had some curious ways.[5] For a start, all the fighting was done by the officers, together with senior non-commissioned officers who were entitled to wear wings on their chests, though not wings on their sleeves. Airmen do not fly. Officer ranks are based on those of the Royal Navy. The most junior is an acting pilot officer. Next up, the flying officer is equivalent to an army lieutenant. A flight lieutenant is a commander of a flight – equivalent to an army captain – and so on to air marshals, of whom there are many. By the end of World War II, when numbers were highest, just 17.5 per cent of the service was aircrew; the remaining 82.5 per cent were there to protect them and get them ready for battle.[6]

There was a delay of some three months before Bob was called up to begin his training, but after that his progress was rapid: through ground training at Aberystwyth in Wales; basic flying training at a civilian flying school at Fairoaks just outside London; advanced flying at Kidlington in Oxfordshire, followed by operational training on Hurricanes at Debden in Essex. In the brief memoir he left us, Bob says nothing about learning to fly – yet he loved flying and took every opportunity to do it well into his fifties. He leaves no description of his first flight. No sense of what it was like to be ordered about during square-bashing. Nothing about those months in the summer of 1940 when heroes were made in the sky and the Royal Air Force came of age as the saviour of British freedoms. An awful lot was happening during the four months he spent waiting to be called up.

All summer, while he waited for orders, waited for transfers and waited to be assigned to flying training, the air above was rent by vapour trails. The world's first major air battle was being fought above South East England. It was a battle of attrition. The speed with which Bob was trained as a fighter pilot was a measure of the scale of losses and the need for more pilots to secure the skies above Britain. The threatened skies were blue. It was a beautiful summer. The sun shone on the harvest. The hops ripened in rows along the Vale of Kent. But German barges were being assembled in ports across the channel. Göring's Luftwaffe had bases in north-west France, Belgium and Holland. He had 3,500 aircraft. Facing them were 700 British fighters. Two-thirds were Hawker Hurricanes, tasked with stopping the bombers getting through. After the air battles of the summer of 1940 the RAF pilots became pin-up boys. Churchill's words 'never have so many owed so much to so few' echoed in newsreels and newspaper headlines. The fighter boys were true heroes.

Bob's flying training began in September 1940 as the battle overhead was easing. He was at Fairoaks, a small airfield near London. Soon all the flying training would happen abroad – in Canada, America or in the relative safety of British colonies in Africa and Australia. Fairoaks airfield is still there, tucked away among outer London's stockbroker belt of clipped hedges and smooth lawns, brick houses with mock Tudor beams. Now it is within the Heathrow zone. Small aircraft make careful approaches beneath intercontinental airliners carrying hundreds of thousands of passengers a year. Only the well-to-do could afford air transport 70 years ago. For the rest of the population, flying meant circus acts and seaside rides. Aeroplanes were, in some ways, more visible than they are today. Sir Alan Cobham's flying circus entertained the crowds from local fields. There were annual pageants and a race around Britain by little biplanes and monoplanes.[7] It would be decades before air travel was affordable. Flying was for the elite. Bob doesn't say why he was so keen to take to the air. Did he, as a boy, wonder how birds could fly? Did he watch seagulls wheeling on thermals or pulling out of fast dives? Or had he already, as a scientist, learned about aerodynamics?

Bob's first flight was in a Miles M.9 Master. This was a two-seat monoplane powered by a Rolls-Royce engine, built as a trainer for the RAF and the Fleet Air Arm. On 29 September 1940 he left earth behind and entered the third dimension, slipping away into another world where the ground looks small and unimportant and the aircraft feels motionless in space. His ear took in his instructor's voice as he calmly talked him through the cockpit layout and the effect of various controls. Initial flying training followed a relatively simple course: after breakfast there would be a morning flying lesson, then lunch, then afternoon lectures. Evenings could be spent in the pub. They were taught the art of stalling, gliding, straight and level flying, approaches and landing, taxiing and emergency action.[8] His progress was fast. In less than a month following his first flight, with just 12 hours in the air, he was flying solo. Soon it was cross-country flights with a map tucked in the pocket of his flying suit to learn navigation techniques. Then exams. Assessments. Bob had a natural aptitude for flying. But it would be many more months before he would be operational – ready to fight in the sky.

The RAF motto is 'Per ardua ad astra' (through hard work to the stars). Discipline, professionalism, good standards of behaviour and a sense of formality were expected from men who had been educated mainly at public (fee-paying) schools. From 1940, officers no longer had to wear mess kit (a form of fancy evening dress) for dinner and a simplified uniform was introduced. Officers were looked after by a batman, a relationship not unlike that between a student and his bedder or scout at university or a gentleman and his valet. The new wartime recruits often shared a batman, who woke them with a cup of strong tea in the morning and put out their uniform ready to wear. Basic uniform was supplied in a kitbag, a white canvas bag with a rope tie like those used by sailors in the Royal Navy. Refinements such as the famous leather flying jackets, which were never worn while flying, were bought out of pay, which was £264 per annum for the most junior officer – the equivalent to £30,000 today. It was sufficient to pay mess bills and run an old car. Travel was mainly by steam train. Railway lines criss-crossed the country. Bob travelled by train to Kidlington near Oxford for advance training. Just 50 miles away, the bombardment of London known as 'the Blitz' had begun.

From the autumn of 1940 through to the spring of 1941, the period when Bob was being trained to be a fighter pilot, the cities of Britain were pummelled by bombs. London suffered sustained attacks over 57 consecutive nights. Refugees spewed from the big port cities – Plymouth, Liverpool, Hull, Clydebank and Belfast. Londoners went underground. Other cities emptied into the countryside. England began to look like a land of stragglers carrying all they could from their ruined homes. On 24 April 1941, perhaps 50,000 people walked out of Plymouth. London was devastated by incendiary bombs. On one night, 19 March 1941, 500 planes dropped 122,000 incendiaries and 470 tons of high explosives in six hours.[9] The worst day of all was 10 May 1941 when, on a clear, cloudless night with a full moon, many of Britain's most iconic buildings were hit, including the Houses of Parliament, Law Courts, Mansion House, Westminster Abbey and 14 hospitals, the water mains, churches and more than 5,000 houses – the smoke from the fires could be seen for miles. It was a terrifying experience and one that Bob was not far from experiencing first hand.

During his training, Bob got engaged to a girl he had known since they were both at school. Alice Arnold lived on Chatham Hill in a detached house with a large garden. She was as good as a boy on the tennis court and counted as one of the group of friends who picnicked and sailed together. She had been residing in London while she trained as a teacher and had already experienced the terrors of bombing. She was living in digs, renting a room and sharing house facilities with the owner, in South London. Bob visited her as frequently as he could. Alice had stayed in London because she was committed to her classes of primary-age children. Sometimes Alice and the children spent the whole night in shelters. Every night they could hear the bangs and crumps of bombs bringing death and destruction. Into this world came another uneasy realisation: that Bob's chances of survival as an inexperienced front-line pilot were slim. They married, despite parental reservations due mainly to their youth. Bob was 20. Alice not quite 21. A brief honeymoon was spent in a hotel in London. There were no wedding pictures of them in the house on Chatham Hill.

Alice was one of eight – seven sisters and a brother who was in the Royal Navy. Her older sisters and their husbands looked out from ornate frames in the family home. The wedding dresses elaborate, speaking of lavish ceremonies. Not so for Alice. 'It was the war', she would reply when asked. She had a small photo of a girl in a pale suit on the arm of a young man scarcely more than a boy in the uniform of an RAF officer. His pilot wings shone new and bright above the chest pocket.

Even in the desperate days of war only half of the hopeful young men who had begun training with Bob actually attained the prized RAF wings. By the time he got his in April, Bob had 160 flying hours in his logbook and quite a few of those were at night. 'Only birds and fools fly by day and only owls and bloody fools fly by night' was the much-quoted saying. Wartime England at night was very, very dark. The blackout prohibited any lights in any building, street or railway. All familiar landmarks were blotted out unless there was a full moon. Instructors told their pupils:

'... the moment you leave the ground and are off the flare path do not, repeat do not, no matter how tempted, try to look outside the cockpit ... it will be very black and you will have no horizon or any means of orientation whatsoever and so we have to rely on our instruments. This is the whole secret of night flying.'[10]

Night flying was like taking off into a black void. The pilot had to keep his eyes fixed on the cockpit instruments in front of him. The most vital information the instruments provided was an artificial horizon, rate of climb, air-speed indicator and a directional gyro.[11] It required a huge effort of concentration.

Preparing for the wings test gave young pilots the chance to show off their aerobatics skills. Knowing just how far to push the plane, how tight to make the turns, how fast to spin, were essential life-saving skills. They might be hurtling around in the sky when the examiner suddenly cut the throttle in a simulated engine failure to force a landing. Trying not to panic, the pilot would have to find a suitable place to land, and quickly. If they were lucky it would be an airfield, one of many grass strips that had appeared over southern England. After the flying test there were two days of written tests. Questions might require knowledge of fuel systems, hydraulics and engine data – such as correct revs and manifold pressure for all procedures, including landing and taking off – as well as a certain amount of Air Law and RAF regulations. Eventually, the great day for Bob arrived with results. By the time he returned to his room the wings had already been sewn on to his uniform by his batman. The final stage in the making of a fighter pilot involved gunnery practice, air-to-air and air-to-ground, with live ammunition. Bob did rather well. It was time for him to move on.

Bob flew his first Hurricane on 27 April 1941. He was delighted. Pilots invariably spoke warmly of the aeroplane. They said it inspired confidence, was responsive, strong, stable and forgiving. It was also a great platform for guns – a brutal machine. The Hurricane, designed by Sydney Camm, first flew in 1935. It was

13

an immediate success with the RAF, which ordered 600 on the spot. Those early Hurricanes were constructed along the lines of the biplanes they replaced. They had a girder-like fuselage, covered in doped (varnished) linen and fabric-covered wings. The 'canvas, string and sticks' design made them very easy to assemble and mend, though they looked rather old-fashioned. Modifications were constant. By 1939, fabric wings were replaced by metal ones that could stand greater stress loads – while diving, for instance.[12] The sloping nose gave the pilot good visibility – a factor in making it the choice for night sorties. When used for fighting, the Hurricane could manage tighter turns than most German aircraft, which was much appreciated during the Battle of Britain, in which the Hurricane outnumbered the Spitfire by three to two.[13]

The Spitfire, designed to the same brief by Reginald Mitchell, was immediately recognisable. It had beautiful lines, a slim fuselage, a graceful elliptical wing. The Battle of Britain became known as the 'Spitfire Summer' after Lord Beaverbrook used his newspapers to engage in a PR exercise, 'Saucepans for Spitfires', which encouraged housewives to give up their aluminium for the cause. Spitfire funds were set up in towns and villages all over the country and abroad – there was a Jamaica Plane fund, a Gold Coast fund, a Singapore fund. More than 20,000 were eventually built. The Spitfire caught the public's imagination but throughout the war it was the Hurricane that earned a reputation as a go-anywhere, do-anything fighter – an aircraft that 'could be danced in the air'.

The newest Hurricanes with their Merlin engines took their pilots higher and faster than was possible before. In his last few weeks of training Bob had to learn to master the new aircraft, flying it in formation, air firing, night flying, formation aerobatics, practising dogfights. Hurricane pilots describe 'testing the limits, height climbs, the tightest possible turns ...

14

"greying out", sustaining a turn until "blacking out", learning to tighten the stomach muscles, and tensing up to increase one's "black out" threshold'.[14] World War II fighter pilots had to learn just how steep a climb they could afford to make. It was dangerous. Too steep and the pilot could lose his colour vision. Much too steep and he risked losing vision completely. Tightening the stomach muscles acted to force the blood back to the brain. Levelling out also had an immediate effect. Twisting and turning in the sky, they had to judge these forces while dodging bullets. It took courage, bravery and a lot of professionalism to be a fighter pilot.

It was summer, 1 June 1941, when Bob was commissioned as a pilot officer in the RAFVR and received his first posting – to 1 Squadron. He was delighted. It was one of the most prestigious fighter squadrons in the RAF. Formed in 1912 out of the Army's 1 Company, the term 'squadron' was adopted from its use in the cavalry. 1 Company had distinguished itself in World War I and the war in Iraq in the 1920s. At the time that Bob joined, it had a hard core of surviving veterans from the brief battles in France, over Dunkirk and over London, during the Battle of Britain and the Blitz. They flew Hurricanes from Redhill, a small grass airfield some 15 miles south of London.

In the winter of 1941 tactics began to change. After months of being on the defensive, the RAF took to the offensive in a series of raids code named *Rhubarb*. The style of the raids appealed to young fighter pilots in their new, fast, well-armed machines. In pairs or two pairs they set off across the Channel and harassed any obvious German positions on the French coast. The first pair from 1 Squadron set out on New Year's Day and, making use of low cloud cover, shot up various installations in the Boulogne area. It was not very efficient, extremely dangerous and the Luftwaffe often refused the bait and laid low to avoid revealing their positions. *Rhubarb* sorties were abandoned later in the year.

A more effective form of harassment, code named *Circus*, involved dispatching, in daylight, small formations of Blenheim light bombers with a fighter escort to bomb airfields, railways and other military installations in the Pas-de-Calais area. There were four types or layers of bomber escort: close escort surrounding the bombers; escort for the close fighters; high cover to protect the lower layers from enemy fighters; and finally top cover – tied to the bombers' route 'with a roving commission to sweep the skies clear of enemy fighters threatening the immediate area of the bomber attack'.[15] In some cases up to 200 fighters were involved in the escort of one bomber. The bomber might survive but at a cost in fighters. It was a tactic copied from the Luftwaffe but in this case the bombing was incidental. The main object was to entice the Luftwaffe positioned in France and the Low Countries into the air. It also forced the Germans to keep a disproportionate number of fighters in north-west Europe, drawing them away from the Eastern/Russian Front. It was a tactic, Bob noted, that to be successful involved large numbers of British fighters.

One unintended consequence was that air battles were frequently fought over the Channel. Air-sea rescue was in its infancy. Without a dinghy pack (dinghies became standard issue later in the summer), survival in the cold sea could be counted in minutes. German fighter pilots were issued with dinghies and a pack that stained the water around bright green so they could easily be spotted. The British pilots made do with a 'Mae West' lifejacket. Within the year, the RAF and Navy co-operated to develop an efficient air-sea rescue service. Pilots in danger of ditching in the sea were urged to turn their radios to Channel C and give the emergency call 'Mayday, Mayday, Mayday'. This had been invented by a radio operator at Croydon Airport in 1923 and comes from the French *'m'aider'* or *'venez m'aider'* meaning 'come and help me'. The call triggered rescue aircraft and launches to search the area. It proved very effective.

All the squadrons flew convoy patrols to protect essential shipping from marauding German bombers and fighters. 1 Squadron were flying on convoy patrol in the late afternoon of 19 March when:

> '… between Dungeness and Hastings, two Me109s from l.LG2 zipped in from the south and engaged the Hurricanes … Tony Kershaw was hit, dived, and baled out too late. His body was later picked up by a minesweeper's whaler and brought ashore. Sergeant Stefan's machine was also hit but he crash landed without injury although his Hurricane was a write-off.'[16]

Squadron combat reports reveal how every day brought aerial fights, some lost, some won. As soon as they landed, the pilots would report to an officer from Y-service, the RAF signals and tactical intelligence service. He was the only person entitled to confirm whether there had been a 'kill' – an enemy aircraft shot down. The squadron flew day and night. In May 1941, the Luftwaffe renewed their blitz on London. On one night, 10/11 May, 12 pilots from 1 Squadron took off in pairs and fought through the night, only returning to refuel. Bob felt very much the new boy as he joined this experienced team.

An unusual feature of 1 Hurricane Squadron at this time was the many nationalities of its pilots. With the exception of the squadron commander and three or four others, who were either British or from one of the Dominions or Colonies, all were either Polish or Czech or, in one case, a Lithuanian. The squadron was divided into two flights. Initially Bob was in A Flight, which, without him, would have been entirely Czech, under Flt Lt Velebnovsky. He remembers one Sgt Plt Kuttelwascher, known as 'Kut' – a formidable fighter with a number of claimed kills. 'Sergeant Kuttelwascher, acting as top weaver on the way out, saw four 109's [sic] attack two Hurricanes and dived on the rearmost, firing two bursts from 50 yards. The 109 went down out of control pouring smoke.'[17] A few months later, Kut was commissioned and led the flight. Flying at night without the benefit of radar, he specialised in raiding German airfields in France and picking off the German bombers as they landed or took off. On one occasion he got three in four minutes.[18] The Czechs and Poles were all veteran pilots from their own countries and had already fought for a month or so after they reached England and enlisted in the RAF. Bob remembered:

'Their enthusiasm for pursuing the hated Boches often led not only to success but sometimes to failure due to foolhardiness. It was like learning to survive in what was practically a foreign air force, whose members, in time of stress or excitement in the air, often resorted to using their native language over the R/T.'[19]

Integrating a newly trained pilot into an operational unit had its problems. When rookie pilot Geoffrey Wellum was posted to 92 Squadron, the commanding officer looked at his logbook and said:

'So at least you've flown something that folds up, undercarriage, flaps and that sort of thing? ... Well that's the only thing in your favour, but even so you are not much use to the squadron. I pay little attention to an assessment made after a hundred-odd hours' flying... half-trained youngsters who think they know all the answers are just a pain in the neck in an operational squadron in time of war.'[20]

Bob Allen said he thought his complete greenness actually helped his survival. When he first joined the squadron he was kept out of the night operations and flew only daylight sorties, convoy patrols, escorts and sweeps, and Channel patrols meeting the Blenheims as they came home. He flew as number two to one of the experienced section leaders.

On 12 June 1941, Colin Gray, a New Zealander with a Distinguished Flying Cross (DFC), took over A Flight. A fighter ace credited with 15 aircraft destroyed, he was one of the highest-scoring pilots in the RAF. Bob was appointed his number two. Bob described his briefings in his memoir: 'Oral briefings were usually to follow the leader in loose formation, keep a good lookout, give warning over the R/T of any enemy aircraft and, if necessary, to turn towards and attack any fighters that came at them.'[21] In fact, in his early days, all Bob *could* do was to follow his leader in loose formation, to stay with him while any engagement took place and return home to base afterwards, preferably with his leader. However, to achieve this was quite a major feat, especially when the more experienced members of the squadron threw their aircraft all over the sky either chasing German fighters or evading them.

On 16 June Bob recalled: 'We found an He59 over the Channel and shot it down. It didn't carry any Red Cross markings. I was no2 to Colin Gray and there were also ten or a dozen Me109s about who were naturally very aggressive. I took a shot at them, more in haste than in anger I have to say.'[22] The next day Bob wrote to his wife from the officers' mess, Redhill.

'My Dear Alice, As I write this tonight I am feeling very pleased with myself. I became an operational pilot yesterday afternoon and since then I have been very busy. Up to this evening we have had several patrols but saw nothing. Tonight however the whole squadron was sent off and we had a wizard show. We ran into some 109s in the Channel off Folkestone and did we

give them hell! I saw a 109 diving at me from the side
so I turned into him and gave him a burst but he went
past me too quickly to notice any effect – THEN about
4 of us saw a Hun sea plane stooging along at about
100' and we filled him really full of lead and he finally
burst into flames and crashed. After that we were all
split up so I raced home. We lost one plane but the pilot
although burnt a little is safe in an English hospital.
Other squadrons did well today – Jerry certainly has
had a shaking! We have had 2 bottles of champagne for
dinner tonight – everyone is very cheerful.'[23]

Officer pilots lived in a large house near the airfield, once
owned by the Goldsmiths Company. Bob shared a room with
the Lithuanian pilot Romualdas 'Rene' Marcinkus – the only
Lithuanian pilot to serve in the RAF during World War II.
He had been a football champion before rising to the rank of
captain in the Lithuanian Air Force. In spring 1934, Marcinkus
and three colleagues flew a Lithuanian-designed aircraft on a
promotional tour of 12 European capitals and became well
known outside his own country. In 1940, he left Lithuania to
join the French Air Force, a short-lived exploit. When France
fell and he applied to the RAF, gossip has it that he took three
years off his age or he would have been too old. He was posted
to 1 Squadron just weeks before Bob Allen. Marcinkus wrote in
a letter:

'I was transferred to night fighters – at that time the most
dangerous kind of military aviation But I like danger – I
faced danger during my entire life, in flying, sports, and
personal life. With this I am satisfied, but … I am lacking
warmth and the comfort of my personal life in this country
of cold slob weather and so called correctness.'[24]

Other colleagues describe Marcinkus as a friendly guy, a good character with a phenomenal memory. This would come in useful later when he was forced to ditch his plane in the sea, and was picked up by the Germans and taken prisoner. He ended up in Stalag Luft III, where he was a principal player in the notorious Great Escape, then was recaptured and was one of the 50 men shot by the Gestapo. But that final dangerous adventure lay two years in the future.

For the remainder of June 1941, 1 Squadron flew day and night. Bob writes:

'The weeks passed quickly. The day began with squadron readiness at first light, which meant rising at 2.30am for breakfast in order to be on stand-by in the crew room near the aircraft by 3.15am. Often the day's activities lasted until last light and sometimes those pilots who had been on stand-by would not get to bed until past midnight.'

On another occasion Bob describes how, when the squadron had been sent out over the Channel to cover the rescue of a bomber crew that had ditched and were reported to be in a dinghy, they ran almost straight into an equal number of ME109s at about 3,000ft. The sky erupted into a melee of diving, turning, climbing fighters and Bob fired his eight machine guns at a yellow-nosed ME109 that came at him almost head on. The encounter was brief. The two aircraft must have passed very close to each other as their paths crossed. Bob, forgetting his briefing to stay with his leader, turned hard to follow his adversary but when he straightened up there was no sign of any aircraft, whether enemy or friendly. He felt very much alone and not a little scared sitting some 1,000ft up in the middle of the Channel. After a brief look around for anyone who he might join up with, feeling rather stupid and still anxious, he pointed his aircraft towards the English coast and returned to base as fast as his Merlin-engine Hurricane could carry him.

Fighter pilots say that no amount of training can prepare you for combat. That there is just one golden rule: 'Never, but never fly straight and level for more than twenty seconds. If you do, you'll die.'[25] If you see tracers flashing past then break hard and fling the aircraft all over the sky. Attempt stall turns. Fire. Gunnery practice was included in operational training but in the chaos of battle there was not much time to adjust one's aim. There was talk of 'deflection shooting'. Reflector sights could be lined up to touch the wing tips of the enemy aeroplane but the pilot still had to judge how much 'lead' or deflection was needed to make a hit at speeds of up to 350mph and closing. Most pilots opened fire far too soon. The best chance of a kill was achieved by approaching the enemy from dead astern and then raking him with all eight machine guns. Expert shots harmonised their guns to give a 'spot' of concentrated power. Air fighting was, after all, relatively new, and there was much discussion over the merits of astern, head-on, beam and quarter attack and the use of sun and cloud cover, or how best to get on the tail of a 109. 'They knew that all depended on teamwork, that they must never fight alone.'[26]

Fighter pilots were never far from death. They had to face the horrors of seeing aircraft blown to bits in the sky. Men falling, turned into burning torches. Friends spiralling uncontrolled into earth or sea. Winston Churchill praised the pilots for 'the canine virtues: vigilance, fidelity, courage and love of the chase'. Perhaps the greatest of these was courage. Courage supported by loyalty to tightly knit groups of officers and men in the squadron. Bob Allen was a newly married 20-year-old who admitted later that his 'preoccupation with a demanding schedule and keenness to do well in flying to match the skill and enthusiasm of the others gave him little time to think about his wife'.[27]

Setting up a home was virtually impossible. Like many other couples, they lived apart with occasional brief meetings. Many wartime brides were obliged to live in the parental home. Alice, however, continued to live 'in digs' and teach at a school in Bexley. There were just a few opportunities to do 'normal' things, such as going to the cinema or taking a walk in the countryside. Alice was resourceful. Through a series of contacts and gossip at the local shop she heard of a couple, the husband in the navy, who wanted to share their house by letting off three rooms and sharing the bathroom. While waiting to move, Alice narrowly escaped being killed by a bomb landing in her back garden without exploding and had to spend the night in the community shelter. She always said it was down to chance; in one house the whole family was killed, in another a baby survived being buried in rubble. She tried not to think about the dangers her husband was facing. Then something happened that changed everything.

One sunny morning towards the end of June, Bob was sent for by the squadron adjutant. The squadron had been detailed to nominate one British pilot officer to join a new Hurricane squadron that was being formed in Africa. Because most of the other pilot officers were either Czech or Polish, there was little choice. Bob would have to go. He was devastated. He'd survived the most dangerous first few weeks of operational flying and was now a valued member of the team. He could not believe that he would have to begin all over again overseas. And of course he would not be able to tell his wife or family where he was going. He pleaded long and hard, first with the adjutant, then the flight commander and lastly with the squadron commander, but to no avail. He even brought up his marriage, but this cut no ice with anyone. He had to go. Compassionate leave was granted.

He was given two days before embarking. He was anxious to provide Alice with enough funds and spent some time explaining that he had set up a joint account. They sat and listened to the wireless. He tried to reassure his wife that the place he was going to would be less dangerous. It might well be a blessing in disguise, since life on a front-line squadron was short. He promised to write. Next morning he left.

2

Overseas

THE 'GREAT SCOT' PULLED out of Euston Station at precisely 10am, as it did every morning.[1] Steam and smoke masked wives, family and friends as they waved their goodbyes. Bob watched them. Would they meet again? Where were they going?

The train was crowded. There was barely standing room in Third Class. The officers sat in the First Class dining car. The food was a great deal better than Bob had eaten for quite a few days. It had been a shock, leaving a front-line officers' mess and finding himself back in a Personnel Dispatch Unit (PDU). There were several along the Lancashire coast close enough to reach the great ports of Liverpool and Glasgow. The PDU was a makeshift barracks for processing hundreds of men, officers, NCOs and airmen to their various overseas destinations. Bob had been told he was going to Africa. Nothing more. He was issued with some hopelessly out-of-date tropical dress, including a khaki solar topee and shorts that hung below the knees. There was no way he could look smart in that outfit. Then he was vaccinated and inoculated against typhoid, tetanus and yellow fever. Within hours he could barely lift his arm.

It was several days before he was told that his destination would be Sierra Leone, where a new flight was being formed, initially under 95 Squadron Coastal Command. His morale, already pretty low, sunk yet further. He would not even be in Fighter Command. Coastal Command was looked on as the

Cinderella of the RAF. It had outmoded aircraft and none of the glamour. There seemed to be no one else heading in the same direction as him. Bob's new unit would be at flight strength, just four aircraft, with a flight lieutenant in command, and he had not yet reported in. Two days late and still hung-over from overenthusiastic farewell celebrations, the flight lieutenant finally turned up. Those two days saved both their lives.

It was over evening drinks in the bar that Bob and his new CO first met and almost at once established a rapport. John Ignatius 'Killy' Kilmartin wore the ribbon of the Distinguished Flying Cross (DFC) and had served both in France and in the Battle of Britain. He was slightly older than the average pilot and seven years older than Bob. On that first night Bob learned that the last year had been difficult for Killy. He had been in 1 Squadron during the blitzkrieg, the Battle for France, where he was in the thick of the fighting. He had 11 destroyed and two shared kills, which put him just outside the Aces, who had 12 or more destroyed. After three weeks of continuous combat, 1 Squadron had been pulled back on 24 May to give the pilots a rest.[2] Kilmartin was transferred to 43 Squadron based at Tangmere. The Battle of Britain was about to begin. It was a brutal time for the fighters, culminating in a terrible battle on 7 September. When he was told of two more lost pilots, Killy, ashen faced, could only mutter 'My God, My God'.[3] Yet he went on fighting and claimed two more destroyed before being posted away to a less stressful arena. In the last two months he had been with 602 Squadron in Ayre and 313 Polish Squadron in Catterick. Now he looked at his instructions and found that his flight would be just him and Bob with four sergeant pilots and 50 ground crew. They had passed through the PDU a week before and were already en route.

On the long train journey north, Bob learned a little more of Killy's background. It was unusual. He was born in Dundalk,

Eire, one of eight children. His father died when he was nine and Killy was sent to Australia on a 'Big Brother' scheme. This was designed to attract upright, clean-cut, well-mannered middle-class young boys to work on the land. Killy went to a cattle station. 'Big Brother' remained responsible for his moral and general welfare until he was 21, when he left Australia to live with an aunt in Shanghai. While he was in China he worked as a bank clerk and registered as a professional jockey. Killy didn't reveal to Bob when or why he decided to fly, only that he travelled to Britain with a group of Japanese sumo wrestlers on the Trans-Siberian railway. He joined the RAF in 1937 and would remain in service for 20 years.[4]

For Bob and Killy, the journey north was through an England muted by fear of invasion. All place names on stations had been painted out. All signposts had been removed from roads and anything that might identify a village covered up. At night all was dark. It made travel something of a mystery tour.[5] The passengers could see how much damage had been done in the last month or so. The Luftwaffe had been pounding Britain's western ports – Swansea, Bristol, Liverpool and Glasgow – in an attempt to destroy sea trade, just as they had hit big industrial cities. In Merseyside in one May week 1,900 people were killed, 1,450 seriously wounded, 66,000 houses destroyed and some 70,000 people made homeless.[6] The scale of destruction was shocking. When Bob and Killy reached Glasgow, once thought to be out of range of the Luftwaffe, they could see that acres and acres of the city had been flattened. (At the time official figures did not admit to the severity of the destruction.) Glasgow was Britain's second-biggest city with a concentration of heavy industry and shipbuilding yards.[7] To the west of Glasgow lies Greenock, then the base of the Home Fleet and assembly point for Atlantic convoys. It too was badly hit in early May 1941. In what became known locally as the 'Greenock Blitz', many thousands of homes were damaged and 1,000 totally destroyed. On one night, 7 May, incendiaries hit the town's whisky distillery, sugar refinery and foundries. The blaze this caused had shown the way across the city for the Germans to drop wave after wave of high-explosive bombs and parachute land mines.

Bob and Killy left the train at Gourock on the Clyde. This was the railway terminus that met ferries to the Scottish islands. It had been a traditional fishing port with sheds for herring curing and rope making. It was also the perfect place to throw a boom across the Clyde to Dunoon on the northern Argyll shore. The boom was made up of two lines of torpedo nets laid with depth charges. A guard ship at either side was ready to open or close the nets. This system provided anchorage for dozens of vessels that was safe from marauding U-boats or warships. The two pilots expected their troop carrier to be waiting for them in the safety of the Clyde. By the time they arrived it had gone.

Standing on the docks with all their gear, the two airmen had to confront an irate rail transport officer (RTO) who challenged them to explain why they were at least two days late for embarkation. Their ship, the SS *Anselm*, was part of a large convoy due to sail that night. It had already raised anchor. Now there wasn't enough time to jetty the two late arrivals to their ship. Bob recalled how Killy's Irish temper came to their aid. He left the RTO in no doubt about how he viewed his lack of initiative and, furthermore, that if the captain failed to get them aboard some ship in the convoy, all hell would be let loose.[8] It was all very well, but there would be serious consequences if they missed the convoy. They waited, getting more anxious as darkness came.

The RTO finally reappeared to say they were to embark on the Royal Navy cruiser that was to be the convoy's principal escort. It was in almost total darkness that they took an uncomfortable trip in a launch across an inky black sea. Killy and Bob, together with their assortment of cases and kitbags, were deposited rather unceremoniously on the deck of HMS *Galatea*. They were in luck.

HMS *Galatea* was one of the Navy's fastest, newest cruisers. They were met by the officer of the day, a young sub-lieutenant, and immediately made welcome in the wardroom (the naval equivalent of an officers' mess) already crowded with a large number of naval officers travelling as passengers. The presence of the two RAF pilots was a novelty and instead of being asked to sleep in hammocks as they had expected, Killy was shown to a single cabin while Bob, the junior officer, was escorted much further below decks to a rabbit hutch of a cabin with just room for a single bunk. Worse than its cramped size, this particular cabin was situated just above one of the ship's propellers and, at sea, the noise of the screws and the motion of the ship made it necessary not only to wear earplugs but also to hold on tightly to the bunk supports to avoid being thrown to the floor.[9] Bob soon got used to his cabin and reckoned he was fortunate to have his own space. He was also delighted to be travelling on a warship. After his experiences in the PDU, the wardroom on board was a palace; food was plentiful and well cooked and there were ample supplies of duty free drinks. Killy quickly made himself at home in the bar and, in view of his experiences, particularly in the Battle of Britain, he was something of a celebrity. Much of the voyage would be spent trading stories with the naval officers who had been involved in hunting the German battleship *Bismarck*. The two RAF men settled in and began to enjoy themselves.

For three days and nights they seemed to be going in the wrong direction for Africa. On the third morning, Bob went up on deck and was amazed to see that the cruiser had become part of a large convoy of merchant ships stretching almost as far as the eye could see. On the horizon, destroyers and corvettes fussed around, shepherding ships that were having difficulty maintaining their stations.

Convoys were seen as the safest way of protecting Britain's supply routes. They brought weapons, aircraft, machine tools, coal and food and took men and weapons to Africa, India and the Far East. Before the well-named 'Battle of the Atlantic' came to dominate British anxieties, the first convoy of eight ships bound for Cape Town set out from Gibraltar the day before war was declared.[10] Within months, 63 ships had been sunk. Once the imminent threat of invasion had passed, the War Cabinet switched resources to trade protection. By mid-1941, convoys typically contained 40–50 ships arranged in parallel columns with escort ships patrolling the perimeters. This made it more difficult for marauding U-boats, German destroyers or aircraft, but there were never enough escorts. In a big convoy the perimeter might extend to 30 sea miles.

Convoy WS9B left Liverpool on 27 June. It sailed north to meet up with more ships off Oversay in the Outer Hebrides and then turned south. The enemy lay in wait in ports and airfields along the Atlantic coast of occupied Europe and parts of West Africa. The convoy was protected by six Royal Navy ships and an armed merchant ship. Four of the escorts were recently acquired 'Flower' class corvettes – so called because they were named after flowers. They were small, robust ships based on Atlantic whalers but their top speed was 15 knots – too slow for chasing U-boats.

At this point, summer 1941, the war in Europe was changing fast. Russia had entered the conflict and Italy was losing ground in the Mediterranean. FM Erwin Rommel was sent to North Africa where successful campaigns would earn him the title 'Desert Fox'. Back in February, Hitler had issued his Directive 23 demanding greater efforts to destroy the British economy by targeting merchant shipping. 'The sinking of merchantmen is more important than attacks on enemy warships,' he wrote. 'Not only will the blockade, which is decisive to the war, be intensified, but enemy operations in Europe and Africa will be impeded.'[11] Churchill identified the danger and called it the Battle of the Atlantic. 'Herr Hitler will do his utmost to prey upon our shipping.' Just a few days later, the commander-in-chief of the German fleet, sailing in the *Gneisenau* and with the battleship *Scharnhorst*, spotted an unescorted group of British merchant ships off Newfoundland. They sank five before sailing back across the Atlantic to the Cape Verde Islands and the coast of Africa.

Convoy WS9B had its escorts but it was unwieldy, so it split into two groups. The faster ships were carrying military equipment and troops destined for the Middle East. Because of the situation in the Mediterranean, they had to go the length of Africa and around the Cape of Good Hope. It took on average 16 days to sail from Liverpool to Freetown. The 'fast' convoy was travelling at a mean speed of 12 knots and sailed in a zigzag pattern roughly south. The weather changed dramatically, giving way to clear skies and warm, even hot, sunshine. Looking back on the convoy, it seemed to Bob that several of the merchant ships were having difficulty keeping up and some were already beginning to fall behind. One very ancient freighter in particular soon began to recede into the distance and by the following morning could no longer be seen on the horizon behind the convoy. That night, the cruiser that Bob was on went to 'Action Stations' and sped off into the darkness at high speed for several hours.[12]

At breakfast in the wardroom next morning the talk was of several U-boats seen in the vicinity, and that the relatively fast speed of the convoy had kept most of it from attack. Not so the stragglers. Killy gave Bob the news. The ancient freighter they had seen was the SS *Anselm*. She had been torpedoed. Worse, this was the ship carrying all the ground crew and two sergeant pilots of their new squadron. But for Killy's tardy arrival at the PDU, he and Bob would have been on board. Reports were flashed by signal lamps from two escorting corvettes. A large number of survivors had been picked up either from the deck of the stricken ship or from lifeboats and rafts, and of these many had been transferred to the armed merchant ship SS *Cathay*. It was a shocking reminder of the dangers of their mission. Life aboard the cruiser had become a matter of routine, even pleasure. Now the two pilots were faced with the reality that if it hadn't been for their luck in missing their scheduled ship they too could have been lost or, if lucky, one of the survivors.

In many ways what happened on the night of 5 July 1941 was typical of the dangers encountered on convoy duty.[13] SS *Anselm* and its escorts were approximately 300 miles south of the Azores in fog. The HMS survey vessel *Challenger* was ahead with two corvettes, *Lavender* and *Petunia*. A third corvette, *Starwort*, was in line astern behind the *Anselm*. The SS *Anselm* was not ancient; she had been built as a cargo and passenger liner in 1935 but being coal fired she carried huge bunkers of coal to fuel four steam engines, which may have made her look old-fashioned. In 1940 she was requisitioned as a troop ship, her passenger accommodation given to officers and the holds to other ranks, up to 500 of them, stacked in hammocks. Reports say that on this trip she was heavily overloaded with about 1,200 troops, of which 175 were RAF, including the men destined for Bob's squadron.[14] At about 3.50am the fog cleared and they began to zigzag again. However, a Luftwaffe Focke-Wulf Fw 200 Condor patrol had reported the convoy's position. At 4.26am the German submarine U-96 came to the surface and fired four torpedoes at *Challenger* and *Anselm*.[15] They missed *Challenger* but caught *Anselm* on the port side amidships. It was a huge blow that momentarily blasted the troop ship out of the water. U-96 dived immediately, under attack by the two corvettes. *Lavender* fired six depth charges and *Petunia* 20.

In danger of catching survivors, however, they broke off their attack. The German submarine was badly damaged and gave up its attack, opting to return to the Saint-Nazaire base in France for repairs.

Anselm was able to launch all but one of her lifeboats. *Challenger*, which was half a nautical mile ahead, manoeuvred close and took off 60 or more survivors as the ship's bow settled in the water. Officers in the passenger accommodation got out on to the boat deck. Men packed into the holds had a more difficult time because many of the overheads had collapsed and ladders were wrecked. The ship sank within 22 minutes with the loss of four crew and 250 troops – a fearsome loss. Yet, more than a thousand men were rescued[16] – many from the water, others from lifeboats or life rafts. The corvettes and *Challenger* were dangerously overloaded so they transferred some survivors to HMS *Cathay*. Meanwhile, Bob and Killy sailed on, unaware of the effect the sinking of the *Anselm* would have on their task ahead.

Zigzagging from time to time to fool potential attackers, HMS *Galatea* and the faster boats steamed on for another week. The men on board changed into tropical uniform: the naval officers whiter than white, the RAF duo in rather baggy khaki. The sea was calm. They saw schools of dolphins and swarms of flying fish. The nights were beautiful. A whole range of new stars rose in the equatorial sky. Early one morning, Bob went on deck. There, in the first light of a tropical dawn, he saw a large harbour with many great ships at anchor. It was very hot and humid and a heavy smell hung in the air. Graham Greene describes arriving at Freetown with a novelist's eye:

'From here the port was always beautiful; the thin layers of houses sparkled in the sun like quartz or lay in the shadow of the great swollen hills … the destroyers and corvettes sat around like dogs: signal flaps rippled and helio flashed. The fishing boats rested on the broad bay under their brown butterfly sails.'[17]

He describes, too, the smell – a 'sweet hot smell' from the land.

Soon after breakfast, a smart-looking RAF launch came alongside and it was time for Killy and Bob to disembark. They said their goodbyes to their fellow passengers, who had many weeks of voyage ahead as they set off again for Cape Town and East Africa, and to the ship's officers with whom they had established such a good rapport.

The launch ferried them through shoals of small boats, some no more than dugout canoes. Everywhere there were fishermen, small boys begging for pennies and boys and girls selling bananas. They were to be taken to the headquarters of a flying boat squadron, whose Sunderlands could be seen at their moorings in a small bay just off the shoreline. First, they had lunch in the officers' mess. The resident officers looked sunburned and smart in well-tailored khaki drill bush shirts and shorts. Bob felt self-conscious and ill at ease. Too much the new boy. Both the newcomers were pale, despite sunbathing on the voyage, and dressed in regulation issue shirts and ridiculously long shorts. They had noticed as soon as they landed that topees were not worn and quickly unpacked their service blue dress hats. The newcomers were assured that the local tailors would make smart, well-cut tropical uniforms for a very modest price and the mess laundry service would produce daily supplies of freshly starched and laundered khaki. It would not take long before Bob learned of many such local amenities in his strange new environment. After lunch, preceded by several drinks, Killy and Bob and their kit were driven 10 miles inland to the Royal Navy air station that was to be their home for many months to come.

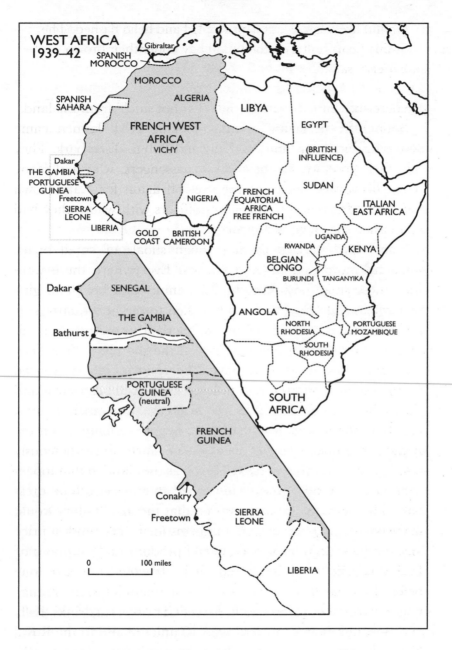

WEST AFRICA
1939–42

Gibraltar

SPANISH
MOROCCO

MOROCCO

SPANISH
SAHARA

ALGERIA

LIBYA

EGYPT

FRENCH WEST
AFRICA
VICHY

(BRITISH
INFLUENCE)

Dakar

THE GAMBIA
PORTUGUESE
GUINEA

Freetown

SIERRA
LEONE

LIBERIA

GOLD
COAST

NIGERIA

SUDAN

FRENCH
EQUATORIAL
AFRICA
FREE FRENCH

ITALIAN
EAST AFRICA

BRITISH
CAMEROON

UGANDA

RWANDA

KENYA

BELGIAN
CONGO

BURUNDI

TANGANYIKA

Dakar

SENEGAL

ANGOLA

THE GAMBIA

Bathurst

NORTH
RHODESIA

PORTUGUESE
MOZAMBIQUE

SOUTH
RHODESIA

PORTUGUESE
GUINEA
(neutral)

SOUTH
AFRICA

FRENCH
GUINEA

Conakry

Freetown

SIERRA
LEONE

0   100 miles

LIBERIA

The drive through Freetown gave Bob his first experience of Africa. He was both fascinated and apprehensive. Sierra Leone and the other countries around the bulge of West Africa had a reputation for being 'the white man's grave'. Beyond Atlantic breakers and sandy beaches lay thick mangrove swamps, tropical forest and, in the winter months, dusty grasslands. July, when Bob first arrived, was the middle of the rainy season. Torrential rains turned the grasslands and hills green, encouraged mildew on anything left for a day or two, and brought mosquitoes everywhere.

Freetown has one of the finest harbours in the world after Rio and Sydney. A natural deep-water channel off a broad bay 5 miles wide, it has huge anchorage. The first Europeans to visit the area were Portuguese who named the peninsula *Serra Lyoa* – 'lion mountain'. Some 300 years later, a group of anti-slavers landed and named their settlement Freetown. It became a Crown Colony in 1807 and was used by the British Navy as a base against the slave trade and pirate ships.[18] By 1941, Freetown showed the results of more than a hundred years of colonisation. There was a red Anglican cathedral in a prominent position. Several churches and chapels. Streets of gabled bungalows with tin or corrugated-iron rather than thatch roofs. Houses built of brick to the first floor and a clapboard second storey. Wide verandahs and overhanging eaves copied from the West Indies. Two-storey shops run by Lebanese or Syrian traders. Government buildings solidly Edwardian. Everywhere bougainvillea and hibiscus. Gaudily dressed locals. Open-air stalls selling peanuts, pineapples and other exotic tropical fruits.

The two pilots travelled by truck. Once they left the town they were on dirt roads, speeding inland bump by bump, rut to rut. They passed through many villages made up of round grass-roofed homes. People waved cheerfully but Bob was totally unprepared for his first sight of real poverty. There were old men and women with crippling diseases, in particular elephantiasis. Naked children. And 'dusky bare breasted maidens bathing in a wayside pool below a waterfall caused heads to turn as the truck passed by'.[19] Around the next corner women were weeding rice paddies. Some had babies strapped to their backs.

The naval station appeared in almost laughable contrast. White picket fencing. A guard hut and barrier. Neat, white-painted, fly-proofed buildings and, most comical of all, sailors, white-uniformed and bearded, far from the sea yet determinedly on board ship at their stone-frigate shore-base. The RAF officers were shown to their quarters. The rooms had fans, fly guards at the windows and mosquito nets over the beds. It was appallingly hot. Sweat dripped from the smallest effort. At tea in the wardroom they met the captain of this 'ship' – a veteran flyer of World War I. His task now was to receive amphibious flying boats from their mother ship when it came into port and to operate anti-submarine patrols. Killy asked for news of his squadron and aeroplanes but was met by blank looks. It seemed no one had any idea what had happened or where they might be. The fate of their squadron would have to wait until morning.

That first night in Africa was strange to the point of surreal. Darkness within minutes. Night noise of insects painful to unaccustomed ears. Feeling rather scruffy without well-laundered uniforms, Killy and Bob joined the naval officers for pre-dinner drinks in the wardroom. They were told the form was that the whole mess sat down to dinner at the same time but never before the captain decided it was time to dine. After a while, Bob and some of the younger officers found this irksome since the captain never permitted dinner to be served until he had drunk a large number of pink gins and then taken his place, sometimes a little unsteadily, at the head of the table, from where he peered down to see who might be misbehaving. Bob, not used to the drinking culture of the services, finding that there was no beer, asked for a lime juice. He was approached by a middle-aged naval doctor who invited him to have a drink. When Bob asked for another lime juice the doctor looked hard at him and said, 'If you carry on drinking that muck, within six months I shall be invaliding you home from this God-forsaken hole with malaria, dysentery or both. Try something stronger'.[20] Reluctant to ignore such medical advice, Bob asked for a whisky. One whisky was an impossibility in such company. There would be several more both before and after dinner. His recollections of that first evening were vague. Goodness knows how he got back to his room, or his cabin as it was called, on this earthbound ship.

At 6am the next morning it was still dark when Bob was woken by an orderly. The officers worked a tropical daily routine of 7am to 1pm. Bob was not feeling very well. He had to put on a brave face. Get up. Shower. Dress in newly laundered uniform and join Killy for breakfast. It was a full English: eggs, bacon, toast, tea and, as a concession to the location, a plate of tropical fruit. Bob was in no state to appreciate it but Killy showed no outward signs of the previous evening's activities. He told Bob that he was going back into Freetown to the Royal Air Force Headquarters close to the port, since he needed to make enquiries about the fate of his squadron and the whereabouts of their aircraft. He was also concerned about the state of the available runway and its suitability for use by their Hurricanes – if and when they were located. Killy thus took off in a borrowed naval staff car, driving himself.

For the first time since he'd left England, Bob was alone. The naval officers were all at work. It was sticky and quiet save for the occasional thump as a lazy vulture landed on the roof. Bob was suddenly overwhelmed by homesickness. Apart from one letter, which he had posted as soon as he had arrived in port, he had been unable to write home. Despite enquiries at the base's post office, there was no mail from home for him. His wife kept the letter he had written from the ship on 30 June:

'Well here's another day gone by and all I seem to have done is eat, sleep and read. I am feeling quite fit except that I wish we could get more exercise and I would feel a lot happier in my mind if we could get that blasted u-boat which is following us!! Already I am feeling homesick and am beginning to long for green fields and another glimpse of England. How are you feeling my dear? I am very anxious to hear from you to know what you are doing but best of all I wish you were here with me.'[21]

It is the letter of a young man, just 20, newly married, who has been torn from his wife, his home (in another letter he asks his wife to call on his mother) and his country. Little wonder, then, that having decided the airfield could wait, his first task should be to write long letters home to his wife and his mother. He immediately felt better and set off to look around, asking a naval rating to direct him to the runway. The bearded stalwart, in immaculate white shirt and shorts, looked hard at him before replying that if he meant the grass strip the naval aircraft used then it was over there, beyond the hangar.

Bob set off, trudging on in the heat of the tropical morning. When he rounded the corner of the only hangar, his worst fears were realised. There was no proper runway, only a grass strip, bare in the middle, some 800 yards long. He imagined trying to land a Hurricane. The approach from one direction was from hills about 2,000ft high. They looked ominously close. The other end of the runway ended in a water-filled creek overgrown with mangrove trees and bushes. This runway had been hacked out of the bush just a few months earlier. He saw another hangar under construction at the far end of the airfield. There was someone in the control tower. Trying not to look too disconsolate, Bob walked purposefully across the airfield and up the steps of the tower. A naval air traffic controller confirmed that the new hangar was to be for a newly formed RAF squadron but until it was ready they would be sharing with the Navy. Bob spent the rest of the morning in the tower watching Fleet Air Arm aircraft, mainly Walrus amphibians, doing circuits and bumps (take-off and landing). They were much slower and of lower performance than the expected Hurricanes but they seemed to manage well. He began to get a better perspective on the airfield and its limitations, though he was still apprehensive about landing a Hurricane on such a short strip.

Killy arrived back after dark. It was yet another occasion when Bob marvelled at his boss's robust constitution. He had obviously been well entertained at Air Headquarters and then negotiated the tortuous bumpy road back to the airfield without damaging the borrowed staff car. Bob had to wait until after dinner to hear the latest; it was not done to discuss work matters in the mess. The news was grave but not as bad as it could have been. Most of the squadron ground crew had survived the sinking of the *Anselm* but some were in hospital. All had lost their personal kit, even their clothes. All, except those in hospital, would be arriving at the airfield in two days' time. There was good news about their aeroplanes, though. Three Hurricanes packed in large wooden crates had already been offloaded from a ship in port on to a lighter, which would be towed up the creek close to the airfield. The crates could be used as working space for ground personnel and aircrew until the squadron hangar and office accommodation were finished. Killy's instruction from Air Headquarters was to get the three aircraft flying as soon as possible. They were to provide further air defence of the port, which was such a vital link on the important round-the-Cape

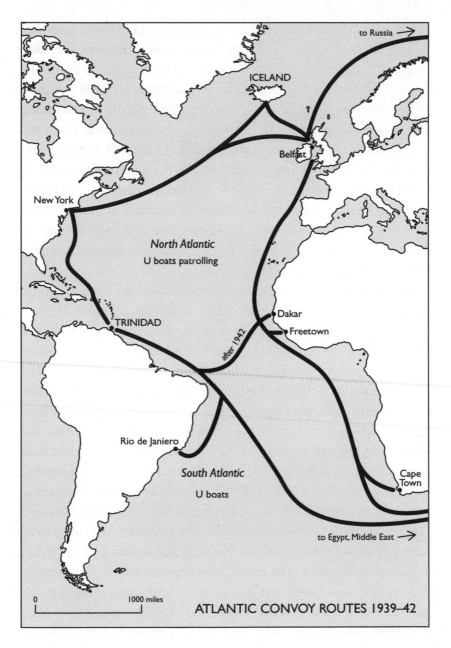

to Russia →

ICELAND

Belfast

New York

North Atlantic
U boats patrolling

to Russia →

TRINIDAD

after 1942

Dakar

Freetown

Rio de Janiero

South Atlantic

U boats

Cape
Town

to Egypt, Middle East →

0   1000 miles

ATLANTIC CONVOY ROUTES 1939–42

shipping route. In particular, they were to prevent or discourage any aerial reconnaissance by hostile aircraft when convoys were in port.

What none of them could know was just how crucial their work would be to the Battle of the Atlantic. In April, U-boats had sunk 43 ships. In May, 58, of which half were in the Freetown area. The German naval commander Admiral Karl Dönitz had achieved this carnage with just six U-boats by adopting the tactics of the 'wolf pack' – often attacking, as he had the *Anselm*, on the surface and at night. In June they sank a further 61 ships. It seemed for a while that the U-boat might succeed where the Luftwaffe had failed.[22] There was a critical shortage of ships at a time when vital raw materials, troops and their equipment had to be moved around the world. On average, 29,000 British service men needed to be relocated each month. Meanwhile, at home, imports, many of them food, had shrunk by almost half. Rations were cut again and some fresh foods, including fruit and vegetables, were prohibited. Admiral Dönitz claimed that given 300 U-boats he could starve Britain into submission.

Even without knowing the full importance of his role, it struck Bob as a daunting task. How could they operate from a substandard grass-strip runway? How would they be able to locate and destroy hostile aircraft without the help of radar-assisted ground control? To Bob, still very young and inexperienced, it all seemed utterly hopeless. That night he was close to despair. Torrential rain thundered outside. Here he was in a stinking, tropical climate, forced to sleep under a mosquito net to avoid malaria, living in a Fleet Air Arm station run as if it were a ship at sea. Just three weeks before he had been a member of one of the RAF's foremost fighter squadrons operating from a well-organised airfield in mid-summer England. During stand-down he had travelled home and spent short periods with his wife. He was anxious. Worried about life at home. There were no encouraging letters. Eventually he fell asleep, exhausted at the futility of it all.

Next morning the rain had stopped. The air was bright and cool and clear. Bob woke up feeling quite different about his situation. After all, he might not have to stay long as the climate was considered so bad that tours of duty rarely lasted a year. He should make the most of the experience presented to him. First, he must see to the aircraft, which had to be dragged ashore in crates and assembled by ground crew who had just suffered a forced swim in the Atlantic Ocean. Later in the morning, a technical flight sergeant and the two sergeant pilots who had travelled on the *Anselm* arrived by truck. They were accommodated in the chief petty officer's mess. Now, for the first time, Bob heard in detail about the loss of the *Anselm*. It was terrible. And it was to have a direct impact on Bob's task in West Africa.

The squadron ground crew were in their hammocks several decks down when the *Anselm* was attacked just before first light. Several were injured in the explosion. The survivors escaped by climbing gangways and vertical ladders up to the deck. A few were lucky and were able to jump across on to the deck of a corvette that came alongside the stricken ship, but as she began to settle further the escort had to cast off. Many of the wounded, who had either been carried or had managed to make their way up to the deck, could not be transferred in time. As the *Anselm* sank further they were swept away by the overwhelming sea. Some were rescued from rafts or by clinging on to debris but most of the badly injured were lost.

As the ship's bow settled lower in the water, an RAF padre showed extraordinary bravery and selflessness, for which he was awarded the George Cross. His story did not fully emerge until after the war, when the *Anselm's* survivors spoke out. Cecil Pugh was a South African who had served in World War I as a medical orderly, trained as a minister of the Congregational Church and joined the RAF at the beginning of World War II as a chaplain. The troop ship was taking him to a new posting in the Gold Coast (now Ghana). When the torpedo hit, he was asleep in his cabin on the upper deck where the officers were accommodated. He immediately lent a hand, helping to launch the lifeboats and life rafts, but then he heard the screams of injured men trapped below decks in one of the converted holds. The reports say that he told some marines to lower him down into the hold on a rope in order to be with his men. The marines tried to dissuade him but Pugh insisted, 'My love of God is greater than my fear of death.'[23] Once in the hold he knelt to pray with the trapped men. He was seen with seawater up to his shoulders.[24]

An appalling 250 troops and four crew were killed when the *Anselm* sank, though 92 of her crew and 965 troops were rescued, having scrambled up nets to board the naval escorts *Challenger* and *Starwort*. Around 900 of the men were transferred to HMS *Cathay*, the armed merchant cruiser. The two young sergeant pilots made light of their own experiences. By the time they had reached the deck of the *Anselm* the corvette had stood off and the sinking ship was already at a steep angle. They were both poor swimmers so they clambered up the steepening deck to the stern. As the ship sank further they began to tower above the water. Rather than dive off the side, they were forced to jump some 50ft off the by-then near-vertical stern of the ship. They managed to stay together and found some wreckage to cling to. A boat from the corvette came to their rescue. Bob, also a non-swimmer, listened to their story. They had no physical injury but to Bob it was obvious they were still shocked by their experience.

Bob found himself, at the tender age of 20, being the only other officer, appointed to be adjutant of the squadron or, to be more accurate, the flight. His instructions were to look after the ground crew when they arrived and to get them working, under direction of the flight sergeant, to offload and assemble the aircraft. In normal circumstances this would have presented little difficulty. The Navy had provided a heavy crane and transport to unload the enormous crates from the lighter. However, when the ground crew who were fit enough to travel arrived the next day, after a bumpy ride from the port in an open lorry, he realised he had a morale problem.

Bob described it as 'reluctance to accept that they should do the job they had been ordered to do was an understatement of the first order. Having recently nearly lost their lives and most of their possessions, it was apparent that they thought that they should be sent home on the next boat.' So it was that around 100 disgruntled, frightened men arrived in the safety of the white-painted, well-organised naval station. Fortunately, they were satisfied with their accommodation and the food was the best they'd had in weeks, which did much to relieve their depression, general bolshiness and reluctance to do anything but lie on their beds. By the time Bob saw them again the next day, the immediate crisis had been averted.

'Apparently, they had been royally welcomed by the Naval ratings. In addition to unlimited supplies of cold beer, which they were able to buy duty free with the pay they had been given at the port, there had been the added attraction of a liberal, daily, free Naval rum ration for which all non-commissioned RAF personal also qualified.'[25]

Bob set the ground crew to work right away. The crane offloaded the crates on to a heavy vehicle. Slowly, agonisingly slowly, the precious cargo was transported down a narrow unmade road to the airfield. When they opened the crates they found the propellers and wings had been removed and packed flat separately from the fuselage. The tools and ground equipment to reassemble the aircraft had been offloaded from another ship in the convoy. Within a few days of opening the initial crate, the first Hurricane was ready to fly. Bob was amazed at the skill and dedication of the technical airmen. There was a core of pre-war regulars in the crew with expertise and experience. As the time drew near for the aircraft to be tested, the earlier resentment of the ground crew had been replaced by a sense of pride, squadron spirit and good morale. Much of this was due to the leadership and example of the senior NCOs but Bob, unable to make a technical contribution, had played his part by his general concern for their health and welfare. There was another factor, too: much friendly rivalry between the Navy and the RAF. They began to boast that anything the Navy could do ashore the RAF could do better – especially operating aircraft. They were about to put this to the test.

Another great boost to morale was the arrival of the first mail from home. Bob received three letters from his wife, all of them very cheerful. What could these letters tell? Alice was still teaching in London. She visited her family in Kent at the weekends. She spoke of making do with rationing, visiting the cinema and keeping spirits up. One of her sisters just shut the door on her bombed home and continued to live in the remaining rooms. All the family were involved in the war effort.

What Alice didn't tell Bob, or her family, was that one night her train to London, full of servicemen returning home, had been hit. Also in her carriage had been two women, one of whom was obviously pregnant. She'd noticed a great fire along the Tilbury docks that seemed to spread along the whole river. Suddenly the train had stopped. They'd flung themselves on the floor of the carriage. Thudding bombs. Explosions. Windows shattered. Alice had thought this was strange. 'I always thought Bobbie would be killed, now it's going to be me.'[26] It was an uncanny feeling. A fatalistic acceptance of the inevitable. When the dust settled there was absolute silence. The passengers helped each other. Some hot, sweet tea was shared around. It was London. Wartime. Yet Alice could not share this with her husband, so far away – somewhere tropical. The sweethearts, so recently married, could only write 'I love you'. And do so often. Bob renewed his resolve to write at least two letters a week and to tell Alice as much as the censor would permit.

Back in Freetown, the intense tropical heat and high humidity began to cause health problems. Despite an efficient laundry service, which enabled uniforms and underwear to be changed daily, everyone suffered prickly heat and other irritating skin diseases. Cases of malaria and dysentery appeared, mainly due to mosquito nets not being issued for the ground crew when they first disembarked. The naval sick bay looked after minor complaints while the more seriously ill were taken to a military hospital on a hill overlooking the port. It was time for another boost to morale.

14 July was the day on which the flight sergeant declared the first newly assembled Hurricane fit to fly. Killy stepped up and, watched by a large crowd of RAF and RN men, took off with stylish ease, leaving a cloud of dust from the runway behind him. He disappeared in the direction of the harbour, then buzzed the harbour and flew low over a recently arrived convoy, causing heads to turn. Back over the airfield, in true fighter-pilot style, he executed some low-level aerobatics, which drew some sharp intakes of breath from those who had just toiled to assemble the aircraft. It wasn't a perfect landing – the runway was too bumpy – but he was smiling broadly and giving everyone the thumbs up, which raised a cheer.

While the aircraft was being refuelled and inspected, Killy told his young officer to take it up for a second trip. That would be enough for the day, so the sergeant pilots would have to wait until the morrow for their turns. Bob could feel the excitement bubbling up. It wasn't until he was strapping himself into the cockpit that he realised how rusty his flying was. Unlike his experienced squadron commander, he took a long time to start the engine and taxi to the take-off point. Opening the throttle cautiously, he was expecting to be airborne but no, there were a couple of embarrassing kangaroo-like hops across the rough surface before he made it into the air. He decided on a sedate cruise round the harbour, which looked even more impressive from the air, and toured the local area before returning to base.

The hills near the airfield, covered in tropical vegetation, were free from cloud when he came in to land and he realised that they were much further away than they appeared from the ground. Still cautious, he made two practice approaches before finally landing, and was really pleased to finish his landing run with only an average amount of braking. Taxiing back to dispersal, he felt elated. He was flying, doing the job for which he had been trained. He climbed out of the plane and received congratulations from the ground crew. They approved of their young officer.

3

At war in West Africa

I N AUGUST IT RAINED. Heavy downpours that left huge
puddles on the runway. It was hot and so humid that
clothes never felt dry. There were many mosquitoes.
Aircraft continued to arrive by sea to be assembled, flight-tested
and put into operation. The two sergeant pilots who had survived
the sinking of the *Anselm* had been sent overseas directly from
their operational training unit in England. They had even less
experience than Bob. Landings were hair-raising, especially after
the rains. Killy set up a programme of flying training. Weeks
went by without accident. It was a quiet, even dull routine.

One morning, while on a training sortie, Bob was radioed by
the airfield controller. A hostile aircraft had been spotted flying
over the airfield and was now over the harbour. Bob immediately
turned and saw puffs of smoke from anti-aircraft fire from the
harbour-shore batteries. By the time he was over the shipping
there was nothing to be seen. Indeed, even if he had seen the
intruder it was far too late to manage to intercept him. He
turned for home. When he landed he was told that the enemy
aircraft had made one high-level run over the airfield and then
dived down at great speed across the harbour. It disappeared at
a very low level out to sea in a northerly direction. So there was
an enemy in the air. However, the chances of catching him were
remote without either radar or a ground station to advise them.
No intruder would hang around waiting to be intercepted. For
the next few weeks they kept one aircraft and pilot on permanent

readiness during daylight hours. That meant ready to take off and pursue hostile aircraft whenever they were sighted by the airfield control tower or AA gun batteries. It was a long, boring wait. No intruders appeared.

There were times when despair returned. Letters from home tended to arrive in batches with weeks in between. Bob carried a small piece of paper in his wallet. Alice kept hers in her purse. It was a poem written as though it were a telegram.

```
TOGETHER AND APART.
I THOUGHT TO LIVE WITHOUT YOU
WAS A THING I COULD NOT DO –
TILL SUDDENLY I REMEMBERED
THAT I WAS PART OF YOU.
SO IF YOU'RE FEELING LONELY
WHEREVER YOU MAY BE
WILL YOU PLEASE DEAR REMEMBER
THAT YOU ARE PART OF ME.
SO WE'LL ALWAYS BE TOGETHER
ALTHOUGH WE ARE NOT NEAR
FOR I AM WITH YOU DARLING.
AND YOU ARE WITH ME DEAR...
```

Homesickness was very real among the men serving abroad. For those in active theatres of war such as Malta, the sadness of personal loss and chronic homesickness could lead to depression and feelings of friendlessness. One young pilot wrote from Malta: 'Must we lose everything we love and everything that promises fair in life. I am twenty-two years old. I have spent a few short weeks with my very young wife – is this then our future?'[1]

For Bob, though, the future was suddenly full of promise. The mail brought a letter from Alice.

'Darling, We're going to have a baby. I hope you are as
happy as I am. I feel absolutely, wonderfully fit and all
is well. Don't worry about me at all. I shall take care
of myself and do as the doctor tells me. I have written
just to tell you this. Please answer my letter quickly.
All my love, Alice.'

It would be six weeks before she received Bob's telegraphic reply:

'DEAREST, HAVE JUST RECEIVED YOUR LETTER
WITH THE NEWS. I AM SIMPLY OVERJOYED AND
CANNOT BELIEVE THAT I AM TO BE A FATHER.
TAKE CARE OF YOURSELF AND SEND ME ALL NEWS.
I THINK OF YOU ALWAYS. YOUR LOVING HUSBAND,
BOBBIE'[2]

Bob was delighted. He was also secretly pleased that his chances of
surviving his tour of duty in West Africa and of seeing his son or
daughter were much greater than they would have been if he had
been flying elsewhere. The arrival of two very experienced pilots
from Malta to join the squadron reminded them of the benefits of a
quiet posting. The Malta pilots had been through terrible, exhausting
times. For them, West Africa would seem like a rest home.

There was still work to do. A mobile radar station was sent out
from the UK. It was sited overlooking the harbour and manned
by two experienced officers – also from Malta. The radar was
also called Range and Direction Finding (RDF). It could pinpoint
an intruder up to 60 miles away. On 11 August, Sgt Todd, an
ex-Malta pilot, was flying over the harbour when he was called
up by the ground controller. There was an unidentified, possibly
hostile aircraft at 5,000ft. Turning and climbing hard he got a
clear view of the intruder silhouetted against the clear blue sky.
By flying his Hurricane to the limit he managed to get astern

just as the pilot of the twin-engine light bomber decided it was time to go home. He dived away from the harbour. Too late. A single burst from the eight machine guns mounted in the wings of the Hurricane had a devastating effect. Pieces of metal flew off the intruder and smoke, followed by fire, appeared from both engines. The dive steepened. When last seen the aircraft was engulfed in smoke and would certainly crash a few miles inland.[3]

To disable the enemy. That is why they were sitting in West Africa, so far from home. There was much rejoicing that evening to celebrate the squadron's first success. Killy wasn't among them. He had been called to HQ and ordered to locate the crash site and recover anything of importance. When he returned he was not his usual jovial, carefree self. He told Bob that with the help of a local army unit he had easily located the crashed aircraft near a village, but the search party had then had to extricate the charred bodies of the four-man crew from the wreckage. The bodies were already starting to decompose in the heat so they decided to bury them where they had fallen. Apart from some maps, which enabled the home base of the aircraft to be identified, and a camera that confirmed its reconnaissance role, there was little that could be salvaged except a bicycle of French manufacture and the trade mark 'Le Pyramide' of Casablanca. One of the bike's steel wheels had bullet damage but it could be ridden. Killy reported back to Air HQ and thought that was the end of the incident.

Not at all. The next day, Killy was ordered to return to the crash site, disinter the victims and return with their remains to the airfield for burial under military funeral arrangements. He protested. To no avail. After lunch he set off in a small convoy of vehicles with a party of volunteers and three coffins. Bob offered to go too, but Killy declined. Killy was next seen that evening in the wardroom, very, very drunk. The names and religion of the dead aircrew had been established from their identity discs.

The following morning a ceremony was conducted by both Anglican and Catholic priests. It had a powerful effect on all who attended. The rights and wrongs of recovering the remains were debated long after the event. In retrospect, despite the appalling unpleasantness of the disinterment, there was general agreement that the right decision had been made: honour the dead.

One of the surprises about Bob's time in West Africa is that 'the enemy' was French in this war against Germany. For centuries the British had been the traditional enemy of the French but latterly they had become allies. With the fall of France to Nazi Germany, the French empire, and in some ways France itself, had been divided against itself, split between Vichy loyalism and Free French republicanism.[4] The sinking of the French fleet at Oran, the failure of the Dieppe raid and the unsuccesful British attempt on Dakar put the erstwhile allies at loggerheads. The relationship between British and French colonies, once comfortably symbiotic, had become fractious and tense.

The British colonies Gambia and Sierra Leone were surrounded by French West Africa. Afrique-Occidentale Française (AOF) was ruled as a homogenous unit from Dakar but was in fact unwieldy, massive and diverse'.[5] It ran from the coasts of Senegal and Côte d'Ivoire to the huge landlocked territories of Mauritania, French Sudan, Niger, French Equatorial Africa and links between them and Morocco and Algeria. The colonised peoples were hugely diverse in culture, language, religion and economic activity, yet French colonial administration in West Africa was surprisingly cohesive. The British colonies were right to feel nervous of their neighbours.

Dakar was the most important French imperial port. Freetown was the most important British colonial port. The French continued to assist the Germans. The British set a blockade on Dakar. Beyond the coast lay the Atlantic and the vital convoys supplying Britain. Since 1940 there had been a considerable French Army presence in Senegal. There were ten companies of soldiers, 14 motorised units, 1,500 trained pilots and 700 aircraft including Glenn Martin bombers and 298 torpedo bombers.[6] Fortunately for the Allies, their blockade was effective in depriving these machines of fuel. In 1940 in Dakar, Pierre Boisson, Governor-General of French West Africa, was offered terms by the British: neutralise your ships or face the consequences. On 5 July 1940, British intelligence intercepted a French signal ordering all French vessels to 'Meet attacks from the English enemy with the utmost ferocity'.[7] One of those vessels was the French battleship the *Richelieu* with eight 15in. guns. In a daring raid, worthy of James Bond, Cdr Bobby Bristow got alongside the battleship in a black-painted motorboat and loosed four depth charges. Unluckily for Bristow, they did not go off at once. However, a torpedo dropped by a Swordfish aircraft detonated them, tearing a huge hole in the hull.[8] The *Richelieu* could not sail but remained in Dakar harbour, guns in place.

Gallic pride was challenged. The Vichy government managed to persuade the Germans and Italians to let them re-arm. Within a few months there were Vichy units, including 200 French fighters and assorted bombers and reconnaissance units in North Africa – in Morocco, Syria and Lebanon – and in West Africa in Senegal, as well as small forces in Madagascar and Indochina. Gnl de Gaulle was trying to persuade all of them to join him in the Free French service. At the end of September 1940, a Free French officer, Cdt Hettier de Boislambert, wearing civilian clothes, set out for Dakar intent on persuading the garrison to defect. They were not to be persuaded by talk. Maybe a show of force? Code named Operation *Menace*, it was a dismal and embarrassing failure, especially as it involved HMS *Ark Royal* and a large force of British and Australian marines. The exchange of signals was bellicose. De Gaulle stated that 'Once fire has begun it will continue until the fortifications at Dakar are entirely destroyed'. The response from Governor-General Boisson on the *Richelieu*: 'France has entrusted me Dakar. I shall defend Dakar to the end.'[9] The French in Dakar showed no signs of surrender and fought back, putting the British fleet at risk. They retaliated with an attack on Gibraltar led by Vichy bombers operating out of Morocco. Only a few months earlier the British and French were on the same side. Now they were pitted against one another. The French naval attaché in Madrid made it quite clear that it was Gibraltar for Dakar. The British withdrew and the Vichy government declared victory.

A year after these events, in the summer of 1941, when Bob Allen arrived, Dakar was a constant threat to its neighbours in the south: Gambia, Sierra Leone, Liberia, Ghana and Nigeria. These were countries that had no intention of becoming 'slaves under Hitler'. De Gaulle had the support of Gnl Félix Éboué of Chad (then the Cameroons, adjacent to Nigeria) and French Equatorial Africa (Côte d'Ivoire) to the east. All these countries supplied labour, troops and raw materials to the Allies throughout the war: 240,000 fighting men and many thousands of labourers and carriers. Goods including palm oil, groundnuts, iron, diamonds, cocoa, manganese, wood, tin and a war fund of a million pounds were contributed by rulers, including the Asantehene (the ruler of the Kingdom of Ashanti, in Ghana). The people of Ondo, Nigeria, contributed £1,400 for a Spitfire. Radios and newspapers carried anti-German propaganda pitting fascist 'racist' Germans against strongly democratic Brits. Lagos, fearing attack, brought in a blackout.[10] And there was another important reason for the protection of this now-vital coast: it was to be a supply route for war materials and foodstuffs for the Allies in the Middle East.

The route began in Takoradi on the Gold Coast (Ghana). For almost two years it had been impossible for the Allies to supply the Middle East from the Mediterranean. Rather than rounding the Cape, they opened up an old Imperial Airways route from Takoradi to Khartoum, a move that had first been considered as early as 1925. Takoradi was 3 miles from the nearest township and had a well-developed port. The plan involved flying aircraft and supplies across the vast scrub and sandy wastes of the Sahara desert via a set of staging posts, landing sites and fuel dumps. The initial group of 350 men and 25 ferry pilots under the command of Gp Capt Henry Karslake Thorold arrived at Takoradi on 24 August 1940. The first aeroplanes (six Hurricanes and six Blenheims) arrived in crates from the UK on 5 September. The very next day, a further 30 Hurricanes arrived on HMS *Argus*. The foremost group set off with a BOAC navigator on board for the 3,800-mile journey. All but one made it, despite some of the aircraft being battle-scarred veterans of Dunkirk and the Battle of Britain, ill fitted for heat and sand.[11] The route first took the 378 miles along the coast from Takoradi to Lagos. Thereafter it was 525 miles from Lagos to Kano (over forest), 325 miles from Kano to Maiduguri (over savannah), 689 miles from Maiduguri to Geneina in the Sudan (desert) and finally a whopping 754 miles (over desert) to Khartoum, with one refuelling stop at El Fasher.[12]

No fewer than a thousand aircraft – Blenheims, Hurricanes and Spitfires – were shipped from the UK, assembled at Takoradi and flown via this route in 1941–42. Despite fears of attack from Vichy, Italian or German forces, there was only one successful disruption – in January 1942, when a small German/ Italian force from Campo Uno in the Libyan desert supported a Heinkel He111H in a daring attack on the fuel dumps at Fort Lamy. In a single bombing run, Lt Bohnsack destroyed eight Hurricanes and 80,000 gallons of fuel. On his return north he had to force-land in the desert, his fuel exhausted after a ten-and-a-half-hour flight. A week later, a Junkers Ju 52 landed close by and refuelled the Heinkel, which then flew safely back to Tripoli. This one raid closed the Takoradi route for weeks while fuel was ferried overland across the desert and more than 50 Hurricanes waited at Takoradi.[13] Once the Americans got involved, a further 2,000-plus aircraft arrived from the USA via Brazil and Ascension Island and were ferried along this route.

Air HQ West Africa, based in Freetown, co-ordinated all RAF activities from the Gambia to the Gold Coast. There was a weekly communications flight between Bathurst, Freetown, Takoradi and Accra and Lagos.[14] Bob Allen does not say much about his day-to-day life in Sierra Leone but one of his contemporaries left a vivid account. The novelist Graham Greene, appointed by MI6 to cover intelligence matters, including counter-espionage, was also based in Freetown. He took the flight to Lagos. Greene's account of expat life in Freetown is famously grim and depressing. Lagos was luxurious by comparison. There were lavatories to flush and you could drink the water from the tap. Moreover, in addition to a cinema there was plenty of nightlife – dancing, drinking and 'sugar babies'. Back in Freetown his house had taps but no water. Rain, 147in. per year, turned the scrub around his bungalow into a swamp. Vultures sat on his roof 'like old broken umbrellas'. Houseflies, cockroaches, spiders and ants moved freely through his rooms.

Greene's brief was to keep an eye on the battleship *Richelieu* in Dakar. 'I think MI6 at that period was a little hazy in their geography because I was well over a thousand miles away from Dakar.'[15] He suggested they set up a brothel in Bissau to snag visiting French. London turned him down. An American reported that in November 1942 the *Richelieu* had little damage, just a bent propeller shaft and a hole in the engine-room floor. He reckoned even in that condition it could have managed at least 26 knots and would have been a serious threat to British shipping.[16] Greene, meanwhile, got information out of Vichy-run

French Guinea and from Portuguese boats smuggling diamonds through Freetown harbour. Three years into the war, Germany was running seriously short of the industrial diamonds needed for precision-tooling new weapons, including rockets. Every liner and freighter stopping in Freetown was therefore searched for diamonds and information. In *The Heart of the Matter*, Greene's anti-hero Scobie searches the captain's cabin right down 'to the squalor and intimacy of a man's suitcase'. Distasteful it might have been, but it was necessary. German spies were passing on intelligence about British shipping to German submarines. Freetown was essential to the Battle of the Atlantic. It was in a key position from which to monitor enemy movements up and down the West African coast.

Bob's flight had been doing little else but test newly assembled aircraft and fly short reconnaissance missions along the border with French Guinea when an order came from HQ to install cameras in the fuselage of one of their aircraft. To make space, compensate for the extra weight and protect the balance of the Hurricane, they took all the ammunition out of the gun bays. Bob volunteered to test-fly the aircraft as soon as it was ready. He found it had to be handled very gently or it lurched and became unstable. After a number of practice runs he found that by flying very straight and true, back and forth, he could take overlapping photographs of the ground from up to 10,000ft. He was charged with photographing some 20 square miles of land and mangrove swamp that was near the port but sufficiently far from the hills to be considered suitable for a new civil airport. Without any previous training, but with great enthusiasm and a certain relief at having a specific job to do, Bob devised a method of producing a photographic mosaic from the series of overlapping prints. It took several days and a large number of sorties to complete, but it worked. Bob became known as the local expert in aerial photography and received congratulations from Air HQ. His 'expertise' would be called upon again.

Life at the base had become very tedious. There was no action. The climate and the unhealthy location of the airfield took its toll on all but a few hardy souls. Despite vigorous anti-malarial precautions, including taking quinine tablets, the daily sickness rate rose to 50 per cent. Killy and Bob somehow escaped both malaria and dysentery. Not so the two sergeant pilots who had already had a rough time getting out to Sierra Leone on the SS *Anselm* and who had never regained their full strength. It took two near-accidents before this was properly realised.

The first incident happened when one of the pilots was airborne. He called up on the radio transmitter (RT) in a rather faint voice saying that he was feeling unwell and was returning to base. As he came in to land the ground crews were dismayed to see that instead of a normal landing, the plane was being held some 10ft above the runway until it stalled. A wing tip just missed striking the ground. The undercarriage held. A very white and shaky pilot climbed slowly out of the cockpit, helped by the crash vehicle crew that had been called out. He was feverish with a temperature of 103°F and was suffering an attack of malaria. After this incident the doctors insisted that all pilots had a daily blood sample taken and were examined for malaria. The pilot was repatriated on medical grounds soon afterwards.

The second incident was less easily explained and might have had more tragic consequences. Late one afternoon, a Hurricane was called on to make a practice interception on a friendly passenger aircraft arriving from the north. He didn't find it, so the pilot was recalled to base. He was told to look out for the passenger aircraft, a Dakota, which was now making a long, straight and low approach to the runway. The Hurricane pilot did a quick half-circuit of the airfield, lowered his undercarriage and made a steep curving approach. To those on the ground watching, including Bob, it was obvious that unless the Dakota turned away, there would be a collision. Realising the danger, the runway controller fired a Very flare as a warning. It was too late. With mounting horror, the spectators saw the Hurricane straighten up for landing just above the Dakota, which had to approach lower over a creek. Neither pilot was aware of what was happening. The Hurricane landed on top of the Dakota just as it began landing. The result was incredible. The Hurricane bounced off and landed on one side of the runway with its undercarriage broken off. The Dakota, also with a broken undercarriage, slithered to a halt in a cloud of dust. Neither aircraft caught fire. When the crash crew arrived they found nobody injured except the Hurricane pilot, who had a 6in. gash on his head. That evening the accident was summed up drily by other members of the flight: 'This was not the way to intercept a friendly aircraft.'

On 7 October 1941 the flight had 15 Hurricane Mk11s.[17] It was almost up to strength and would now be identified as 128 Fighter Squadron. The two sergeant pilots from Malta were promoted and commissioned as pilot officers. Bob was promoted to flying officer, though the news did not come through for several months. The new squadron got a new commander. John 'Killy' Kilmartin was promoted to squadron leader and sent to Air HQ in Freetown. His place was taken by an old friend of his, also a squadron leader, Billy Drake.

Billy Drake was a direct descendant of Sir Francis – the Elizabethan sea captain who famously played bowls on Plymouth Hoe before confronting the Spanish Armada.[18] Billy Drake was born in London in 1917, so he was just three years older than Bob, but from a very different background. Drake spent his early childhood in Australia, and was schooled at the French *lycée* in Tangiers and then Prior Park College in Bath, which was at the time run by ferocious Christian brothers chiefly remembered for their use of the leather strap. He described himself as a loner, given to long rides on his bicycle. His father taught him how to use a shotgun and calculate deflection. His next school was in Switzerland, run by Swiss-German Catholics. Here, Drake found himself and his country the butt of Fascistic boys' jokes. He brushed up his boxing skills and challenged every one of them.[19] He finished his formal education in a French-Swiss school in Geneva.

Ever since he had visited Alan Cobham's Flying Circus as a small boy, Drake had wanted to fly. He spent his pocket money on *Aeroplane* magazine and as soon as he was 18 he applied for the RAF. He was posted to 1 Squadron (he had left by the time Bob Allen joined) and fought in the Battle of France and the Battle of Britain with 43 Squadron, where he met Killy. He was a good shot. His boyhood spent shooting birds and understanding deflection came in handy; he soon had a record of kills: five confirmed, four probable and three damaged. It was this 25-year-old veteran who found himself bound for West Africa.

Drake arrived in Freetown on board the SS *Nakuda*, part of a large convoy en route to South Africa. He was put in charge of the booze – 2,500 bottles of gin and 2,000 bottles of whisky – a duty he says he carried out with a 'suitable degree of responsibility and seriousness'. The ship was manned as it might have been in peacetime and carried a number of women among the passengers.[20] When Drake arrived at Hastings he was dismayed. 'Hastings was a tatty runway from which we took off towards jungle covered hills. Duties were convoy protection and defence of Freetown.'[21] Billy Drake was a big personality and in no time he had his signature cartoon, a big boot aimed at a cloudburst, painted on the nose of one of the Hurricanes. He seems to have enjoyed his time socialising with Killy in Freetown, which he described as: 'Whilst a long way from the main focus of the war, it was none the less an interesting and important outpost of Empire to the observer, and I was to meet the Syrian merchant and the padre immortalised in Graham Greene's book.'[22]

There was another famous English writer in Freetown at the same time as Bob. In November 1941, Terence Rattigan was posted to 95 Squadron, the parent squadron of the Freetown Defence Flight, and subsequently to 128 Squadron. Bob's squadron. Rattigan had had a smash hit with the play *French Without Tears* and was a darling of the theatrical West End when he was struck by writer's block. He wrote nothing for three years. In response, he consulted a psychiatrist, Keith Newman, who prescribed a dose of discipline and suggested joining the RAF. Like Bob Allen, Rattigan went through basic training while the Battle of Britain raged overhead. He was accepted as an officer and trained as a rear gunner and wireless operator. He found the whole experience utterly absorbing and wrote to his psychiatrist:

'The concentration is so enormous that from the moment one fell into the plane till the moment that one jumped out and leant nonchalantly against the plane in the hope that someone on the road would think one was a fighter pilot, one was utterly and completely oblivious of one's surroundings and conscious only of that infuriating medley of knobs and dials before one's face.'[23]

Rattigan was posted to Coastal Command. As an air-gunner wireless operator he spent 12–18 hours at a time in the back of a Sunderland flying boat over the Atlantic in search of German submarines. It was a concentrated, dangerous mission for the whole crew. Many had never met a writer before. Rattigan was friendly and well-liked and proved himself as tough as anyone. He found the subject of his next play in these men – their courage, their fears and the effect of the war on their lives and those close to them – and he began writing his next play in

Calshot on the Solent while his aeroplane was grounded with bad weather. The first act was complete when they set off for West Africa, whereupon they were pounced upon by a Heinkel over the Bay of Biscay and had to put into Gibraltar for repairs. Act two was completed. Halfway into the last leg of the journey off the coast of Spanish Morocco, one of their engines died. Their only chance of avoiding internment was to fly on – in the hope of reaching the Gambia. To lighten the plane's load as much as possible they threw everything they had overboard to try to maintain height. Rattigan even tore the covers off his notebooks and stuffed the loose pages into his flying jacket. Luckily, a tailwind blew up and they made it into Bathurst (the Gambia) with two minutes of fuel left. The play's third act was written in Bathurst while they waited for repairs.

Once in Freetown, Rattigan set to making a copy of his play in longhand before sending it off to his agent with someone flying home. He found nowhere to work in private; even the officers were crowded four to a room. So he sat out on the verandah of the officers' mess and wrote there. Later he was interviewed about it by the BBC, and said:

> 'It was a verandah of a former school with monkeys
> clambering about and everybody drinking gins and tonics
> going spectacularly to pieces in the White Man's Grave – all
> of them looking over my shoulder while I wrote the thing…
> I say, Rattigan, that's not a very good line, is it.'[24]

It was Newman, the psychiatrist, who suggested a title for the play. 'It should illuminate the world … It must be called after those lights that show aeroplanes where to land – a flare path.'[25] *Flare Path* duly opened in London in August 1942, attended by a nervous Rattigan in uniform surrounded by RAF high-rankers including Air Chief Marshal Sir Charles Portal. Sir Charles liked the play. *Flare Path* was a success and ran to 670 performances. Rattigan had caught the mood of the moment. He'd also caught something of the tension in those who flew operational missions. An officer in the same squadron as Rattigan said: 'I felt it was too true. Something in me, something in all of us who had flown, was exposed ... he was talking about us, he was demonstrating us, our lives and the way we worked in war.' Rattigan used his own near-miss experience in the play:

> 'You don't know what it's like to feel frightened. You get a beastly bitter taste in the mouth, and your tongue goes dry and you feel sick, and all the time you are saying – this isn't happening – it can't be happening – I'll wake up. But you know you won't wake up ... and you pretend you're not afraid, that's what's so awful...'[26]

Much later, *Flare Path* would be the basis of a successful Hollywood film, *The Way to the Stars*. Rattigan also wrote a screenplay for *Journey Together*, made by the RAF Production Unit for Flying Training Command, which looked again at the emotional problems of very young men with ambitions to pilot aircraft and who have yet to learn the stringent disciplines involved in wartime operations.

In November 1941 Bob Allen celebrated his 21st birthday. The squadron presented him with a large wooden key, 21in. long, inscribed in blue ink: 'To Pilot Officer R Allen. Congratulations on your 21st from the Officers, NCOs and airmen of 128 Squadron.' There must have been celebrating in the mess that night, accompanied no doubt by the music hall song 'I'm 21 today' and 'For he's a jolly good fellow'. Bob leaves no record but he kept the key as a memento all his life. It was a symbol of adulthood – 21 was the age of majority, the age of consent, the age to vote, in the USA the age to drink alcohol, and the age to have a key to a house. He had now been in Sierra Leone for six months. He began to hope for a posting back home. News was slow. He could not know that Alice had been taken into hospital, the Royal Naval nursing home, with complications in her pregnancy.

Alice was living with her sister Rose and Rose's baby son in Kent, near to the rest of her family. She helped her father with his shop when he was on Home Guard duty. However, one day her face, hands and ankles became swollen. The doctors diagnosed a kidney malfunction that could endanger mother and child, and asked her permission to induce the baby. Alice's sister advised her to agree. While she was in the nursing home there were frequent air raids. One bomb exploded near the front entrance. Anti-aircraft guns seemed to clatter all night long but people slept through. In the early hours of the morning of 14 November a little girl was born. Alice arranged for a special telegram to go to Bob. She had no idea where he was. Just that it was somewhere hot. An anxious week passed as she wondered if he had received the news. Then one afternoon a telegram came:

'DARLING, WONDERFUL NEWS. TAKE CARE OF YOURSELF. LOVE TO YOU BOTH. BOBBIE.'

More days and weeks passed by. Then a letter arrived for Alice that had been posted in England by one of Bob's friends who had been detailed to ferry an aircraft back home. Bob's excitement is palpable.

'My dear wife and daughter, 27 Nov
     Your telegram came as a complete surprise and when I saw Nov. 14ᵗʰ I was amazed. That telegram took 12 days to come darling and there I was a father and didn't know it! What is she like darling and are you

O.K. my sweet? I am so anxious to hear all about it that I can hardly wait. Just think a baby girl – how much did she weigh Alice?

As you see my love I'm bubbling over with joy and, my darling, I must say thank you and well done. You have been 100% wife and I love you and love you and love you!

Let me have a photo of Suzanne Alice won't you darling and also another one of you. I must see you now darling. I hope you are just the same my love.

Oh my darling I'm just too full for words tonight and I will be a very impatient husband and father from now onwards.

All my love and kisses to you darling

from Bobbie xxxxxxx

PS The bag and material are for you my love and there is a small parcel for Rose and another for Mum

A big hug to Suzanne from her proud father.'

It would be more than a year before Bob would see his daughter.

Thousands of miles away, in a location secret from his family, Bob was engaged in the camera tests on the Hurricane I and testing out the new Hurricane IIs that had arrived with Billy Drake. Now that there were so many RAF crew, they moved out of the naval station into their own quarters. Though it was quiet, they remained on standby as the enemy, the Vichy French, attempted an occasional reconnaissance of their airfields or the port. The French had American Glenn Martin 167F attack bombers based in Dakar. They were fast enough and had the range to reach Freetown. One morning, an intruder was spotted by Sgt Todd in the vicinity of Port Loko. He chased after it. Bob Allen was sent after him and could report that it had been pursued back to Conakry in Vichy-controlled French

Guinea. Conakry had two aerodromes, a landing strip, new hangars under construction and a large concentration of enemy fighters. Todd returned to Hastings airfield with just 5 gallons of fuel left. But that was not the end of the incident.

A couple of hours later they heard gunfire. Bob was scrambled again and describes climbing to 10,000ft up-sun of the reported gunfire. He continued to patrol but saw nothing. His CO Billy Drake takes up the story:

'On 13 December 1941 – a Sunday, as I recall – I had been scrambled on the approach of one such intruder, and was patrolling over the harbour when he appeared, I flew up alongside him and indicated that he should land at our airfield, which he refused to do. This left me no alternative but to do my stuff, and shoot him down – which I did, although I did not like having to do so at all.'[27]

There were no further fatal incidents before Drake was posted to the Middle East in March 1942. From there he was posted to a Kittyhawk squadron as a supernumerary. The Americans copied the British by painting a shark insignia on their aeroplanes. Drake was for evermore called 'Shark leader'. On his departure, 128 Squadron was handed back to 'Killy' Kilmartin.

By January 1942 there were 392 men in 128 Squadron: 31 officers, one warrant officer, five flight sergeants, 75 sergeants, 262 other ranks and 65 civilians. Army co-operation had been added to their duties. The field at Hastings was too short for most aircraft to land on. The outlying hills inhibited large transport planes, so another airfield was built at Waterloo, 20 miles east of Freetown. All these activities, including the expansion of the port at Freetown, involved the recruitment of large numbers of local men and women. An intelligence report worried about security. At times there might be 8,000 labourers around the aerodrome at Hastings. The hangars, petrol stores and other important buildings were guarded by native troops or naval ratings but they were not equipped to deal with sabotage or large-scale insurgencies. Several attempts had been made by 'native labour to cause minor riots and disturbances – usually when they feel they have a grievance over wages or at being paid off by the Contractors'.[28] The report said the contractors were held at bay with sticks and brickbats. There were suspicions that several houses were deliberately set on fire in the village of Hastings, but nothing was proven. There was a risk, it was thought, that if the locals were properly organised they would be capable of attacking the aerodrome from several directions during the dry season (November to March) when surrounding creeks were not flooded. The RAF and naval personnel were on the alert for trouble.

There was always information to be traded. Labourers were brought by train or bus to Hastings from Freetown each day, so there was plenty of opportunity to report back movements of aircraft or general information about the station. In the port 'the native grapevine' acted as a speedy and efficient telegraph, getting reports as far as Dakar. Ill-advised chat at the City Hotel bar leaked information on ship movements and convoys. Local servants seemed to be able to find out when the latest convoy was due to arrive. The Europeans tucked up on the hill or out in the stations had little idea or little interest in the impact caused by the war and their presence on the country they had colonised.

During the time that Bob spent in West Africa, every part of the economy was mobilised to support the war effort. Most of the countries were dependent on commodity prices. Money poured in. Black markets flourished. There was a massive increase in the cost of living. Then, in 1942, the rains failed.[29] From the outbreak of war the colonies had been expected to support the Imperial government by raising taxes, limiting imports and providing shipping. Sierra Leone co-operated by contributing to the expense of the new infrastructure, the port area, roads, railways and airfields. The government withdrew peasants from farms and plantations to put them into construction. There was plenty of scope for unrest. Major grievances included low pay, long hours, unfair treatment, poor medical attention and compulsory overtime. Within months, however, all the labour leaders and trade unionists had been arrested.

Agricultural products were subject to centralised purchase and export through a Control Board. Rice, a staple foodstuff, was subject to quotas. Productivity dropped. Feeding the thousands of troops and labourers in the city was a problem.[30] By 1942–43, the shortage of rice was so severe that many labourers were malnourished and could not physically work hard all day. Freetown had 10,000 labourers in 1939; by 1943 there were 45,000. The sheer numbers put a huge strain on accommodation. Governor Stevenson wanted a Military Labour Corps. 'I am appalled at the standard of labour in Freetown at present. I have watched a number of gangs engaged in different work and all were moving and working so slowly that it was obvious that they were deliberately making an effort to do as little work as possible.' Lord Swinton reported that port labour in Freetown was 'a study of African still life'. Maybe it was just too hot and they were just too malnourished. There were many desertions, especially in the farming season; several hundred men sleeping on the streets of Bathurst were press-ganged into the army in November 1942.[31]

Rattigan doesn't say much about his experience in Sierra Leone. He enjoyed the flying but not the climate in Freetown. He wrote that the flying was a relief:

'It does at least get me out of this spot, which is, to put it frankly, torture … Infested not only by 95 Squadron but by lizards, giant spiders, giant centipedes, mosquitoes (not giant but not any the less pleasant), bats, bugs that nest under your

skin and a particularly delightful monkey … the town itself
is better not visited and certainly there is no reason to do so,
although it boasts of one Officers' club and one brothel.'[32]

He was also alarmed by how quickly his manners slipped. When
recalling how he spoke to his servant, he says:

'After a few days of "I say would you mind awfully" etc. I
have now firmly descended to "Fetchem master's shaving
water plenty chop chop or master whip black boy's hide
plenty bloody quick". Even then the shaving water is not
brought unless the treat is accompanied by the gift of a small
coin – necessarily small because the recipient has stolen all
the larger coins already.'[33]

Graham Greene, who wrote so disparagingly about the white
colonials, has Scobie say: 'This isn't the climate for emotion.
It's a climate for meanness, malice and snobbery.' 'Greeneland'
as Greene's West Africa has been called – with its prostitutes,
thieves and men on the make – is not evident in the accounts
of servicemen who spent a few months or even a year or so in
the country. There were things to like. Greene 'loved' Africa …
the Africa of the exotic, chiefs, witch doctors, bush schools and
spirits. By contrast, when he returned to Britain, Bob Allen never
talked of his time in Africa save to mention the sweetness of the
paw-paw (fruit). However, he did bring home with him a book,
White Africans and Black, filled with drawings of the different
peoples of West Africa,[34] whose authors sought to convey the
beauty, dignity and intelligence of the African peoples.

Bob had few opportunities to go upcountry but on one
occasion he took the road to Marampa. This was little more than
a dusty track through forests of palm trees and 10ft-high sword
grass. They came to a river with a pull-ferry. Marampa was home

to a Mende chief, and court officials wore red fezzes and black coats with brass buttons. There was food aplenty, including eggs, ducks and chickens, fruit and local cloths and silks. In honour of the visitors, tom-tom drums beat all night.[35]

The seasonal rhythms of Sierra Leone's customary life persisted, albeit in a reduced form. November is a time for singing, dancing, cool weather, green land. Yams ready to harvest as well as ginger and cocoa, a time for feasting, rejoicing and gaiety. December is the marriage month. January is devoted to house-building. February to tree-felling and burning. April to sowing. May is when the rains begin again. The young pilots waiting on standby or practising chases, formation flying and aerobatics grew increasingly restless. At the end of January, two aircraft carrying Killy Kilmartin and Bob Allen flew to Bathurst, where they spent a few days attached to 200 Squadron at Jeswang. It was their first time out of Sierra Leone in nine months. It would be the first of several trips 'up north' for Bob, which would lead him into a whole new experience, a new phase of operations for which he had already shown some aptitude – photo reconnaissance.

4

Eyes in the sky

I N 1938, COLONEL-GENERAL OF the German Army, Generaloberst Werner von Fritsch, forecast: 'The military organisation which has the most efficient reconnaissance unit will win the next war.'[1]

Bob and the Hurricanes of 95 Squadron (now renumbered 128 Squadron) had been in West Africa for six months before their reconnaissance flights involved photography. The value of getting pictures from the air had been proved in World War I, when it was used as tactical intelligence to guide and spot artillery. Its use in strategic planning, however, was yet to be realised. There was no particular need for this in Freetown, but further north, where the enemy had airfields and ports, photographic evidence of planes, ships and troops could prove invaluable. The Hurricanes were out of range from Freetown. So, Killy Kilmartin and Bob Allen were sent on two weeks' forward reconnaissance to Hastings in the Gambia, where they were within 60 miles of the enemy in Dakar. When they arrived back in Freetown they had new orders. For the next six months they were to prepare pilots and aircraft for their new task, since photographic reconnaissance was in its infancy; there was much to learn.

Between the wars, every country with a sizeable army had someone lobbying for more funds for research and deployment of aerial reconnaissance. In Britain, the RAF had Wg Cdr Frederick Winterbotham, chief of air intelligence in the Secret Service.

In the late 1930s, he had recruited Frederick Cotton, an Australian pilot with experience of photo reconnaissance in World War I, to take clandestine aerial photographs of the German military build-up. Cotton was by this time a wealthy film producer with his own aircraft. On the eve of war, pretending that he was looking for film locations, he overflew German military airfields with a senior Luftwaffe officer, Albert Kesselring, at the controls, while he took photos with a concealed camera.[2]

With the outbreak of war, Cotton joined the RAF as a wing commander and headed 1 Photographic Development Unit (PDU) flying Blenheims at Heston Aerodrome near the present Heathrow airport. Later, the whole unit would move to Benson in Oxfordshire. Nicknamed 'Cotton's Club' they pioneered high-altitude, high-speed stereoscopic photography. A young flight lieutenant, Maurice Longbottom, was one of the unit. In August 1939, Longbottom produced a remarkable memorandum on the value of strategic reconnaissance. He suggested that using a single light bomber such as the Blenheim was extremely dangerous as it was too slow. What they needed was a specially adapted Spitfire that could outrun enemy fighters. Air Chief Marshal Dowding, facing the immense demands of the Battle of Britain, reluctantly gave them two Spitfires. The precious Spitfires were stripped of all 'unnecessary' equipment, including armament. The engines were modified to allow climbs to 40,000ft. Cockpit visibility was improved. Various paint colours – pale pink, light blue, duck-egg green – were tried out for the best sky-camouflage, until eventually dark blue was chosen. Extra fuel tanks were fitted. Two F24 cameras with 5in. lenses were mounted in the wings and synchronised to provide overlapping photos.[3] By 26 January 1940, one of these Spitfires had photographed 5,000 square miles of enemy territory. It was a huge success. When they had used Blenheims they'd lost 16 aircraft covering just half that area. Nonetheless, even with

Spitfires there were problems. At high altitudes the cameras froze, lenses fogged and film cracked. Then there was the whole business of interpretation. What did the photos reveal?

In Britain, a Central Intelligence Unit had been set up in a country house in Medmenham, Buckinghamshire, to 'derive strategic intelligence from reconnaissance photography'.[4] The interpreters scrutinised pairs of vertical photos through a stereoscope that made buildings and other objects stand out in 3D. Shadows helped them to calculate height. Together with the code breakers at Bletchley Park, the photo interpreters provided the chiefs of staff with intelligence throughout the war. They depended on the efforts of pilots and aircrew who flew the missions. Flying alone. Flying high where the air was cold. Flying without radio contact, with just a map and a compass, deep into enemy territory. Finding the target and then getting safely home. They might be above cloud for hours or have to burn fuel flying zigzags to avoid being spotted. At 35,000ft it was freezing and oxygen was low. They must not leave a telltale contrail (the condensation left behind the aircraft).[5] It was dangerous work and required rather special talents from the pilots. Bob proved to have the talent to be one of them.

Photo reconnaissance was first used in West Africa during the abortive Operation *Menace* –a joint British and Free French attempt to persuade Dakar to join the Allied cause, which took place before Bob arrived in West Africa. The expedition included four French airmen photographers equipped with RAF F24 cameras and a J-type photographic trailer with the equipment for developing and printing the negatives. They all set out in HMS *Pennland* on 30 August 1940. When the mission failed, the *Pennland* continued to Nigeria, where the photographers were transferred to another ship to take them to Doula in the French Cameroons, one of the few colonies to commit to the Free rather than Vichy French. The photographer in charge was Bernard Lefebvre.[6]

The trailer was supposed to have air conditioning but it didn't work. It was so hot the film melted. Despite these problems, the Free French maintained two reconnaissance squadrons in French Equatorial Africa throughout the war.

In early 1941 the RAF equipped the Sunderland flying boats of 95 Squadron with cameras and established an interpretation unit in Freetown under the command of Gp Capt Ronald H. Carter from the Central Intelligence Unit back home.[7] A proper photographic system was set up, with interpreters in both Sierra Leone and the Gambia. It was as unpleasant as it had been for Lefebvre in the Cameroons. They had to work in sweltering dark rooms without air conditioning in 100 per cent humidity. They were plagued by insects and threatened with malaria and yellow fever. Food was poor quality and few events disturbed the monotony. The average posting was restricted to three months. Despite the conditions, though, they produced good results.

Carter wanted to replace the Sunderlands with Hudsons. He got them in March 1942, attached to 200 Squadron in the Gambia. Meanwhile, two Hurricanes were converted and began work. Bob Allen was one of the pilots who flew from Sierra Leone to the Gambia in a DC3.

The Gambia is a slip of a country following the contours of a wide river between Senegal and the Portuguese neutral colony of Guinea Bissau. The Gambia had been granted to the British in 1816 to keep control of the slave trade. It would be decades before the story of Kunta Kinte and the heritage of so many black Americans was made famous by Alex Haley in his book *Roots*. The Gambia he describes – the seasons rainy and dry, the women farming rice, men farming groundnuts and couscous, the gentle Muslim headmen in white robes and pillbox hats – was the rural Gambia of World War II.[8] Bathurst, now Banjul, was the main town. Surrounded by saltwater wetlands and mudflats, it had none of the sophistication of colonial Freetown. In 1942, settlements in the town reflected its early history. Descendants of the West Indian Regiments and Royal Africa Corps lived in Soldier Town, with artisans and mechanics from the Wolof ethnic group in Jollof Town, the Akus group in Melville, and mulatto descendants of mixed African/Portuguese heritage in Portuguese Town. The poorest and migrant labourers tended to be found in Half-Die Bay, named after a cholera epidemic in 1869. It was a spur of land at the mouth of the Gambia River. This was where the Sunderlands were based, and where Bob and Killy would be accommodated.

Sunderlands were known as the 'queen of boats'. They had been adapted from C-Class Empire flying boats operated by Imperial Airways. Their main role was in coastal command, guarding merchant shipping, seeking U-boats. Because of the power-operated gun turret the Germans called it 'the flying porcupine'.[9] They were first built in Gillingham, Bob Allen's home town, and flown out of nearby Rochester to destinations around the world. The Gambia was one of the more uncomfortable of these. Crews of the Sunderland flying boats were called 'web-footed warriors'. They lived on board.[10] A crew of between seven and 11. Eating and sleeping. Flying and patrolling for hour after hour.

At Half-Die Bay they used the SS *Dumana* and the SS *Manela* as planning rooms and for additional accommodation. Bob and Killy stayed on the ship while in Bathurst. Nothing could mitigate the climate. Rainfall of 50in. Temperature up to 105°F. For six months there was rain every day with fogs and huge storms out at sea. Then from June to October it was dry, very dry. The ground like talcum powder. An easterly harmattan wind blowing dust up to 10,000ft. Visibility reduced to a few hundred feet so pilots were forced to fly on instruments only, even in daytime. Aircraft became too hot to touch so maintenance crews had to work in the very early morning and late evening.

Fuel evaporated. Ground crews complained about the terrible conditions, especially the food. 'No fruit and veg, only peanuts,' said airman Derek Anderson. 'Stinking heat day and night, permanently damp kit, never ending sweats, work and more work. Nowhere to go off-duty. Water getting into everything. Never dry.'[11]

Most of the time the flying boats went on patrol and saw nothing. When there was action it came suddenly. In September 1941, Fg Off Ken Dart was the skipper on a recce of the north-west of Dakar. He passed the coast at zero altitude, crossed a main road and almost ran into the Vichy French battleship *Richelieu* and a cruiser moored in the harbour. He flew over the town at rooftop height to avoid the fire from the warships and got caught by four fighters. Dart managed to get home and beach his plane. The crew escaped but the plane had 74 bullet holes, a punctured fuel tank and a smashed rear turret. Dart was awarded the DFC.[12]

By 1942, the need to protect Atlantic convoys and keep an eye on the Vichy French was urgent. However, the Sunderland production line in Belfast was hit by strikes and threats of strikes. In response, the RAF commissioned a new light bomber ideal for coastal reconnaissance – the Hudson.

The Hudson had originally been designed as an airliner by Lockheed. It was adapted for its wartime maritime role in a remarkable co-operation between the British Purchasing Commission and the relatively new American company. The RAF wanted the planes now. Plans and details on armament were carried between continents in the diplomatic bag. Agreement on the design was achieved within 80 hours. Within months it was on the production line and hundreds were being made. The Hudson swiftly became the aircraft for Coastal Command worldwide.[13] It was big: 44ft long with a wingspan of 65ft and it took a crew of five. It had a range of 1,700 nautical miles and a ceiling of

24,500ft. Pilots liked it because it was manoeuvrable and had a tight turning circle. They named it the 'old boomerang' for its ability to survive enemy fire and return home safely.

Hudsons were also used for photo reconnaissance. In the Gambia, the Hudsons of 200 Squadron had their base at Jeswang, just a few miles from Bathurst – an airfield modified from a civilian landing ground. While he was there, Bob co-piloted a Hudson on convoy patrol. They were now close enough to Dakar to appreciate the threat of enemy naval vessels and aircraft taking off from any one of the 30-odd airfields or landing strips in Vichy control. The Hudsons were just too slow; they needed fighter aircraft, preferably Hurricanes.

In February 1942 Bob recorded in his flying logbook: 'Photo-recco 14,000 with "F" of French Senegal landing grounds Sealion –Zuguchmor-Bignona.'[14] 'Sealion' refers to the aborted German invasion plans for taking England in 1940. 'Zuguchmor' is correctly spelled 'Ziguinchor'. These were towns in the Casamance area of Senegal, south of the Gambia River. It seemed likely that a new invasion plan was being prepared for the Gambia and there was some anxiety about military build-up. The British airfields in the Gambia were surrounded. It would be a few months before the squadron of Hurricanes arrived.

Meanwhile, Bob and Killy flew back to Hastings, Sierra Leone. Being back at home base felt like a rest cure and they were supplied with good food and plenty of duty-free drinks by the Royal Navy. Bob even had time to write home.

Saturday May 2nd 1942
My dear, darling wife Alice,
Saturday evening once more! One of those evenings when I just sit and think of all the glorious Saturdays that have passed; of Rugby in the afternoon or cricket – with tea at your house or straight to the pictures and

a late supper and of the tender goodnights with both of us feeling so weary yet happy to the last degree.

I think darling that you have a convinced sentimentalist for a husband but I know that my wife is the same so I don't care at all.

As I sit in my room tonight – long sleeved shirt and long trousers on, with perspiration running down my back, I look back with envious thoughts on those long walks we used to take when we were both at school; nights when we snuggled together for warmth and our noses went dead with cold. Nights when every star in the heavens was lit for our benefit.

It's strange how one remembers details so clearly. Tonight for instance, a thousand separate incidents are running through my mind, each of them so clear as if we had a cine camera record of each of them. I could ramble on and on tonight sweetheart but I know that you have an echo for all my memories.

One of my most precious memories is that night when for the first time in my life I knew the answer to all those irresistable impulses which govern a man's life. I don't know how you felt my dear, but I know that I felt as if I had just started to live.

Even as great as our love was in those days Alice darling, it is a thousandfold more at this moment. My heart is longing for the moment when yours will be beating against it, with my arms around you and all our desires and emotions satisfied.

I expect you realise that tonight my darling I am writing to you for companionship; my nerves seem to be strained to the breaking point and I have to pour my heart and soul out to you to prevent myself from screaming out aloud. I expect you think that I an a nitwit darling talking like this but it's just the natural reaction to this bloody hole! Physically I seem to be as sound as a bell, but very often the craving for your company reaches the utmost limits. I felt the old Saturday evening feeling coming on before dinner and as the only cure is to either drink myself into another mood or write a passionate love letter to you, I chose the latter.

It's not very often that I write to you solely in this strain but tonight, my dear love, I feel my love for you in such a manner that it is useless to try to prevent myself writing down anything that enters my mind.

I do hope that you receive this letter when you are feeling sentimental my sweet, perhaps just before you are going to bed so that you can read it and sleep with it close to your heart. Oh my darling, I love you with a determination that knows no limits; to me you are the queen of my world.

I will close this short, but most sincere letter with my love and kisses from your everloving sweetheart, husband and pal

Bobbie

P.S. I feel a hundred times better after writing to you darling.

News had been arriving from England – subject to official censorship and to sincere attempts to reassure loved ones far away. Alice and baby Suzanne continued to live with Alice's sister Rose and her baby son, Alan. Rose's husband, Hector, was in the Navy. The arrangement suited both sisters and they were close enough to the rest of the family. Their youngest sister, Joan, arrived in her ATS uniform with news of the raids on London. The House of Commons had been hit. The people of London were sticking it out. Helping each other. Planes passed over their house. When there was an air-raid alert, Rose took her son down to the Morrison shelter but Alice preferred to stay upstairs. She often slept through a night of air raids. She discussed the war with her father. They both felt that if help didn't come soon Britain would be starved out. These were not matters to be shared with a husband in danger somewhere out there in a hot country. They hoped that the inclement posting might mean that Bob would be back home soon.

The general upheaval of the war meant that there were plenty of furnished houses to let for short periods. Alice began to look for a home of her own. She found one belonging to a pilot who had been posted to Rhodesia. It was just under a mile from Rose and it backed on to a golf course. It was her first home as a married woman with a child. She would have to wait many months before Bob could share it with them.

One day there was terrible news. Rose received a telegram from the Admiralty saying that Hector was posted 'missing, presumed killed at sea'.[15] Rose was devastated, almost to the point of collapse. After the first shock she seemed not to recognise the information. She spoke about the time Hector would come home, clinging on to the phrase 'missing'. Maybe he would be found as a prisoner of war. Later, the confirmation of his death was equally shocking. Hector had been in the engine room of the cruiser when it was hit by a torpedo. He had been blown to bits. A friend of Hector had been on the ship, which though damaged had managed to limp into port. There could be no doubt. Hector, one of the gentlest of men, had been 'blown to bits'. It was too much for Rose to hear. The trauma of war bore a heavy cost among the innocent. When Alice wrote to Bob she stuck to the original report, 'missing presumed killed'. She feared for the day these dread words might come to her.

During May 1942, Bob was required to take a Hurricane from Jeswang to photograph Dakar harbour. He met enemy aircraft and flak on almost every outing. He dubbed the operation the 'milk run' since the best time of day for getting good, clear photographs was early in the morning. He went out every day for a week. Same place, same time. The request from intelligence was for medium-level shots of the harbour and its nearby airfields. The Hurricane was not ideal for the task since it had two downward-facing cameras in the fuselage and no guns. Above 10,000ft it could ignore flak from the ground or sea but it would never be able to evade fast fighters coming from the air. The cameras made the plane unstable in a tight turn. Bob was hoping to set out before dawn but the specialists wanted the photographs within two hours of dawn. He set out at 7.30am and headed north. It would take 40 minutes to arrive. He flew at low level to avoid radar. Then, as he neared the target, he climbed to 15,000ft and, approaching from the north, swept into a shallow dive to level out across the airfields and port with both cameras running in a straight line at 12,000ft. Time over target: ten minutes. While the cameras were turning he had to fly on instruments to keep a steady course and height. His only hope if he was intercepted was to dive, increase speed and hope to outrun his pursuers.

On the first run he completely forgot about the flak and fighters. He was checking his instruments for the home run when he turned to see if there had been any reaction to his fly-past. He was down-sun and had a perfect view of the shipping, including warships in the harbour. There were big puffs of black smoke. It took but a second to realise that he was being fired at by heavy anti-aircraft guns on the battleship. It was of course the *Richelieu*. What about fighter planes? Suddenly he felt very vulnerable. They must have seen him. His mission was complete. He needed to get the hell out of it. He turned his aircraft towards home, lowered the nose and let speed build up until he was flying very fast at wave-top level. He remembered chasing enemy planes when he was with 1 Squadron. Was he being hunted? Keeping low, he cautiously turned first one way and then the other to see if he was being pursued. Nothing. Half an hour later he flew over some native fishing boats. They were waving. Or were they shaking their fists? Whether friendly or not, they were people close to home. He relaxed a little. It had been a lonely, vulnerable run home. Elated to see his airfield, he managed to curb the impulse to fly low and perform some aerobatics to announce his safe return. He landed instead, and was met by a special vehicle sent from the Photographic Unit, which would process and interpret the photos. Some hours later, Bob received a phone call. The mission was a complete success. The cover was perfect. The photographs were of good quality. And, by the way, could he repeat the mission the following morning...

Not surprisingly, Bob's annual report for that year noted that he was 'an above average fighter pilot'. By that time he had been in Sierra Leone a year. He had high expectations of being sent home. It was not to be. Instead, when the new Hurricanes arrived he was promoted to flight lieutenant and put in charge of B Flight. It was a surprise as he had only just been made a pilot officer. At this time, 128 Squadron was still based at Hastings near Freetown with two or sometimes four aircraft on detachment to Jeswang in the Gambia. It was on one of his last sorties from Hastings that Bob once more confronted the enemy, and scored a fatal hit. The story of war in the air is unlike any other for it is a ruthless personal combat, man versus man, machine versus machine, man versus death. As J. R. D. Braham wrote, 'It was the most exciting, dangerous and highly skilled form of duelling ever devised.'[16] Out in West Africa there were few opportunities to 'duel in the sky', yet every encounter with the enemy was potentially lethal.

11 October 1942. It was an ordinary afternoon. Bob was on standby with another pilot when they heard 'Scramble'. Radar

had picked up an unidentified aircraft approaching the port from the north – where the enemy reconnaissance aircraft were based. Almost as soon as he was airborne, Bob's RT crackled into life and he was told there was an unidentified aircraft over the harbour. Looking around desperately, he caught sight of a twin-engined aircraft several feet above him. He turned and climbed at full power, followed by his number two. As he turned, so did the enemy, which dived across in front of them. Bob recognised it as a Vichy Glenn Martin, the same mark as a hostile recce aircraft they had shot down the year before. He turned again and gave chase. The intruder was faster as it continued to dive. Bob fired several bursts at long range. The fleeing aircraft had reached the wave tops and appeared undamaged. Bob pulled his throttle to override – allowing the engine to exceed its normal limits – and gradually began to gain. It was some 15 minutes before he was able to creep within close firing range.

He was now alone with the enemy. His number two radioed that he had to return to base with engine trouble. Bob did not acknowledge. His whole attention was on the aircraft in front of him, which had crossed Freetown harbour, seen what was there and photographed it. He was determined that they should not escape. He was so close that the plane's wingspan filled his windscreen. Easing his Hurricane out of the slipstream and steadying it so that the optical gunsight covered the target, he pressed the firing button on the control column. There was a dull thud. To his astonishment and fury, nothing happened. No guns fired. He tried again and again with no result. He must have used all his ammunition earlier in the chase. By now he was speedy enough to overtake his quarry. He tried to force him into the sea by flying his aircraft almost on top of him. When this did not succeed he dropped behind and even considered touching the tailplane with his propellor. Luckily, common sense prevailed over blind frustration and he broke away. As he did so he noticed an inert figure in red-and-white overalls in the rear enclosed cockpit of the enemy plane.

Once he had given up the chase, Bob began to think about getting safely back to base. His engine, used under prolonged emergency power, had overheated badly. His fuel gauges, which he had disregarded, showed that it would be touch and go whether he managed to get back. He throttled back to the most economical cruising power setting and climbed gently in the general direction of the base in the hope of catching a homing signal. His blind determination to catch the enemy had pushed his aircraft to its limit. The thought of running out of fuel and crash-landing in failing light either in a jungle clearing or on a sandy beach or, worse still, having to take to his parachute while his aircraft crashed into the sea or jungle sent cold shivers down his somewhat overheated spine. It was a subdued Bob who, with the aid of homing bearings received over his RT, thankfully sighted his airfield and landed with both his fuel tanks reading zero. The ground crew could see that his guns had been fired. They took off the covers and saw that the guns had not fired at the critical moment because of a malfunction. There was at least half the ammunition to each gun left in the wing. Bob felt sick. So near and yet. When he was debriefed by the intelligence officer he mentioned that the rear gunner might have been killed or wounded. There was no return fire even when they were very close. That evening Bob didn't feel like celebrating. He felt he had missed an opportunity to make his reputation; he had been close enough to see the man he had killed or injured. He had to admire his opponent, though – the pilot who had handled his aircraft with skill and determination.

Several days later a report came through intelligence sources that a senior Vichy officer, flying as an observer on a reconnaissance

Bob Allen aged 18.

Bob joins up in April 1940 aged 19.

Bob Allen (far left) with fellow trainees in the mess during flying training in 1940.

Bob and his wife Alice in 1941. This is the first photograph of him wearing his wings.

Hurricanes being removed from their crate on arrival in West Africa in 1941.

Bob and fellow airmen in West Africa in 1941.

One of Bob's photographs of a village in Sierra Leone, West Africa, 1941.

Bob and Killy Kilmartin wearing their inflatable vests. Sierra Leone, 1941.

A Hurricane preparing for take-off at Hastings, Sierra Leone, 1942.

95 Squadron's Short Sunderland moored up in the Gambia river.

SINGLE-ENGINE AIRCRAFT				MULTI-ENGINE AIRCRAFT						PA
DAY		NIGHT		DAY			NIGHT			ENG
DUAL	PILOT	DUAL	PILOT	DUAL	1ST PILOT	2ND PILOT	DUAL	1ST PILOT	2ND PILOT	
(1)	(2)	(3)	(4)	(5)	(6)	(7)	(8)	(9)	(10)	(11)
10	210·15			31·35	38·00	6·05	2·40	2·10		8·05
	·25									
	1·20	P. R.	Dakar							
	3									3·00
	·35									
	·45									
	1·00									
	16·50									
·40	214·20			31·35	38·00	6·05	2·40	2·10		11·05
(1)	(2)	(3)	(4)	(5)	(6)	(7)	(8)	(9)	(10)	(11)

Complimented personally by
on results of all Dakar so

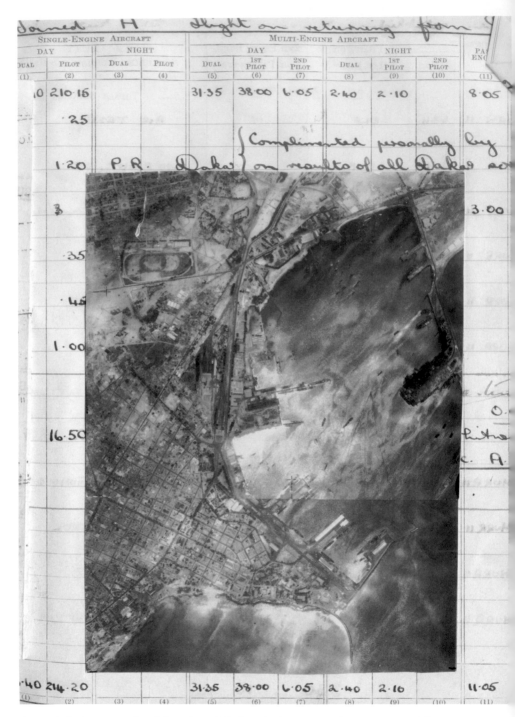

An aerial photograph of the city of Dakar, in Senegal, taken on an aerial
reconnaisance mission in 1941.

Billy Drake with his aircraft showing his emblem of a great boot aimed at a cloud burst.

Killy Kilmartin in his Hurricane, Jeswang, the Gambia, 1942.

Bob, baby Suzanne and Alice in 1943.

Bob talking to workers on a factory visit in 1943.

mission, had been killed in an air battle over Freetown harbour and had been buried with full military honours. The pilot who had managed to get his damaged aircraft home with a VIP dead on board reported that a mad British pilot had tried to force him into the sea. Bob's daring moment was effective. It was a long time before the enemy was seen reconnoitering the airfield or the harbour again.

Bob would not be in Sierra Leone for much longer. Soon after he took over B Flight he heard that half the squadron was to be posted to the Gambia on an operational photographic mission. Bob immediately volunteered and his offer was accepted. There was much to be done. More aircraft had to be converted to take cameras, long-range tanks needed to be installed and tested, and all the other detailed preparations undertaken to ensure a successful transfer to the new base had to be made. They left on 31 October, with Bob leading four aircraft north over the sea past neutral and hostile territory. He was familiar with their destination but it was the first time he had made such a long flight with responsibility for other aircraft. He was quite apprehensive. Fortunately, the weather was perfect. He flew nearer to the coast of neutral Guinea Bissau than planned in order to check on his navigation. There were no incidents. With some relief he sighted Jeswang, his destination. He called his flight into close formation and swept across the runway of their new home at low level before breaking formation to complete the usual fighter 'stream landing'. This was not appreciated by the resident Coastal Command squadron. As he climbed out of his cockpit, Bob was greeted by a red-faced wing commander and berated for flying in formation over the airfield while the Air Officer Commanding (AOC) was making an inspection. And what the hell did he think he was playing at landing more than one aircraft at a time on the runway. 'Glory be,' thought Bob, 'what a reception.'[17]

It was soon clear that life at the new airfield would be pretty uncomfortable. All the men were accommodated in tents with minimal camp-type furniture. Washing facilities were primitive. A daily shower consisted of standing under a 4-gallon tin can, previously used for transporting petrol, filled with cold water that sprinkled through holes pierced in the bottom. The officers' mess was a dilapidated building that had once been a garage. It was nothing more than a tin-roofed hut with a concrete floor, furnished with trestle tables and wooden chairs. Worst of all was the food. It consisted of army rations made worse by poor preparation and cooking by some of the local people employed to assist one or two ill-trained, sullen RAF cooks. Bob's ground crew, who had been flown ahead in a transport plane, appeared to be better off. They too were housed in tents but there were some reasonably fly-proofed huts that served as messes for the senior non-commissioned officers and airmen. Fortunately, the rains had stopped, but it was now the season of heat and dust. Compared to their home base with its links to HMS *Spurwing*, it was grim. But for Bob, given his first command at the age of 21, it was an exciting time – a chance to exercise leadership and management without the day-to-day supervision of his squadron commander.

He wrote home in October:

My dear wife Alice,
    Hello my darling this is the first ime I have written to you for approximately 10–14 days – and the reason being that we were under orders for home and have been retained for the time being. Thank God I didn't rush off and send that long awaited telegram or else your hopes would have been raised as mine were and then dashed. I can't tell you the reason for the postponement my darling but I have been promised that it will be for another month only.

Please don't worry about me dear love because I am
still very fit and well. I'm very busy, even more than
ever before but am doing my job as a Flight Lieutenant
to the best of my ability and as far as I know to
everybody's satisfaction. I feel very unhappy to think
my darling that you are worried so keep your chin up
my dear and let me know that you are smiling because
then I can carry on here with a contented mind.

I have been receiving your mail very regularly my
dear and was very unhappy when I heard of Hector's
death. Poor Rose! Please convey my deepest regards
and sympathies my dear. The only thing that is
keeping me going my love is to know that very soon I
shall be in your arms again kissing you and loving as
we did before. Oh my darling how I long for you to be
by my side when I go to bed so that I could kiss you
and cuddle until we both fall asleep in the ecstasy of
knowing that we were one again.

Please give Suzanne a big hug for me darling and
tell her that Daddy won't be long now and God willing
we shall all three be together for Christmas. I'd love
to have at least one Xmas pud! I haven't had time to
write to mum as well my darling but please give her
all the news and say that I will write as soon as I can.
I am so tired tonight that I can hardly see the paper so
I think I will roll into bed very soon.

Goodnight my dear darling wife sleep with this
next to your heart and you will feel me close to you.
Goodnight and God Bless, Bobbie xxx

Alice read this letter with mixed feelings. It was sweet and
comforting, but Bob had been away for such a long time.
Suzanne had had her first birthday without meeting her father;

Alice resigned herself to planning another Christmas without him. The government approved extra rations, including sultanas and raisins. She made a small cake. One evening, there was a knock at the door. Her brother, Bill, stood smiling down at her. He was a lieutenant in the Royal Navy. He had gone away – goodness knows where – at the same time as Bob. When the men came home they said nothing of where they had been, what they had been doing or what they had experienced. Alice knew that his ship had seen action in the Mediterranean but after that… Now Bill beamed at his niece Suzanne, declared her a beauty and Bob a lucky chap. He had a daughter of his own, whom he had seen only once as a tiny baby. He was anxious about his sister Rose, who was still shocked with grief. They went to see her. Bill didn't know when he would be home again. The family, five sisters living within a mile or two of the parents, planned Christmas lunch hoping that their men – son, uncle, brother, husband, father – might be back home. Some had been at war for three years already.

Bob had no time to think about Christmas. After his initial, less-than-friendly reception by the station commander at Jeswang, he got on well with the resident Coastal Command Squadron whose crew included members of British, New Zealand and Australian air forces. Bob's operational task was to maintain at least two Hurricanes on readiness during daylight hours to defend the base and to fly photographic missions over the surrounding 'hostile' territory. The biggest threat was Dakar, with its heavily defended naval base and several airfields. Defence was 'more of a joke' because they had no radar. But they could put on a show. The very next day a twin-engined reconnaissance plane flew across their airfield before either of the standby fighters could get airborne. So now the enemy knew they had arrived. The risk of being intercepted and shot down made each mission highly dangerous.

There was much speculation among the pilots about future missions. What could they expect when they overflew a harbour that contained a hostile battleship, two cruisers, a number of destroyers and submarines, and shore batteries with anti-aircraft guns? Bob had been there. He knew. He took the first sortie. It was the 'milk run' once again. From 1 November he overflew Dakar harbour every day. In fact, he was told that until further notice a daily sortie over the port and airfields would be required. It was a huge risk to Bob and the two other pilots who flew the photo reconnaissance runs. They were not told why it was so important, just that intelligence needed to know of any overnight movements, especially of warships, battleships and submarines, so they could be detected as early as possible each day. The anti-aircraft fire became increasingly accurate, so Bob began to vary the height over the target to make the anti-aircraft gunner's task more difficult. Intelligence declared that the photos were of 'even better quality'. And no one got shot down.

Unknown to Bob and his pilots in West Africa, their daily 'milk' run was part of an Allied operation to retake Vichy North Africa. Things had become pretty desperate in the Mediterranean. Malta had been under bombardment for three years. The pilots from Malta who joined Bob's squadron could confirm the terrible conditions. In March and April 1942, twice as many bombs were dropped on Malta as were dropped on London throughout the Blitz.[18] Survivors were starving. In August 1942, Operation *Pedestal* was launched to take oil, aircraft and food to the stricken island. Only five out of the 14 merchantmen who set out made it. Churchill wanted to strike at the 'underbelly' of the enemy. If the coasts of North West Africa could be in Allied hands then the Mediterranean would be a safer place. He persuaded his American allies to prepare for an invasion of Vichy-French Morocco and Algeria.

Planning for what came to be called Operation *Torch* may have begun as early as Christmas 1941 at the Arcadia Conference in Washington. The Americans were keen on an invasion of Northern Europe. The British resisted, saying that they had neither the manpower nor the boats for confronting the German Army in Continental Europe. On 25 July 1942, Churchill had a private meeting with American President Roosevelt and persuaded him to agree to invading North West Africa. On 3 August, Churchill was in Cairo with his generals. The operation to save Malta had begun. Rommel had been repulsed in the first battle of El Alamein. The second crucial battle at El Alamein was planned for late October. 8 November was the date set for Operation *Torch*.

Historian Andrew Roberts has described *Torch* as the greatest amphibious operation since Xerxes crossed the Hellespont in 480 BC.[19] It was hugely risky and top secret, involving meticulous planning, right down to the increased photo reconnaissance in Dakar. *Torch* would comprise close on 100,000 troops, 430 tanks, 300 warships and many other assorted vessels.[20] US Gen Dwight D. Eisenhower planned the whole operation from tunnels under the Rock of Gibraltar. Somehow, despite a need-to-know list of around 800 mainly military personnel, the plan came as a complete surprise to both Vichy and Germans. German intelligence had picked up rumours that included a possible action against Dakar but only the Italians came close to guessing that it would be at the beginning of November and would involve Casablanca, Oran and Algiers. Almost to the last minute the Americans thought the Vichy French and the Arabs could be persuaded to agree to terms. Along with bazookas and rocket-launchers and other essentials – such as 750,000 bottles of mosquito repellent, $100,000 in gold, '5 pounds of rat poison per company, 7,000 tons of coal, 3,000 vehicles and 60 tons of maps' – the Americans took along 6 tons of women's stockings and lingerie with which to bribe the Arabs or the French.[21]

On the morning of 8 November (his 22nd birthday), Bob was about to take off on his routine run when he was told that the Allied invasion of North Africa had begun. Chances of him meeting opposition were likely. His aircraft was unarmed. He would be most vulnerable from attack from above during his run. He took off regardless. Photographs would be his contribution to the bigger plan. The American Task Force 34, led by Gen George S. Patton, crossed the Atlantic and narrowly missed a U-boat wolf pack that had chased after a British convoy heading for Sierra Leone. In all, 12 merchant ships were sunk.[22] In three days all three landing sites were in Allied hands. Algiers, the capital of the French Empire in North Africa, put up little resistance; Oran was successfully overrun with few casualties; at Casablanca, the forces landed unopposed and then met with stiff opposition. A French legionnaire manning a gun battery above Casablanca described his horror as American planes targeted their uncamouflaged positions:

'Out of thirty men and one officer, fifteen men and the
officer were dead; ten more were wounded … I felt a
great bitterness in my soul as I saw my comrades scattered
all around. Ever since the fall of France, we dreamed of
deliverance but we did not want it that way.'[23]

In fierce fighting, 700 French troops were killed and the battleship *Jean Bart* was badly damaged in Dakar harbour.[24] On 10 November, Eisenhower brokered a ceasefire just before Patton attacked the city. Mshl Pétain was issuing orders for continued resistance but the local commander of Vichy forces in Africa, Adml Darlan, deliberated. Darlan was a Frenchman with a great hatred for the British – his grandfather had been killed at the battle of Trafalgar in 1805. Nonetheless, he agreed the ceasefire. The Germans were quick to respond. On 9 November, 17,000 German troops were sent to reinforce Tunis – known as the German capital in Africa because of the acquiescence of its Vichy French resident-general. It would be five more months before the Allies secured Tunisia.[25] Hitler ordered the troops into unoccupied France. In response, the French Adml Jean de Laborde scuttled a big portion of the French fleet: three battleships, seven cruisers, 29 destroyers, 16 submarines and an aircraft carrier sank in Toulon.[26] In Libya, Rommel was in retreat. Montgomery won his battle at El Alamein. On 15 November, Churchill ordered church bells to be rung all over Britain – the first time they had been heard since the invasion scare two years before.

The events in the north had repercussions in West Africa. Adml Darlan had called for an all-out ceasefire of French forces throughout Africa. It was not until the end of November, however, that the countries of French West Africa switched sides and joined the Allies. Even then it did not mean there would be no further need for daily photo reconnaissance of Dakar harbour. In early November, while Bob was flying the 'milk run' out of Jeswang, a new airfield was opened at Yundum, intended to be a base for the photographer pilots and their interpreters. In fact, Bob only landed there twice and his opinion on the condition of the runway and facilities are confined to a sarcastic comment in his logbook: 'Best aerodrome in West Africa!!!' Yundum was closed the following March because once the rains came the airfield turned into a quagmire and the single metal runway was waterlogged.

Most exciting for Bob was the delivery of two Spitfires especially designed to make long-range unarmed photographic missions. Bob had never flown a Spitfire. Now was his chance. He studied the pilots' notes and made a couple of familiarisation flights. The

Spitfire was certainly faster and with a custom-designed camera it had the potential of taking first-class photographs at higher altitudes. That was a big plus as the repetitive mission had made the use of their Hurricanes increasingly hazardous.

On the morning of 28 November, Bob prepared to fly his first long mission in a Spitfire. He was to fly inland checking Vichy airfields to the north for any activity. The wings of the Spitfire had been fitted with extra fuel tanks. While the aircraft was on the ground the wing tips were supported by external jacks to carry the extra weight of the fuel for such a small aircraft. Bob climbed into the cockpit. Checked instruments and set off down the runway. Just as he was gathering speed there was a terrible crunching sound from the propellor. The engine started running roughly. It was obvious it would never take off. All Bob could do was close the throttle and raise the undercarriage to bring the Spitfire to a grinding, sliding halt in a cloud of dust. 'Get out. Get out' was his only thought. Even before the crash crew arrived he leapt out of the cockpit and ran from the aircraft as fast as he could. The crash crew squirted foam over the aircraft. Fuel was spouting out of the punctured wings. The aircraft was soon covered in foam. It didn't catch fire thanks to the crash crew's swift action. Bob watched almost in disbelief.

They drove him to the officers' mess where, despite the early hour, he was given a large neat brandy to steady his nerves. Colleagues were amazed that there had been no fire. Fire was a killer. Too many pilots lost their lives to them. When he thought about it, Bob analysed his reactions to hearing the first crunch. Maybe he had pushed the control column too far forwards during the take-off run to raise the tail into flying position. That might have made one of the blades strike the ground before the aircraft got airborne. One of the crew of the fire tender who had been watching the take-off reported that before the propellor first hit the runway there had been a muffled bang. It turned out that one of the tyres of the undercarriage had burst and disintegrated and it was this that caused the aircraft to sink and reduce the already critical distance between rotating propellor blades and the ground. Many years later, Bob met one of his erstwhile crew at a party and was told that they realised they should have put extra air in the tyres of the heavily laden Spitfire to compensate for the extra weight of the fuel. A few pounds of air pressure had lain between him and a potentially fatal accident.

The next morning, the second Spitfire was prepared for the same long-range sortie. Extra fuel was loaded into the wings. The aircraft was checked and rechecked. Bob lined up for take-off. He felt more than a little apprehensive. The Spitfire rushed clattering along the metal runway and after a slightly longer run it became airborne. Those last moments before leaving the ground are always dangerous. Bob was intensely relieved to be in the air. He set course. His target was St Louis, a coastal airfield deep into recently hostile territory some 250 miles to the north-west. There were few landmarks. He looked for bends in rivers and for hills. His navigation was good. After about an hour's flight he approached the town and airfield he was to photograph from 20,000ft. All went to plan. The cameras, according to the film footage indicators in the cockpit, appeared to be working. There was no anti-aircraft fire. At the end of the return run Bob turned off the master camera switch and made for home. Apart from the distance from base it had been a relatively dull affair.

Ten minutes later Bob was checking the instruments in front of him when he was struck by a thought 'like the proverbial ton of bricks'. His stomach clenched. He realised with sickening concern that he had forgotten to release the lens cover on the camera. There would be nothing but blank film. The lense cover was a piece of metal held over each camera lens by spring clips, which had to be released manually from the cockpit. The covers kept the lens clear and protected from leaking engine oil or anything else that would obscure the photographs. It was up to the pilot to pull the lens cover cable at the last moment before flipping the release switch to run the cameras. No sooner had he realised his mistake than Bob felt a rush of intense anger and frustration. He could see from his film footage indicator that some film was still left in the magazine. More important, he assessed from his fuel gauges that he might be able to return to the target, take one photograph and get home. It was a risky decision. He had only enough fuel to get directly to the target at a minimum cruising speed. Nothing must happen to deviate from a direct course. Later, he admitted that the most prudent thing would have been to cut his losses and continue homewards. However, frustration and anger clouded his judgement and he turned back to the target. Exactly ten minutes later he was flying over the airfield. He jettisoned the lens cover. At the very last moment he switched on the cameras. Agonisingly, he watched the camera footage indicators tick over until they reached and passed zero. He couldn't see any aircaft. The airfield looked occupied. He doubted if one short fly-by would reveal anything useful. The run back home felt long but was uneventful. He landed 20 minutes late but with some fuel remaining. Now he had to explain himself.

The photo-interpretation unit was waiting for the film. Bob reported that most of it would be blank but he hoped they would find something useful at the end of the magazine. While he waited for the results, Bob and his ground crew discussed how to avoid such an oversight. A simple solution was devised. They made a metal label to hang over the master camera switch to remind the pilot to operate the lens cover cable first. Feeling wretched and rather foolish, Bob made his way to the mess. Later there was a phone call for him. One of the photographic interpreters reassured him that although the photos didn't cover the complete runway they could see areas where aircraft had been parked on some of the prints. It would not be necessary to repeat that sortie.

Next day, he was back in the Spitfire over Dakar harbour. There was more than the usual amount of anti-aircraft fire but it was wild and inaccurate. He was nearing the end of his photographic run and watching out for the ak-ak bursts some 2,000–3,000ft below when he saw not one but three enemy fighters climbing up in formation, about to make a turn that would bring them straight at him. It was time to get out of it. Time to think about making a 'dignified but nevertheless hurried departure'. He switched off the cameras, opened the throttle and dived for home. Ah! This was where the Spitfire outdid the Hurricane. It was faster than anything else out there. It was skimming over the water, yet under the threat from above, it felt like crawling. His whole body was tense. After a few more minutes he turned to left and right to look behind him for pursuers. Nobody. He was quite alone. Somehow the rest of the journey home was an anticlimax. The hostile fighters did not reappear.

By the end of November, the Allies were consolidating their invasion of North Africa. The flight at Jeswang received a signal. Their task was complete. After 184 sorties the PRU was to be disbanded.[27] They flew their Hurricanes back to base, leaving the surviving Spitfire to be collected by a ferry pilot who would return it to Takoradi. By 5 December, Bob was back in Sierra Leone, in Freetown. His photographic task was at an end. He had been away from England for more than 20 months. Surely it must be time to return home. Killy had already left and was in England. Only Bob and the two pilots from Malta remained of the original flight. The new squadron commander confirmed that all three would be going soon but it was impossible to forecast when. Two interminable, frustrating weeks passed without any sign of a sea passage becoming available. By then it was 19 December. The three pilots resigned themselves to another Christmas in the tropics.

With Operation *Torch* and the successful Anglo-American landings in Morocco and Algeria, the mood in the French colonies in Africa changed from menacing to benevolent. French antagonism against the British had been such that during Operation *Torch* British soldiers were asked to sew a Stars and Stripes on their shirt sleeves to make them seem American. The countries in North Africa were leafleted by 'Uncle Sam' in the hopes of bringing more of the population to the Allies.[28] The Allies still needed to keep watch on the Atlantic but now the Portuguese were allowing the RAF to use Lajes in the Azores – the runway had been extended to accommodate Gloster Gladiators. In a few months, Churchill would be invoking the oldest operational alliance in history – the Anglo-Portuguese Treaty of 1373 – to reopen the transatlantic route from Brazil to West Africa. The Sunderlands would remain in Freetown to protect convoys and watch out for U-boats. They even checked the bays around the Cape Verde Islands and the Spanish colony of Fernando Po for lurking U-boats.

Overall, the Allied operation was run down. They left behind many material benefits to the region – roads, harbours, communications and practice in administration. Graham Greene said he would remember Freetown:

'... mainly for the sunsets when all the laterite paths
turned suddenly for a few minutes the colour of a rose,
the old slavers' fort with the cannon lying in the grass, the
abandoned railway track with the chickens pecking in and
out of the little empty rotting station, the taste of the first
pink gin at six o'clock.'[29]

Late in the afternoon on 19 December, Bob was called to the telephone. There were two places on a Sunderland leaving early the next morning. The aircraft was due for a major overhaul. Two spaces, but there were three pilots. Bob's case was not as strong as those of the Malta pilots who had been away from England even longer than he had. One of them offered to stay and let the 'married man' go home. There was a major party in the mess that night. Next morning, feeling somewhat hung-over, Bob found himself a passenger in a flying boat bound for Gibraltar. If all went to plan they would arrive in England on 23 December. Bob began to think seriously about being at home with his wife and a baby daughter whom he had never seen. He would be having an English Christmas in a house he had not seen. It would be cold but it would be home.

They landed in Gibraltar harbour and were told they had the day to rest or visit the town. They would take off again soon after dark. It was wise to cross the Bay of Biscay at night since they would be within range of German fighters based in Western France. On the Allied invasion of North Africa, Hitler had sent troops into unoccupied France. He also made overtures to neutral Spain. Tunisia was still in German hands. The Sunderland would have to dodge the enemy to get back home. It taxied out into a choppy sea. As they prepared for take-off it was clear that one engine was not giving enough power. The captain returned to his mooring in the inner harbour. A deflated crew and passengers went ashore for a night's sleep on land. The flight engineer stayed on board to see if he could fix the problem. He joined them for breakfast. The good news was that he had found the fault and was on his way to the airfield for a replacement. With any luck the aircraft would be ready for take-off that evening. Later in the morning, the captain received a phone call. The flight engineer was in hospital. He had been in a truck crossing the airfield when it was struck by an aircraft taking off. Luckily the aircraft managed to land without much damage but the driver of the truck was killed. The flight engineer was badly injured and would not be fit to fly.

The captain of the Sunderland went off to the hospital to visit his injured crew. When he returned, he had not only the part required for the faulty engine but also a fitter to do the repairs and who could travel with them as a substitute flight engineer. They would be taking off for England as soon as the part was in and the engine checked. Bob, his colleague and the rest of the crew sat around the mess waiting for the call to go aboard. It was well after dark before the aircraft was ready. The captain explained that it was now too late to avoid the French coast so they would fly further out to sea to try to avoid hostile interception. It was well past midnight when the heavily laden Sunderland lurched into the air and turned northwards. The two passengers attempted to sleep on improvised beds in the rear cabin but the noise of the engines and the cold made it near impossible. Every hour that passed was an hour nearer home. Dawn broke and the sun came up in a cloudless sky. Not good. Their only hope of avoiding interception was substantial cloud cover.

Bob had just begun to make coffee. Before the water boiled a klaxon blared out 'Action stations' and the aircraft began to dive towards the sea. Two patrolling ME110s had been sighted positioning themselves for attack. Neither passenger could do anything but wait. There were gunners in the waist of the aircraft and in the tail. They opened fire while the flying boat made some violent manoeuvres. As they reached sea level they entered a bank of cloud some 100ft above the sea. It wasn't visible from higher up and was probably lifted fog. It wasn't thick but it was enough to allow the Sunderland to play a game of hide-and-seek with the fighters. Soon enough the fighters broke off the engagement and, perhaps because they were short of fuel, disappeared towards France. As a precaution the captain continued to fly in and out of the broken cloud until it was judged safe to resume course for England. Three tense hours later the passengers were relieved to hear that the English coast had been sighted and they would soon be landing in Plymouth.

It was raining. Cold rain. It was dark. The passengers were given a hurried meal in the officers' mess and rushed by car to catch the London train. Bob had intended to ring Alice after the meal but to do so he would have risked missing the train, so he continued his journey. It was Christmas Eve. The trains were crowded but he managed to get a seat. He had to cross London in time to catch the last train home to Kent. Alice had no idea what a surprise lay in store. She had put Suzanne to bed in her cot next to the double bed where she slept in the large main bedroom of her newly rented home. She had put up a small Christmas tree in the sitting room and had put sprigs of holly along the top of the pictures and a special sprig, with many red berries on it, across the photograph of Bob on the mantelpiece. Now she still had Suzanne's stocking to prepare. She filled it with a small fluffy rabbit, an apple and a packet of dolly mixtures. Tired, she went to sleep.

Bob had already arrived in Gillingham by train. He found himself walking along familiar deserted streets. He had never been to the house his family lived in. His family. His home. It took him some time to find the right number. It seemed to take hours for anyone to answer the doorbell. His kitbag sagged at his feet. Alice heard a loud knocking at the door. She called out in some concern. Who could be calling so late at night? Alarmed, she left Suzanne sleeping and crept downstairs to put the hall light on. She could see a silhouette. She called out. 'Who is it? What is the matter?' When she heard a familiar voice say 'Who do you think it is?' she couldn't believe it. She fumbled shooting back the safety bolts and opening the door. They looked at each other. Why didn't he call? Well he had tried. Then he hugged her.

Bob was home. Tired and crumpled, at 1am on Christmas morning 1942. It had been a long time. Alice offered him tea.

He asked for beer. Luckily she had managed to buy a few bottles but she didn't have an opener. He used his penknife. She was just wondering when he would ask about the baby when he said 'well where's that big daughter of mine?' He went upstairs two at a time. Alice followed slowly. She saw her husband leaning over the cot. Suzanne opened her eyes. 'Dad-dad,' she said quite distinctly and smiled. She put up a tiny hand. Bob gently picked her up.

5

This island home

B OB WOKE HARDLY KNOWING where he was. Quiet. A double bed with sheets and pillows. Birds chirping outside the window. Cold. A sharp overnight frost had iced a glaze of white over the garden. A strange house. Home. Christmas morning. He dressed quickly, putting on two sweaters and a jacket, and went downstairs. 'Dad-dad,' said Suzanne without hesitation. In less than 24 hours he was out of the tropics and into family life. Bob set to making a coal fire in the sitting room. They shared presents: Bob gave Alice a pair of leopard-skin mittens and Suzanne a doll handmade in Sierra Leone. Alice gave Bob a pair of RAF blue woollen socks that she had knitted herself. They were rather long. Then they set out for a series of family visits. Bob began by seeing his stepmother. She had already made plans to spend the day with her brother's family. Christmas lunch was to be at Alice's parents' house. The family had pooled their rations to create a feast, including a turkey and Christmas pudding. Alice had been apprehensive as they hadn't seen him since their hasty marriage just before he was sent to West Africa but Bob was welcomed like a hero. The party was completed by the unexpected appearance of brother Bill, who had managed to hitch a lift on a friend's motorcycle. The whole family gathered around the piano to sing carols and, for Alice's mother, 'When Irish eyes are smiling'.

Over the next two weeks Bob kept smiling and adopted a cheery manner for his wife's sake, but the abrupt change in his life had caused an emotional upheaval that he hoped he had managed to hide. He was not alone in finding the switch from the stress of operational life to home life difficult. RAF Fighter Command thrust a whole generation of young men into the front line to fight for their lives. Yet when they came back from battle they tried to live a near-normal, social, civilised life in quiet villages and towns with their families. After two or three years on the front line they could honestly say the RAF came first, wife and family second.[1] Bob was feeling pretty disappointed to lose his acting rank of flight lieutenant. It is a flying officer who sits smiling with his wife and young child in a formal photograph. The year 1943 was just a few days old when a telegram arrived. Thinking it might be a recall to duty, he tore open the buff envelope with some concern. He read it twice. With a broad grin he handed it to Alice. It was from his previous squadron commander, congratulating him on the award of the Distinguished Flying Cross. Alice jumped with excitement and demanded to know what he had done to earn it. Bob just smiled. He said nothing. The following Friday the local newspaper carried the headline 'Three Kent airmen win DFC'. About Bob they quoted his official citation:

> **'NEVER RETURNED WITHOUT COMPLETING TASK**. Acting Flight Lieutenant Allen has been engaged in photographic reconnaissance duties for some time, and has acquired great skill in these duties. Despite accurate anti-aircraft fire and the efforts of enemy fighters he has never returned to his base without completing his task. He has secured numerous valuable photographs and his determination has been an excellent example.'[2]

The family was hugely proud. Friends rang to congratulate him. He played down his role, saying that it was work carried out by the whole squadron. Alice sewed the purple-and-white ribbon below the wings on his tunic. Now he began to feel that his time abroad, with all its discomforts and difficulties, had been recognised. He had made a contribution and would no longer feel less successful than his contemporaries who had continued to fly in the UK.

Bob had been away for 22 months, from July 1941 to December 1942. At home, austerity had become almost mundane. 'Make Do and Mend.' 'Knitting for the RAF.' 'Dig for Victory.' These slogans were new to Bob. He began to understand the efforts every family had made. Food was a constant preoccupation. By the beginning of 1942, food imports were at half their pre-war level. With the taking of Malaya and Singapore by the Japanese, sources of rice, sugar and tea disappeared. Parks were turned into allotments. Every back garden had chickens. People found how easy it was to keep pigs, feeding them on waste food. The Ministry of Food issued a poem:

'Because of the pail, the scraps were saved,
Because of the scraps, the pigs were saved,
Because of the rations, the ships were saved,
Because of the ships, the island was saved,
Because of the island, the Empire was saved,
And all because of a housewife's pail.'

Fish, potatoes and bread were not rationed, although white bread vanished and was replaced by the 'national wholemeal loaf', which was lumpy and unpopular. Eggs were plentiful, though they did not come in shells but in tins imported from the USA as part of the Lend-Lease deal.[3] At the height of the war the USA was supplying a third of Britain's food, including beans, evaporated milk, oranges and orange juice, canned fruit and dried prunes. Fuel was stringently rationed. Bob and Alice walked everywhere. Pushing the pram. Visiting friends and family.

After a couple of weeks at home, Bob was ready for his next job. He had heard that there was now a surplus of aircrew. The majority of men on his ground-training course had gone to Canada, the USA or Rhodesia for flying training. They had no experience of battle and many did not fly against the enemy until the war was almost over. He became increasingly anxious. When his posting arrived it came in a telephone call. He was astonished, even angry at its content. He was ordered to report to the Air Ministry in Whitehall for duty with the Ministry of Aircraft Production. He was to be one of several teams of operational aircrew who visited factories producing military equipment. When the task was fully explained to him, he appreciated that it was important. In fact he felt slightly underqualified. He had to speak to men and women in the factories, emphasising the importance of their work, giving them some idea of how their particular products were used and generally boost morale. His role came under the term 'Public Relations'.

A small team of RAF personnel arranged visits mainly in the Midlands and south of England. Bob was about to go out on his second visit when he was given a certificate signed by the Secretary of State for Air informing him that he had been 'Mentioned in Despatches' for distinguished services. There was no citation. It had to have been further recognition for his photographic work in West Africa. Since before World War I, the term 'Mentioned in Despatches' had been used by commanders to report acts of bravery or good work. It was usually published in the *London Gazette* and it entitled the bearer to wear a single bronze oak leaf on the campaign medal. Bob was pleased to receive it, but compared to his colleagues, one of whom wore the ribbon of the VC (the Victoria Cross, the highest order of gallantry) for his exploits in Bomber Command, Bob felt rather inexperienced. He should not have worried. The handsome young officer with charming manners was a great success, especially with the many women workers. He showed Alice some photos. She teased him for his 'film star looks' and warned him not to be carried away by all the adulation. He laughed it off and said they would soon get over it if they saw him digging in the garden in his old flannels. The new job took him away during the week but he was back home again at weekends.

Within a few weeks Bob had first-hand knowledge of a broad section of British industry, from cotton mills to coal mines, large pottery factories to small workshops making service buttons, large aluminium smelting works churning out castings for aircraft engines to equally large car plants producing armoured fighting vehicles. There was even a corset factory making parachutes. In all these places, women made up the bulk of the workforce. The change had happened in the two years Bob had been away. Before the start of the war, single women only took the jobs the men could not or would not do – charring (cleaning), for example. In white-collar occupations such as teaching and nursing, women had to resign on marriage. However, by September 1941 a woman without dependents who did not take a job could be sent to prison and by 1943 even grandmothers were compelled to work.[4] Everyone was expected to 'do their bit'. The munitions industry expanded its workforce from 1.25 million in 1939 to 8.5 million in 1943. In the aircraft industry, 40 per cent of the labour force were women. In engineering it was 35 per cent. In chemicals and explosives, 52 per cent. Some ordnance factories were almost entirely staffed by women. Bob was impressed. As impressed as Churchill's deputy, Clement Attlee, who said: 'The work the women are performing in the munitions factories has to be seen to be believed. Precision engineering jobs which a few years ago would have made a skilled turner's hair stand on end are performed with dead accuracy by girls who had no industrial experience.'[5]

One visit stuck fast in Bob's memory. He was in the Birmingham area at a gasworks that also finished off, by heat treating, the metal 20mm cannon clips that kept the ammunition together in belts as it was fed to guns either in turrets or in the wings of fighter aircraft. Two pilots visited the gasworks that day. The other flying officer, Vic Berg, had been on the same operational training course as Bob at Debden two years before. Vic Berg had also been sent to a Hurricane squadron but their subsequent experiences couldn't have been more different. Vic could not walk without crutches because he had serious leg injuries. After his training, he had, like Bob, been told he was being posted abroad. He was issued with tropical clothing, a mosquito net and a pair of Russian-speaking interpreters, which rather gave the game away. He found himself travelling north on HMS *Argus* with his Hurricane, and became part of a hush-hush operation, code named *Benedict*, to support the Soviets with aircraft and training. Two squadrons forming 151 Wing were based at Vaenga, about 15 miles from Murmansk on the Kola Peninsula inside the Arctic Circle. They were part of a lend-lease deal between Churchill and Stalin by which 2,952 Hurricanes were ultimately ferried to Russia.[6]

151 Wing were the advance party, arriving in September 1941. There were 550 RAF aircrew and ground crew set to train Soviet pilots and ground staff. They spent three months in freezing conditions before handing over to the Soviets. There was little or no radar. The enemy made frequent sorties over the airfield. To enable the aircraft to scramble quickly, the ground crews sat on the tailplane while taxiing to avoid the plane tipping forwards on to its propellers. Vic Berg was waiting for take-off. There was snow and ice on the grass runway. Suddenly there were Ju 88s above. Take-off was urgent. He moved forwards. Usually the airmen on the tail jumped off as the aircraft reached the runway, but this time

the Hurricane was moving so fast that the airmen were caught in the slipstream and pinned to the tail. As soon as he took off Vic realised something was badly wrong. The aeroplane was almost uncontrollable. He closed the throttle in an attempt to land straight ahead but the aircraft was so unstable it crashed back on to the runway, killing the airmen.[7] Vic himself had to be cut out of his cockpit, which was miraculously intact, but his legs were shattered and he had a severe head injury. He spent the next 18 months in a succession of hospitals having operations on his legs.

There was a practical reason for including Vic Berg on the factory visits: it enabled him to remain eligible for full pay. Men in 'non-effective' periods of service, such as lengthy hospitalisation, had their pay reduced. Somehow the employees on shift at the gasworks had heard about this iniquitous ruling and presumed it applied to Vic, whose bravery in bearing his injuries had impressed them. Bob and Vic were having a cup of tea in the manager's office when there was a knock at the door. It was one of the women who worked at the factory. Her apron was nearly filled with money, mostly silver, which she explained was from a spontaneous collection made for the benefit of the wounded gentleman. It was impossible to refuse such a generous gesture. With some embarrassment they accepted the gift. With the exception of the cost of two pints of beer drunk on return to their hotel, the balance was donated to the RAF Benevolent Fund.

Bob spent three months, from late January to late March 1943, making factory visits. He began to appreciate that the war was not just about fighting but also about working. Aircraft production had its own separate ministry under Lord Beaverbrook. In 1943 it employed 1,750,000 men and women.[8] Many were on shift work and put in long hours but they earned good money. They were entertained by BBC Radio's daily programmes such as

Workers' Playtime and *Music While You Work* to lessen strain, relieve monotony and increase efficiency. Posters, films, newspapers and magazines all put out the same message – this was a time to pull together. However, it was not an entirely harmonious scene on the home front. March 1943 saw the first wartime strikes in the north of England. The restrictions on food, clothes, petrol and travel in general were irksome. The news was good from North Africa: Tunisia had fallen and the Allies were back in control. The Russians had held Stalingrad and were fighting in the east with material support from Britain and America. Bob was eager to get back to flying duties. He was surprised and disappointed to be told that there were no vacancies in front-line fighter squadrons but he could go to Scotland to a Hurricane Operational Training unit as an instructor.

During the course of the war, most pilots were asked to do a few months as instructors. Especially in Operational Training, the experience of actual combat was invaluable. On the plus side Bob was restored to the rank of flight lieutenant and flight commander. The posting was for six months. He persuaded Alice to come with him if he could find suitable lodgings. So began what they both described as the best and the worst days of their marriage. Bob found his family lodgings with the McBride sisters. The three maiden ladies, who lived in a solidly built house on the main street of Dornoch, had opened their home to the pilots and families from nearby Annan Airfield as part of their war effort. They charged only the cost of food, fuel and light. Miss McBride, the eldest, was about 65. Miss Margaret 60 and Miss Elizabeth 50. They welcomed Bob and his family with a log fire and tea and scones. Alice and Miss Elizabeth became firm friends. It was quiet in the country. Fishermen sat on the banks of the River Annan waiting for salmon to bite. The war seemed a long way away. Most days, Bob cycled the 2 miles to the airfield. Occasionally, when the

McBride sisters undertook to babysit, Alice went with him to have a drink in the officers' mess. Sometimes they walked to the village pub. The McBride sisters were shocked: nice Scottish ladies did not frequent pubs. Alice noticed that the local men also disapproved of women in their pub. Despite this, soon enough other RAF wives joined in and it became a friendly meeting place away from the station.

After a couple of months of living a relatively normal life, Bob was sent on an advanced flying course. He would be away for a month. Bob was delighted. He would be flying Spitfires again and would be gaining skills for getting back on the front line. Alice was dismayed. Bob forgot to ring her on their wedding anniversary. Then he forgot her birthday, though he did ring the next day. On his return he gave her a silk scarf and organised for friends to come to supper as a delayed birthday treat. Small slights grew into big arguments as the young couple tried to adjust to married life where one partner was at home all day with a young child and the other was a wartime fighter pilot committed to the hectic social environment of the RAF. At the beginning of November, Bob went away again on a two-week course, flying Spitfires, at Aston Down. He arrived back in Dornock a day earlier than expected. The McBride sisters were so delighted to see their young lodgers looking happy that they 'discovered' a bottle of whisky and shared a wee dram to celebrate his return. Supper that night was roast chicken and apple pie before sitting to listen to the wireless. Then Bob revealed that he had just one more week in Scotland before being posted to a fighter squadron in the south of England – where the action was. He was very pleased with the posting; 197 was a fighter squadron where he knew at least two of the pilots. He just wanted to get on with fighting the war. For his wife and child, it would mean leaving the small, friendly village in Scotland and returning to the south-east of England and to the continual stress of air raids. But Alice was determined to stay near to him. They knew that once he was back on operations their times together would be very short. She waited for Bob to find them somewhere to live.

When Bob joined 197 Squadron it had just been equipped with a new aircraft – the Hawker Typhoon. This was intended to be a successor to the Hurricane – a versatile dogfighter of an aeroplane. It became a true dive-bombing ground-attack weapon, essential to the liberation of Europe in 1944. In the final year of the war it would be superseded by the Tempest, another of Sydney Camm's aeroplanes, but for the job in hand in 1944 the Typhoon was unsurpassed. Affectionately known as the 'Tiffy', it was a 400mph workhorse.[9] Faster and heavier than its predecessor, it made its reputation at low level, in fast dives, delivering bombs and rockets. The Typhoon was rushed into production when it was realised that the German Focke-Wulf Fw 190 was outperforming the Spitfire Mk V. Roland Beaumont of 609 Squadron had been a test pilot with Hawkers. He declared that at 500ft the Typhoon could intercept any enemy aircraft. The only problem was that it looked very similar to the Fw 190 from some angles and at least one Typhoon was shot down by friendly fire. They thus painted the undersides of the wings with black-and-white stripes, a distinction that was subsequently much copied. Denys Gillam, a distinguished pre-war pilot who flew in the Battle of Britain, was an early advocate for the Typhoon: 'They could hold their own certainly, if someone was misguided enough to try to outfly them downhill, when they were in for a surprise, but they were a terrific gun platform.'[10] The Typhoon was rock steady and it could hold a dive without swinging about. When it was first used for bombing at low level, losses and casualties were high. The dive facility encouraged a change of tactics when dive-bombing – starting the dive at 10,000–12,000ft and releasing bombs at 4,000ft. Bob had to learn this technique.

It was simple, but for the first few missions it was also very frightening.

197 Squadron was based at Tangmere near Chichester. As soon as he arrived, Bob started looking for accommodation for his family. It proved very difficult. One evening he was in the local pub with some friends and began chatting to the barman. After a couple of beers, Bob asked if he had heard of any rooms available for rent. He was in luck. The barman's sister was living in Chichester and knew that her landlady was preparing three rooms to let. Bob took the sister's telephone number. The house was close by and Bob went to look at it right away. It was a large red-brick house in the Pallants in the centre of the town. He stood outside. It looked rather imposing, four storeys high with a brass lamp hanging over a solid oak door. It was evening but not too late. He knocked at the door. It was opened by a small woman, neatly dressed and holding a Scottie dog in her arms. Bob introduced himself and explained his impromptu arrival; he was to be on duty at 5am, and he was on a rather desperate search for accommodation. The landlady, Mrs Hughes, invited him in and showed him the attic flat. It was certainly spartan. There was no running water. Every drop would have to be carried from a bathroom two floors below. But it had three adequate rooms with views over the rooftops and was in a very convenient location. He decided to take it.

Alice travelled down from Scotland on trains filled with soldiers. It was a six-hour journey. Suzanne toddled among the soldiers in the corridors. They were met in London by Alice's sister Joan, now in WAAF uniform, and caught the train to Chichester. On arrival, she had hardly time to notice that Bob was not there to meet them when an airman saluted and asked if she was Mrs Allen. He explained that Bob was on duty and would join them later. It was a brisk reminder, if she needed it, of service life. Married couples had to adjust to conditions without certainties.

For a few months at least, they would be together as Bob managed to get home every other day. Mrs Hughes was happy to babysit so they could meet friends, other pilots and their wives and girlfriends, at the local pub. There was much drinking of beer, singing of songs and good humour during squadron stand-down periods. The war was never discussed. It was a cold winter. Coal was short. Alice filled the pram with twigs and Bob brought home logs. Some mornings there was ice on the inside of the windows. None of them caught cold. Occasionally Alice took Suzanne to the seafront. They could see aeroplanes flying in loose formations towards France. She never knew when Bob was actually flying but sometimes he was away on a course so she knew he was in England.

Bob's task during the winter months of 1944 was to fly over France to locate and dive-bomb launch sites for the terrifying new German weapon, the V1, an unmanned flying bomb. The sites were given the code name *No-Ball* in a combined operation code named *Bodyline*. The cricketing term was later exchanged for code name *Crossbow*. *No-balls* were notoriously difficult to see. They tended to be hidden in woods and consisted of concrete blocks that looked a little like ski jumps. A brilliant use of photo reconnaissance had revealed the German secret weapons in Peenemünde on the Baltic coast in August 1943. It was alarming to find many identified launch sites between the Pas-de-Calais and Cherbourg peninsula all obviously being prepared for an attack on southern England. In his own account, Bob describes a tactic known as the 'ramrod'. The Typhoons flew together, between three and five squadrons (each squadron made up of two flights of four aircraft) flying as a wing led by a wing commander. At a prearranged time, the whole formation would taxi out, squadron by squadron, and line up in pairs on the runway ready for take-off. Once all were on the runway, the wing leader and his number two would take off, followed by all the other pairs. No radio transmission was allowed, to avoid alerting the enemy. Eventually, some 40 aircraft loaded with bombs would be flying in loose formation at around 500ft above the airfield. It was an awesome sight. One morning, there was a lapse in communication with an adjacent airfield and two wings took off at the same time. The air was filled with circling Typhoons in overlapping patterns. The skill of the pilots, luck and an instinct for self-preservation among the inexperienced avoided collisions. Even the hardiest ground staff were shaken by some of the near-misses as aircraft passed each other at high speed.

Once airborne, they flew to France at low level to avoid German radar. Then, as the French coast appeared, the wing would climb steeply to avoid the enemy's deadly light anti-aircraft fire. As the first aircraft approached the target a flak battery would inevitably send up a fierce barrage. It was vital to identify the target as quickly as possible, however cleverly it was concealed. Squadron by squadron they would dive down from between 12,000 and 15,000ft. At a signal from each section leader the pilots would, in turn, roll their aircraft over and dive at an angle of at least 45 degrees at the target.

Bob described this perilous manoeuvre: during the steep and very fast dive, the pilot used his gunsight to seek out the exact aiming point while holding his aircraft steady. At a critical moment, usually at 5,000ft to allow for the trajectory of the bombs, the pilot would move the nose of the aircraft smoothly forwards through the target and release the bombs by pressing a button on the throttle. The aircraft was by now diving at some 500mph. Immediately after the bombs had gone the aircraft had to be pulled out of the dive and, as hard as the stress on the airframe allowed, climb steeply back up to rejoin the aircraft in front. Almost invariably this pull-out resulted in the pilot 'blacking out' for a second or so, but it was important that the pilot of each aircraft quickly located the one in front so that each flight, squadron and, if possible, the whole wing kept in some sort of formation for the return home.[11] If things went wrong after the attack and aircraft lost sight of each other then they would arrive home in dribs and drabs, sometimes with very little fuel in reserve. In his early days on the wing, Bob flew with a number of experienced section leaders before he was proficient at this hair-raising but effective form of pinpoint bombing.

For a while he flew as number two to a wing leader who had a reputation for diving at the target and climbing away so steeply that the number two invariably lost visual contact. More often than not, the wing leader went home unaccompanied and the chances of the wing re-forming were small. On one particular occasion, however, Bob was determined that whatever happened he would not lose sight of his leader. Sure enough, the wing leader rolled his aircraft on to its back and began what seemed to be an almost vertical dive. Bob did the same, keeping his eye firmly on his leader. He saw him pull out of the dive and followed, pulling as much G-force as possible. He blacked out. When his vision returned he was delighted to see his wing leader ahead of him, still climbing fast. At 15,000ft they both levelled out and headed for home with all the aircraft in sight rejoining formation. Bob's elation was short-lived. With some embarrassment, he heard from his wing leader over the RT. Would he like to jettison his bombs over the sea? He was furious with himself. He had forgotten to release the bombs on target at the bottom of the dive. Now he had to waste them over the sea and he had put uncalled-for strain on his aircraft by having the extra weight of two 500lb bombs in the wings as he pushed it through G-forces pulling out of the dive. On return to base, he was congratulated on keeping the formation together. Everyone tactfully avoided mentioning that he had forgotten to release the bombs.

Bob remained with 197 Squadron for three months, from December 1943 to March 1944. The *No-ball* sites were heavily protected by anti-aircraft guns. Each sortie was expensive, with the loss of three or four Typhoons in the wing for every big attack. Some were shot down during the attack or failed to pull out of the dive and were seen to crash in the target area. Others were damaged by flak and were unable to limp home to the English coast. Pilots who had to ditch in the Channel rarely survived, but those who managed to parachute into the sea were rescued and returned to England. In one remarkable rescue, the pilot of a Walrus seaplane flew 80 miles across the Channel, to within easy reach of German coastal guns, to pick up a pilot who had come down in the sea just 3 miles from the coast.[12] Some were picked up by German air-sea rescue and taken prisoners of war. The unlucky were sometimes seen in the water after parachuting out safely and then never heard of again.

During those months, there were days off when Bob could visit his family and stay overnight. The pressures of almost daily sorties were felt by everyone, including the loved ones. Remarkably few men cracked up. A squadron held together by means of leadership, discipline and a great deal of shared partying and drinking. There were always reasons to celebrate: destroying a target, surviving another day, getting promotion. 'There were many reasons why we drank too much,' wrote fighter ace Bob Braham. '… in my own case I think fear was at the root of it. Not only the fear of "buying it" but also the fear of showing fear to others. It was a terrible responsibility that was thrust on a generation of young men, some not much more than boys.'[13] Bob Braham also wrote that short stays at home often led to heated arguments over bringing up the children or even more trivial disagreements. Bob Allen was all too aware of the strain building up as he flew more and more operational sorties. At least he knew his wife and child were safe. The cumulative effect of bombing the V1 sites succeeded in delaying the German missile offensive against southern England.

It was clear to everyone that plans to get back into Europe, even if shrouded in secrecy, were fast developing. For a start, the south of England was full of Americans. They had begun to arrive in January 1942. A year later, there were 770,000 US troops in Britain. By 1944, there was also a vast bomber force of 426,000 US airmen based mainly in East Anglia. US military bases took over 100,000 acres of farmland. It was an invasion. By May 1944, there were 1.5 million US combat troops in the UK.[14] Alice's sister Joan had described the impact of the Americans who arrived at her RAF station. They seemed to have plenty of money, cigarettes, chocolates and booze and were 'quite full of themselves', she said, 'as though we are not as good as they are. But many girls are falling for them.' 'Overfed, overpaid, oversexed and over here' was a most overused epithet. Bob chided Joan, reminding her that the British needed the Americans – their men, their wealth and their goods. Besides, a whole squadron, Eagle Squadron, had been formed by volunteer American airmen.

Several months later, Joan admitted that she had met an American fighter pilot who was determined to marry her. At the time she was a poster girl for the WAAF. The caption on her poster read 'THE WAAF CALLS YOU TO SERVICE'. By Easter she had taken her American home to meet the parents. They were won over by his charm and his adoration of their daughter. Alice first met Freddie Gill when he managed to 'borrow' an aircraft and fly it to Tangmere in order to see Joan, who had contrived to get some leave to visit her sister. Alice couldn't imagine a British pilot doing that, though it had been known.

To marry, they needed various permissions: Joan required her father's, Freddie his commanding officer's. The US authorities tended to regard marriage as 'an impediment to be avoided … a single man undistracted by family responsibilities was considered to be superior military material, more likely to make strong ties with his buddies that generate the selfless and foolhardy courage war demands'.[15] There were no special entitlements to accommodation, travel allowances, medical expenses or goods from the PX (the store where authorised personnel could buy cheap goods). Nor would there be automatic US citizenship for brides. Freddie was determined. He had his girl and he was going to marry her and take her home to Pennsylvania. Within a year they would be gone.

Partnerships were the name of the game in 1944. The planned invasion of Europe, now called *Overlord*, was an Allied Combined Operation. All significant command levels were integrated, starting at the top. Gen Eisenhower was to be supreme Allied commander and Air Mshl Tedder would be his deputy. Eisenhower was determined to make Anglo-American co-operation work. He was probably the least chauvinistic American and least chauvinistic military commander in history.[16] The Allies combined but so did the services. Tedder commented in 1944: 'I do not myself believe that any modern war can be won either at sea or on the land alone or in the air alone … In other words, war has changed to three dimensional, and very few people realise that.'[17] Even within the services the command structures were changing. Bob and his fellow Typhoon pilots found themselves not in Fighter Command but in the 2nd Tactical Air Force. Fighter Command was split into two, with half taking on air defence and the other half offering air cover and tactical support for *Overlord*. (The renaming was not popular and the name 'Fighter Command' was brought back in autumn 1944.) Fighter aircraft carried bombs and used cannon and rockets. They were used for reconnaissance as well as aerial combat. There were mixed roles mostly involving co-operation with the Army.

One day in early March, some three months after joining 197 Squadron, Bob was posted to 266 Squadron as flight commander. In this role, Bob usually led a section of four aircraft and, on occasions when the squadron commander was away, he led the squadron's eight aircraft. Such postings were always a mixed blessing. It was good to have his own flight, but it was to be in a new squadron made up of Rhodesian pilots, none of whom he knew. Moreover, he was based initially in Norfolk, far from his family. 266 Squadron was one of three Rhodesian squadrons flying in the Battle of Britain. It was formed in World War I and fought in the Aegean and in Russia. With the rumours and then the outbreak of war in Europe, the prime minister of Rhodesia, Godfrey Huggins, an English-born physician who had fought in World War I, immediately volunteered his country's services. Rhodesia was first to offer a training scheme, the Empire Training Scheme, which ultimately instructed about 8,235 Allied airmen. Within months of the start of World War II, some 1,600 white Rhodesians had left their country to fight in Europe. In May 1944, when Bob was a flight commander, Prime Minister Huggins paid the squadron a visit. Bob can be seen in the back row of the official photos. Another photo shows Huggins standing in front of a Typhoon donated by the colony's black community. However, pilots were drawn exclusively from the white minority, though black Rhodesians did go to war – in the African Rifles in Burma.[18] The number of Rhodesians on the squadron was not constant. Just after the Battle of Britain at the end of 1941, only 15 of 34 pilots were Rhodesian and 128 of 490 were ground crew. When Bob joined 266, he was almost the only non-Rhodesian and made lifelong friendships with men from the sunny uplands of Africa.[19]

Before taking over his flight, Bob was sent on a course at 4 Fighter Leaders School and had some practice flying the Typhoon with double-tiered rockets attached to the wings. The rocket projectile was a new weapon with fearsome power. A small 25lb rocket could penetrate 4in. of armour – it was ideal for attacking tanks and trains. The Typhoon was steady enough to fire salvos of up to eight pairs. It was to prove deadly. The aircraft could be fitted with both bombs and rockets, just bombs, or just rockets, according to the target.

Within days of Bob's arrival back with the squadron they moved to Needs Oar Point, a new airfield close to the coast opposite the Isle of Wight on a large estate owned by Lord Montagu of Beaulieu. There were new airstrips under construction all over southern England. Needs Oar Point consisted of two prefabricated runways made of interlocking metal plates. There were small canvas hangars for servicing the aircraft and tents and marquees for sleeping and mess accommodation. They were still flying 'ramrods' to bomb the V1 sites. New targets began to figure in their briefings and included railways and rolling stock, bridges and roads behind the coast from Calais to Cherbourg.

In early May, specific radar stations along the coast of northern France began to be included as targets. They were heavily defended. Some, known as giant *Würzburgs* – with names such as 'Mammut', 'Wasserman' and 'Freya' – required carefully co-ordinated attacks by rockets and bombs. Others, among the 92 strung along the coast, could be put out of action in a single attack. Both sides attempted to deceive. The Allies wanted the Germans to think they would attack at the Pas-de-Calais. The Germans made it look as if even damaged radar was still operating in order to attract more attacks into a well-defended site. Bob and his squadron attacked the radar at Cap d'Antifer and put almost all radar beyond repair on the first strike, but such was the success of German deception that the Allies were drawn back to attack it six more times.[20] On each occasion they suffered casualties, until losses amounted to 10 per cent of the sorties flown.[21] Still, replacement aircraft and pilots arrived quickly from the pool of trained reserves.

Now there was little time for social activities. During squadron stand-down, usually for bad weather, the pilots repaired to a nearby pub or, if lucky, they were invited into the homes of local residents for a bath and a drink. Bob and his squadron commander were welcomed into one particular house on several occasions. One evening, the squadron commander bagged a brace of pheasants en route, and left them in his car while he waited for a suitable moment to present them to his host. While the squadron commander and another officer went to have a bath, Bob was ushered into the drawing room where, to his consternation, he found his host talking to a Home Guard sergeant who just happened to be his Lordship's gamekeeper. He was complaining about ruffians from the airfield shooting pheasant indiscriminately and out of season. Bob had heard that to avoid the sound of gunfire the Rhodesians sometimes did their pheasant shooting with a bow and arrow. He had visions of his squadron commander appearing in the doorway, bathed and full of bonhomie, with the brace of pheasants in hand ready for the grand presentation to his hosts. At the first available opportunity Bob excused himself, went to the car and covered up the incriminating evidence. Back at the house he just managed to intercept the squadron commander. Once the sergeant, or gamekeeper in disguise, had left, they solemnly presented their gift, claiming the age-old excuse that the birds had been struck by their car. In the days of severe meat rationing this windfall was most welcome, and their story was not questioned, though their host had a twinkle in his eye as he carried off the birds to the kitchen. There were similar tales of pilots 'dining on partridge and pheasant up and down the south coast where they poached with complete abandon'.[22] When Bob returned to the airfield that evening he was in high spirits. It was a beautiful sunset. He went back to his tent, which as a flight commander he did not have to share, and wriggled into his kapok-filled sleeping bag on a low camp bed. He was asleep within minutes.

Next morning he was due at briefing at 5am. His orderly woke him at 4am. Breakfast was ready in the mess tent. Bob raised the tent flap and took a look at the weather. There was a thick fog. That would cause a delay. He rolled over and went back to sleep. When he woke he could hear activity near his tent. Needing to answer an early morning call of nature he emerged from his snug cocoon, only to find that the 'fog' was a layer of ground mist about 4ft deep and everyone in the adjacent tents was fully dressed and piling into trucks to go to the briefing. Shouting for them to wait, he flung on his uniform and, without pausing to shave, jumped into the remaining truck. Luckily for him, take-off was put back an hour and he found time to shave and have a substantial breakfast. It turned out to be a memorable day. Their task was to attack and destroy a radar site behind the coast on the extreme northern tip of the Cherbourg peninsula. The Typhoons took off with a roar, skimming over the waters of the Solent and, setting out for France, climbed to their usual height. All was quiet. At the French coast, batteries of anti-aircraft guns started firing at them, many from the port of Cherbourg itself. Their target was just beyond. Bob, leading his section of four aircraft, kept a close watch on the squadron commander and his four aircraft ahead while scanning the sky above for hostile fighters and checking the ground 15,000ft below for landmarks. A map with the target highlighted was strapped to his knee.

Suddenly, puffs of black smoke appeared. Black puffs of anti-aircraft fire in front and at the same height. To reach the target they had to fly on. He heard explosions of heavy shells far too close for comfort. A heavy crunch rocked the aircraft.

He had been hit. The engine was still functioning normally. The squadron leader called on his RT. Target in sight. Attack formation to dive-bombing. Bob could see the target area. It was covered in smoke and fires from an earlier attack. It was his turn to go in. He dived, rolling his aircraft over, got the target in his gunsight. Pressed the button to fire his 20mm cannon. Then, at an exact point in the dive, released his bombs. As he pulled up he could see the results. There were more fires in the target area and flashes of bombs exploding. Heavy fires sent palls of smoke high into the sky. He led his flight high away from the area, back to base. The squadron had survived with no losses but the ground crew pointed out several large holes in Bob's aircraft. One or two heavy flak fragments had punctured the metal just behind the cockpit and penetrated to a few feet from his head. That day, other squadrons were not so fortunate. Debriefing revealed that four aircraft in the preceding wave had been shot down in the dive. Some of the heavy fires Bob had seen could have been where they crashed.

No sooner had 266 Squadron adjusted to the rhythm of operational life than they were withdrawn temporarily to be trained to lay smoke at low level. They were sent to Snaith, a heavy bomber station on the east coast of Yorkshire. Their Typhoons were fitted with canisters of smoke-laying liquid under the wings instead of explosive bombs. The plan for invasion included low-flying Typhoons laying smoke over the beaches at first light to protect troops approaching in landing craft. It was a flawed plan. After a few hair-raising sorties over an estuary close to the airfield, it was abandoned. The problem was that to be effective the smoke had to be laid no more than 50ft above the ground. However, it was almost impossible for pilots to judge their height accurately while travelling at some 288mph in the semi-darkness of first light, even in good weather. There were several near disasters on the practice runs. Over enemy territory they would face devastating low-level anti-aircraft fire. The squadron was ordered to return to their familiar if primitive surroundings down south.

They had been away for just over a week and in that time the tempo of air operations against targets in the north and west of France had increased considerably. Typhoon squadrons were sent out daily to 'blind' the enemy by knocking out their radar. Some 100 heavy bombers demolished the enemy communications centre at Berneval-le-Grand. For the first time with 266 Squadron, Bob was sent to penetrate deep into France to attack a Panzer division near Rouen. The target area was well wooded. They couldn't see even a glint of a tank or vehicle. As they dive-bombed the general area the anti-aircraft fire started up. It was the most intense they had ever experienced. It also proved that the division was hidden in the woods, cleverly camouflaged. On several occasions Bob led the squadron to France and back without losing anyone. He wasn't given a reason but he was pleased to hear that he had once again been 'Mentioned in Despatches' in recognition of his leadership.

By the end of May, preparations for the invasion were almost complete. They were, of course, top secret. Nobody could guess where or when it would actually happen. Bob managed to get a long weekend off to visit his family. They took a bus ride to the sea. The beach was barricaded with barbed wire but there was just enough room on the sand for Suzanne to play. She was just past the toddling stage and attended a small dancing class. She play-acted songs and stories for her father. Bob helped her make sandcastles and threw flat pebbles across the water so they bounced, one, two, three, sometimes four times before sinking. It was a beautiful sunny day. Back at the flat they had cottage pie for supper. It used Alice's entire meat ration for the week. Bob told her to take care of herself. He was expecting to be rather busy and would not be home for a few days. She never liked to see him leave but this time she stood in the window with Suzanne and waved to him until he was out of sight.

Hitler always believed that the attack from the west would begin in Normandy. His generals disagreed and put huge effort into protecting the Pas-de-Calais. German fortifications in France became known as 'the Atlantic Wall'. About 18 million tons of concrete had been poured into deep bunkers. Mines were laid on beaches and in the water. Anti-glider poles were dug into fields. Hundreds of thousands of men were stationed in Norway, Holland, Belgium and around Calais. In an extraordinarily elaborate deception, the Allies flew reconnaissance flights, bombing missions and raids over Calais. They set up a dummy Army Command, which was led by Gen Patton, no less. Designers from Shepperton Studios helped make rubber tanks, fabricated landing craft and fake airfields in the Thames estuary.[23] As just about every 20th-century military commander knew from studying the legendary Chinese master Sun Tzu and *The Art of War*, all warfare is based on deception. The Allies succeeded not only in deceiving the enemy but in somehow keeping the day, the hour and the location of the planned invasion secret.

Bob and the Typhoon squadrons were sent out to 'mop up' the remaining radar stations. The whole wing attacked Cap d'Antifers just north of Le Havre on 2 June. All 16 aircraft arrived back unscathed. Their cannon and bombs had left the radar masts and buildings in ruins. On 5 June, Bob led an attack on a Wehrmacht headquarters in a château in Hermanville-sur-Mer in the Calvados region. Bad weather closed in and they had to abort the mission and jettison their bombs over the French beaches. On their way home, they were amazed to see many large ships and landing craft in the middle of the Channel, including one large merchant ship, full of troops, which was listing and sinking. They circled but had to retain radio silence. It was not until they were back at base for their debriefing that they could report the incident.

Late in the evening of 5 June, the wing was called to a briefing and told in confidence that the invasion of France was scheduled for the next day – 6 June. The long-awaited order was met with whoops, cheers and whistles by American airmen but the British were more reserved. After five years of 'fortress Britain' they were stunned by the sheer size of the whole operation. Desmond Scott, who commanded a wing of four Typhoon squadrons at Tangmere, remarked on:

> 'the airborne assaults, the quantity and variety of shipping, the number of army divisions, the tremendous weight of the air offensive. The scale and the precision of it all made our past efforts look insignificant. When the briefing was over there was no conversation, no laughter. No one lingered and we filed out as if we were leaving church.'[24]

Just before dawn on 6 June, the squadron had its final briefing. When they went to their aircraft they were surprised to find them painted with black-and-white stripes under the wings. There had been a panicky, failed search for brushes so some ground crew had instead used brooms.[25] The stripes were rather crudely painted but at least they would be easily recognised as friendly by air and ground forces at the beachheads. As they set off across the Channel on D-Day they became part of the largest amphibious armada ever seen in the history of warfare. Bob and his squadron arrived over the beaches within 35 minutes of the first troops.

6

Summer in France

RAIN HAMMERED THE WINDOWS of Southwick House, an elegant Regency mansion near Portsmouth. Southwick was headquarters for Operation *Overlord*, the Allies' plan for the invasion of Europe. An Atlantic storm had delayed the invasion by 24 hours. Men had already embarked in landing craft of all shapes and sizes, hidden off mudflats and shallow waters from Shoreham to Lymington. They became seasick as they rocked on storm-tossed water. It would be the next day – 6 June 1944 – that would carry the weight of history and memory. Allied commanders sent messages to their troops. FM Montgomery assured the men of the 21 Army group: 'on the eve of this great adventure' they would be 'striking a blow for freedom which will live in history' and wished his men 'Good luck … and good hunting on the mainland of Europe'.[1] Eisenhower, as Supreme Allied Commander, broadcast his order of the day and sent it out in a letter: 'The freemen of the world are marching together to victory'.[2] He described the invasion as a great crusade. It was his one chance, the Allies' one chance, to regain Europe. The first day was crucial. Speculating on when the invasion might be and where, Rommel summed up the importance of this moment: 'The first twenty four hours of the invasion will be decisive … the fate of Germany depends on the outcome … for the Allies, as well as for Germany, it will be the longest day.'[3]

At daybreak on 6 June, Bob's squadron were given their target – a gun emplacement near Bayeux. It was a heavy rocket-firing gun that was menacing one of the critical invasion beaches. The Typhoons swept inland. Bob could see flames and smoke spouting from US and UK warships as their guns pounded shore installations. Landing craft travelled to and fro delivering troops ashore. The whole shoreline was covered in smoke and explosions. He led the Typhoon pilots in a desperate search for the gun. It had to be silenced. It was firing directly along the line of the invading troops. Not one of the pilots could find it. Aircraft after aircraft dived down, searched for the well-camouflaged weapon, and failed to find it. They directed their bombs at the exact point on the map where they had been briefed to look. Disappointed and with a bitter sense of anticlimax, Bob turned his formation back towards the beaches and home to England.

As they crossed the French coast he saw a battleship firing heavy 15in. guns. The whole ship was enveloped in smoke and flames as each broadside fired. He realised with a jolt that at the height they were flying they were probably crossing the line of flight of the shells as they fell on the coast behind the beaches. He took the squadron down to sea level. As he dived down there were several jolts in the clear air. He saw a blurred object, a shell, hurtling through the air in front of him. Somehow, all of the squadron got home safely. Later in the day they would be back over France. It was the first of daily or twice-daily sorties over France that would last for weeks. 'The longest day' did not achieve all its objectives but it changed the course of the war in Europe.

On that first day, named D-Day (simply meaning D for Day – the chosen day), some 154,000 Allied troops landed in France, 24,000 of them by glider. The RAF flew 13,000 sorties.[4] Air supremacy was crucial to the whole endeavour. Before the first troops landed, more than 1,000 bombers pulverised German

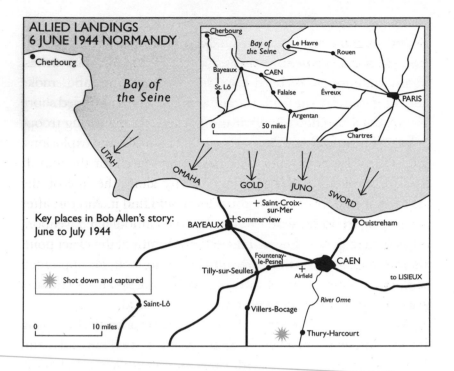

positions behind the beaches. To confuse enemy radar and clear the way for more aerial bombardment, they dropped 'window strips' of metallic paper. Small boats towed big balloons, further confusing radar by appearing as large ships. In the weeks and months before D-Day the squadron had been targeting radar installations.

Attempts had been made to seal off the invasion area. In Normandy, the organisation of railwaymen, Résistance-Fer, passed on crucial information about equipment and numbers of German troops, and disabled trains by derailing them in tunnels. Trains and railheads were a frequent target for the Typhoons' rockets and cannon, putting both friend and foe in danger. The French Resistance had been preparing for this day. They had received coded messages to cut communications on shore. '*Les dés sont sur le tapis*' – 'the dice are down' – was their order to cut cables and telegraph wires. '*Il fait chaud à Suez*' the signal to cut all communications.[5] Curiously, as the Allied troops landed and moved inland, French towns and villages carried on as usual. Shops were open. Richard Dimbleby reported on BBC radio that he saw near the battle area 'a solitary peasant harrowing his field, up and down behind the horses, looking nowhere but before him and the soil'.[6]

On the night of 5 June, southern England was full of men on 24-hour leave. Alice had been helping out at the Toc H, a Christian rest and recreation club.[7] It was full of soldiers, including quite a number of Polish men. No one spoke about it but it seemed obvious that the invasion of France must be imminent. It was late when she finished washing up in the canteen and got home. An unusual noise woke her. It was still dark. She pulled the curtain and looked into the sky. There were hundreds of planes towing gliders – all heading south. It was an extraordinary sight.[8] It was 6 June. Her fourth wedding anniversary. She stayed awake, anxiously waiting for the BBC news. They talked of fighter-bombers dive-bombing German defences. Bob must be among them. She tried not to be worried. She spent the day looking after her three-year-old child. Early editions of the newspapers carried announcements. The headlines were good. The King would make a speech at 9pm. Gen Eisenhower was quoted saying 'the tide has turned'. Alice realised that she would probably not see her husband until the invasion was consolidated. Within a few days, all the men had left the area.

By the time Bob and his squadron of Typhoons flew their second sortie on D-Day, the English Channel was grey with ships delivering troops and equipment. On this occasion Bob's brief was to seek out and destroy enemy troops reported to be advancing towards the beachheads. The Typhoons circled south of Caen and saw a column of troops heading towards the town. The convoy seemed to be stationary, with vehicles nose to tail. Bob dived into the attack, loosing his bombs, and then took a steep turn to come back again.

On the second pass, the squadron of Typhoons strafed the length of the road with devastating 22mm cannon fire. As he manoeuvred, Bob saw the upturned faces of the German troops still embarked in their open troop transports, heading for the front. He was struck by the bravery and remarkable discipline of the men. It must have been terrifying to be attacked at such close quarters. Climbing away, he could see that many of the vehicles were on fire and the road was pockmarked with craters. It was a sobering sight. He had never seen the enemy so close. It made up for what they had thought was their earlier failure to find the gun battery behind the beach. Several days later, they learned that their early morning attack had silenced the rocket gun. They had either destroyed or damaged it. Both their D-Day sorties had therefore been a success. However, the Germans held Caen and that was to cause problems for the liberators for weeks to come. The battle for Normandy had begun.

On D-Day itself, the RAF Typhoon squadrons were given specific targets. They reported to Air Operations Control, which was temporarily based in a tender, or support ship, at sea. By nightfall, the first Fighter Control Centre was operating ashore. Within hours of the troops landing and securing a bridgehead a second Fighter Control Centre had been established by the Americans. In a text-book case of army co-operation, the Allies maintained a 'degree of intimacy' that was astonishingly high.[9] All along the Allied front line, air liaison officers and teams of controllers checked out the position of enemy anti-aircraft guns. They had to be quick. On 7 June, D-Day plus one, the Germans managed to get two flak regiments armed with 88mm guns along the road to Caen. 184 Squadron were sent out to deal with them. It cost the lives of three pilots. Further south, the Germans moved one of their best divisions,

Panzer Lehr, towards the bridgehead by daylight. It was a bad move. Subjected to overwhelming air assaults, they lost all their men and equipment. In future, they moved by night and made greater efforts to remain hidden during the day.

The Allies had another weapon, the existence of which was kept secret for 30 years after the war was over. It was called Ultra, and it made use of the Enigma decoding machine to break the enemy's encrypted radio and teleprinter signals. It had been invaluable in the Battle of the Atlantic. Now it was to prove itself again. The Ultra cryptanalysts identified the headquarters of Panzer Group West at the chateau at La Caine, 12 miles south of Caen. On 10 June, 40 Typhoons from the four squadrons of 83 Group dived into attack. They were followed by 61 Mitchell bombers of 2 Group, dropping 500lb bombs from 12,000ft.[10] In the orchards around the chateau were uncamouflaged office caravans, wireless trucks and a number of staff officers watching through field glasses as the Typhoons swept in. In total 18 were killed, including the chief of staff. The headquarters were pulled back to Paris. It was a serious blow to German plans for a counter-attack.

It was one of the last set-piece attacks by Typhoons. For most of the battle for Normandy, the Typhoons were free-range. Often they would be in 'cab rank' patrols with a small number of Typhoons keeping contact with a radio van travelling among the troops. It was a tactic that had been used very successfully by the Wehrmacht and by the Allies in North Africa and Italy. If ground forces ran into large numbers of enemy infantry or armour, they radioed a map reference and description of the target to the fighters overhead. Sometimes they let off a coloured mortar bomb to indicate their position.[11]

Most days, the Typhoons flew a given sector behind enemy lines at 3,000–5,000ft. They looked for any movement that would indicate German forces. It was a cat-and-mouse game.

Bob and his squadron toured the roads and bridges behind the bridgehead. Anti-aircraft fire from expertly camouflaged gun positions in woods and tall hedgerows betrayed the enemy. Unfortunately, it was often deadly accurate; men and aircraft were lost on every mission. However, overall the tactic was successful. On 12 June, Rommel signalled to FM Keitel:[12]

> 'The enemy is strengthening himself visibly on land under cover of very strong aircraft formations … the enemy has complete command of the air over the battle zone and up to about 100 kilometres behind the front and cuts off by day almost all traffic on roads or in open country.'[13]

On the same day, 12 June, the first V1 flying bomb landed in London. Terror returned to south-east England. Bob managed to ring Alice from his base in Needs Oar Point. Without saying why, he asked her to move downstairs. He thought she would be safer. In fact, Chichester was spared. Over the summer, Londoners took to shelters and to the Underground as 2,419 of these pilotless flying bombs dropped on the capital. Distinguished by their sound and by the quiet that came before they fell, they were nicknamed 'doodlebugs' and killed 5,126 people in London alone. The pressure was on to push forwards into France and overwhelm the launch sites of this deadly weapon. Launch sites that had been targeted for months by the RAF.

Bob and the Typhoon squadrons were flying in 12-hour shifts starting at noon and midnight. There was no stand-down time. The mess kept them well fed with cooked breakfasts, lunches and dinners. They flew almost every day. Only bad weather kept them on the ground; low cloud, rain and heavy ground mists sheltered the enemy and inhibited the airmen. The Typhoons had a range of around 500 miles, which could be extended to 900 miles with additional fuel tanks. Crossing the Channel wasted precious time and miles. They were impatient to get on the ground in France.

By the evening of 7 June, groups of commandos and construction men had built an emergency landing strip. The next day they built another and on 10 June they completed a more substantial ALG (advanced landing ground) at Sainte-Croix-sur-Mer.[14] Spitfires from 144 'Canadian' Wing based at Ford, near Arundel, Sussex, were the first Allied aircraft to put down and refuel for the return to England. By the end of June, 11 temporary airfields had been built – some within reach of enemy artillery fire. What they really needed was to capture Caen with a big enough airfield to support both the RAF and the Army in their plans for advancing into France. Within 36 hours of the invasion, Caen was in ruins. Wave after wave of Allied bombers killed 600 people on 6 June and a further 200 on 7 June. Thousands more were wounded.[15] A warning had been given but came too late for anyone to leave.[16] The raids lasted ten minutes. By evening, a quarter of the city was in flames. Electricity, telephone, water and fire-fighting equipment were all destroyed. People started fleeing to the countryside, some in their nightclothes. By 10 June, British troops were no nearer. German divisions had massed to the north and west, strengthening their perimeter defences. The bombardment continued. The medieval cathedral was smashed to pieces. Citizens sheltered in the stone quarries that had once been used to build their city. Twice Gen Montgomery attempted to bash his way through the German lines and twice he failed.

What happened to Caen was an extreme case of what was occurring across the coastal regions of Normandy. Attacks on roads and railways, attacks on hidden anti-aircraft guns or V1 launch sites – all left the neighbourhoods in trauma. It has been calculated that 19,890 French civilians died. Dozens of hamlets were reduced to rubble. Allied troops found flattened villages, burned orchards and dead animals in a destruction zone reminiscent of the battlefields of the last war. Where the Typhoons had strafed roads, bodies lay awaiting burial. 'Much of the German transport was horse drawn. Dead horses lay in their traces.'[17] The roads were filled with bewildered people dragging their belongings in wheelbarrows and prams, seeking some sort of safety from the fighting. Soldiers tried to barter soap and cigarettes for fresh produce – eggs, potatoes, meat. Some didn't bother to barter and did what occupying armies have done throughout history – looting and ransacking the land as they moved on.

For three weeks, Bob and his squadron kept up daily flights over France. Squadron records log their successes. Targets included petrol bowsers, ammunition trucks, lorries and convoys. They also note 'farmhouse left in flames' in an area that 'showed evidence of heavy bombing'. Their targets were in towns and villages in the Calvados district of Normandy, Lisieux, Tilly-sur-Seulles, Courville, Fontenay-le-Pesnel and the area south of Caen. They went for canal bridges and railway bridges. On 18 June, they took out the northern and centre bridges at Thury-Harcourt. From 19 to 22 June, a violent storm with gale-force winds raged across the Channel, combined with an unusually high tide. More ships and materials were lost than in the invasion.[18] One of the artificial 'Mulberry' harbours was completely smashed. Many air operations were cancelled but Bob's squadron kept on flying. The Americans were attempting to take Cherbourg. It took days. On 25 June they succeeded, but the city was by then a wreck and the port had been destroyed.

The storm had further delayed Montgomery's attempt, code named Operation *Epsom*, to take Caen. His infantry men sat in trenches soaking wet.[19] The clouds were so low that it was all but impossible to provide air cover. The German 21st Panzer Division managed to move forwards. On 27 June, Bob and the whole wing, four squadrons of Typhoons, were given an important target – German Army Headquarters in a chateau at Saint-Aubin-du-Perron. It was easily identifiable. Wave after wave of Typhoons lobbed some 48 500lb bombs into the chateau. Some bombs were fused to explode up to 24 hours later. The main building was destroyed and all the outbuildings razed. Inevitably, one or two of the attacking aircraft were caught by anti-aircraft fire. They no longer had to make the perilous 60-mile crossing back to England. There were airfields within the bridgehead where damaged aircraft could land and get patched up.

Some squadrons had already been moved from their 'temporary' airfields in southern England to a 'temporary' airfield in Normandy. Bob was fully expecting to be one of them. But no. As June ended they learned that they were to be withdrawn from the front line in order to be converted from dive-bombing to rocket-firing. Bob had already practised rocket-firing. His logbook entry contains 'RP' with a couple of underscores, an indication perhaps of his disappointment at being moved from the front line, albeit temporarily.

The squadron flew into an armament practice camp at Eastchurch in Kent. They were once again living in comfort, with hot and cold water, laundry service and a decent mess. There were at least three parties and even a dance during their two weeks there, but no time off or out of camp. Their aircraft were converted to carry eight 60lb armour-piercing high-explosive rockets, four under each wing, mounted on rails fixed where the bombs had previously been carried. The rockets were aimed through an optical gunsight and released by a button. Attacks would be made in dives of between 45 and 15 degrees to the horizontal and at ranges of between 1,500 and 500 yards depending on the angle of the dive. This meant that they would have to dive down to less than 3,000ft to be able to release the rockets at the correct range to hit pinpoint targets such as tanks. It was a novel and exciting new task but the prospect of carrying out such low-level attacks in the Normandy battle area caused concern. They knew the targets were heavily defended by notoriously accurate anti-aircraft fire. They'd completed the course and were preparing to return to their home base when a signal arrived. The squadron was ordered to rejoin 146 Wing in France. The afternoon was heavily overcast with thunderstorms as the squadron took off in pairs and headed at low level for Hurn, an unfamiliar airfield in southern England, near Bournemouth. They spent the night in tents before leaving for France the next morning.

Bastille Day, 14 July, turned out to be another first for 266 Squadron. Instead of making the return journey to France and back, the squadron landed at the temporary airfield on the beachhead at Sainte-Croix-sur-Mer near Bayeux. It was the first Advance Landing Ground (ALG) laid on D-Day. It had an ammo dump and fuel. Ground control was based in the local church. The front line was 11 miles away. From the air, the airfield looked pretty much like their base in the New Forest. Temporary track laid on farmland. But they raised a storm of dust as they touched down and taxied to dispersal. There were no buildings and very few tents to be seen. The unfamiliar ground crews who welcomed them and refuelled the aircraft seemed to be living in trenches and dugouts covered with pieces of corrugated iron and wooden planks from packing cases. The wing's equipment and their ground crew had yet to disembark at the local Mulberry Harbour, a harbour made out of floating concrete blocks that had been towed across the Channel. The pilots spent an uncomfortable night in a deserted farmhouse. They had nothing to eat except Compo – an emergency pack of Army rations. There were no beds or bedding. Pilots slept on the floor wrapped in whatever clothing they had with them in their aircraft. Bob had his greatcoat. He thanked his stars he had something that could serve as both blanket and sleeping bag. An advance party of squadron aircrew arrived the next morning to get the aircraft ready for operations. Within a few hours they were flying over the lines on armed reconnaissance.

It took a few more days before 'order and civilisation'[20] settled the squadron into their new home in Normandy. Tents arrived and were put up by the pilots or whoever was going to occupy them. Field kitchens and messes were installed in marquees. Each night the air was filled with the sound of exploding anti-aircraft shells fired by both sides at hostile aircraft marauding over the beachhead. The newcomers soon realised why seasoned commando-type ground crews preferred to sleep underground protected by corrugated iron. Every night there seemed to be a fair amount of debris falling from the skies. Those with tents were loath to give them up so they compromised by protecting the sleeping area with corrugated metal sheets. Late-night revellers returning to their own tents took to dropping bricks or stones on the improvised shelters. They made a satisfying thud compared to the sprinkling of shrapnel and annoyed the sober early-to-bed sleepers.

There had been little chance of contacting the family, especially under stringent security, though Bob did manage to send Alice a note telling her that he was in France. She was pleased to have received it before she opened the local newspaper and found a picture of Bob and some airmen in what looked like a field with an orchard behind. The caption explained that this was a 'drinking cow' in a tented camp in France. It was a canvas water holder, suspended by rope from a tree. Playing up for the camera, the airmen were pretending to drink straight from the taps. Bob looks on with a wry smile. Alice wrote to the news editor asking for a copy of the photo. He sent her two. She hugged them to herself, praying that Bob would keep safe and come back soon.

On their arrival in France, 266 Squadron had a new squadron commander. Sqn Ldr J. D. 'Barney' Wright, like 95 per cent of the squadron, was a Rhodesian.[21] It would turn out that Barney Wright and Bob Allen's paths would cross again and they would share both misfortune and some good fortune before the end of the war. Now, in July 1944, the new commander caused some concern among the very experienced pilots of 266 Squadron. It had a venerable history. Since it was re-formed at the start of World War II it had been constantly in action. Its insignia, a *bateleur eagle volant*[22] (eagle with outstretched wings) carried the motto *Hlabezulu,* the siNdebele word for 'the stabber of the sky'. It engendered pride in all the men. During the Battle of Britain the squadron had acquitted itself well but suffered terrible losses: three senior officers and five pilots in two days. Since then, for the next three years, if the men were not on a course learning new skills, they were in action. They knew the dangers ahead. Barney Wright announced that he intended to lead sorties over the battle area at a much lower altitude than had hitherto been the norm. He had not yet experienced the intense anti-aircraft fire that greeted any aircraft flying at less than 4,000ft. Bob was not the only pilot to realise that he might be foolhardy enough to try it.

On 18 July, the new commander led the squadron, two flights of four aircraft, on an operational sortie for the first time. Bob was leading the second flight of four aircraft. Their task was familiar: to patrol just south of the battle area and attack any movement on the roads. After about ten minutes, the formation leader called on the RT. There were a number of vehicles on the road below. Ready to attack. The two flights circled to change formation, ready to dive. Bob searched hard for the target his squadron commander had sighted. All Bob could see were a number of horse-drawn vehicles heading away from the front line. He knew that the German army still used horse-drawn transport but this didn't look right. To Bob's experienced eye it looked innocent. Too easy a target. Too good to be true. But the leading flight was already into its dive. Bob was duty-bound to follow.

The attack was a shallow dive. As Bob approached, the rockets from the first flight were already exploding. Not on the road but on adjoining fields. The noise of the explosives terrified the horses. They were rearing and bolting. Bob reached the point of pressing the button to release his rockets. No. This was definitely not a military target. He could see that it was a small convoy of refugees. He didn't fire. He was flying low over a chaotic line of carts. With a final brief close look, his worst fears were confirmed. He called over the RT to his flight not to fire. When they returned to base and landed, they went to the debriefing. This could be awkward. The squadron commander insisted that it was military traffic they had attacked. Bob did not argue. The pilots in his flight were silent. Bob's logbook registers 'attacked with R.P. traffic (?) on roads'. Bob commented later that his confidence in his new leader was not all it should be.[23]

18 July was the day the Allies renewed their efforts to take Caen. Always regarded as essential to the success of the invasion plan, Caen had remained in enemy hands for six weeks. Tension was building up between the Allies, between generals and between the services. The Allies were no further than 20 miles from the sea. The air marshals turned on the Army. Their men had flown 163,403 sorties of which 131,263 were in support of ground forces.[24] They had lost men and aircraft, mostly in Bomber Command. They complained that the Army had dug in rather than moving forwards. As a result, they had 13 landing strips (five in the British sector) rather than the 27 planned for. They had 35 squadrons rather than 81.[25] Gen Montgomery led Operation *Epsom* at the end of June but failed to get further than the ruins of the northern outskirts.

Meanwhile, to the west of Bayeux, the Americans had taken the useful port of Cherbourg on 18 June and now they were aiming south to Saint-Lô, but were bogged down in the bocage. Peculiar terrain notable in this area of Normandy, the bocage is a field system of small pastures enclosed by high hawthorn hedges, bisected by narrow sunken lanes. Roman legions had been halted by it centuries previously. Caesar wrote that the hedgerows 'present a fortification like a wall through which it was not only impossible to enter but even to penetrate with the eye'.[26] The Americans fought field by field, blowing holes in the hedgerows, trying to spot snipers hidden in long grass. The local people waved white cloths as they collected eggs or fetched their animals. Soon all was blown away. It has been estimated that 100,000 cows died in Normandy. Some 400,000 buildings were damaged and many villages had not a building left standing.[27] They reached Saint-Lô on 19 July, the day after Montgomery's next attempt on Caen.

Operation *Goodwood* (another English racetrack for a code name) was intended to take Caen and move on to Falaise. The bombers went in first. In three hours, more than 2,100 bombers dropped 7,000 tons of bombs with the loss of nine aircraft. The British press were reporting victory by the next evening: 'Caen: the big break-through. Mightiest Air blow of all time launches the great offensive. Armour now swarming into open country.'[28] Celebration was premature. At the end of the second day Montgomery broke off the attack. He had lost 500 tanks (a third of British armour in Normandy) and sustained 4,000 casualties.[29] He had taken Caen but it would be many more weeks of destruction before he got Falaise.

On 19 July, Bob's squadron was in the air supporting Operation *Goodwood*. They had been told to expect more resistance from the Luftwaffe. A number of German fighter squadrons had been redeployed from the Russian front. The Typhoon squadrons took turns to wait on their temporary airfield in cockpit readiness. Four aircraft at a time would be waiting for the order to scramble for an instant take-off. Bob's squadron had been on call since first light but his flight of four were not due to take over on the runway until 1pm. He and a few others took the morning to visit a local farm and buy eggs and Camembert cheese. They had an early lunch. Then went out to their aircraft and strapped themselves in, ready to take over duties. He signalled that they were ready. At the same moment, a red Very cartridge fired from aircraft control. It was the signal to scramble. To Bob's surprise, the flight he was about to relieve started engines, taxied out and took off. Bob and his flight were left on the ground feeling somewhat miffed. They had to wait. About 15 minutes later they got the order to scramble. A number of enemy fighters had been seen over the bridgehead. Bob and his flight spent 30 minutes fruitlessly searching. They were ordered to land. At the debriefing there was bad news. The flight that had taken off before them had run into 25 ME109s and got involved in a low-level dogfight. Three of the four Typhoons had been shot down without any of the enemy being destroyed. It was a terrible blow. Since Bob had joined 266 Squadron there had been losses, but no more than one at a time. To lose all but one in a flight was devastating. The Typhoon pilots were simply not used to dogfights; they had been trained for air-to-ground attacks. Experienced ME109 pilots used to flying low-level air-to-air combat would have easily outmanoeuvred the Typhoons. It was the most serious blow to have befallen the squadron. To add to their depression, the weather closed in.

For three days rain 'nailed the air-force to the ground'. Ground crew gave the engines an overhaul under tarpaulins. The sand played havoc with moving parts. The men played cards. Looked forward to their next meal. Suffered from persistent swarms of mosquitoes. Waited for the cloud to lift. Without air cover, the armies battled on. The Americans took Saint-Lô, leaving 80 per cent of the town destroyed and more than 800 citizens dead. They moved on to Coutances. They were ready to begin the next phase, code named Operation *Cobra*, which would take them out of the beachheads and across into central France and the vital ports in Brittany.

On 20 July a rumour started. It turned out to be true. There had been an assassination attempt on Hitler. A group of German military men had planned a coup. Col Claus von Stauffenberg left a bomb intended for Hitler. It killed four and injured many others. Within 24 hours, Von Stauffenberg and 200 other officers were executed, many thousands more were jailed and all Wehrmacht officers were ordered to salute with the stiff-armed 'Heil' rather than the traditional military touch to cap.[30] The resolve of the German Army was stiffened, not shaken, by the failed attempt on their Führer. They would have to be confronted. At last, after three days, the rain stopped but Operation *Cobra* was delayed for a further day. Aerial bombardment came first. On 24 July, the bombers had to turn back because of low cloud but not before they'd dropped enough bombs off target to kill 25 American troops and injure 131. The Typhoons were out attacking tank positions. The next day, 25 July, would be one of the most memorable for the battle of Normandy and for Bob Allen.

American war correspondent Ernie Pyle spent the night of 24 July in an apple orchard near Pont-Hébert. Bob Allen spent a miserable night in his tent being sick. Just before dawn he was called to breakfast and briefing. Ernie Pyle watched fighter-bombers dive in over the battle line. Then he heard a new noise, 'a sound deep and all encompassing with no notes in it – just a gigantic faraway surge of doomlike sound'.[31] Clouds of B-17 and B-24 bombers darkened the sky. Bob was climbing into his aircraft, number MN600. He turned the engine over. It coughed. It would not start. Leaving his parachute in place he climbed out and took over a spare aircraft, R8693. Another pilot had already been through the cockpit drill and left a parachute. Bob struggled to get the clips together. It was tight. He got it fastened as he was taxiing to catch up and take off with the squadron. He took his place leading the second flight. They were to search for a concentration of vehicles in woods close to the Orne River, south of Caen. About 20 miles away to the west, on the Saint-Lô–Périers road, Ernie Pyle took shelter by a stone farmhouse as a huge concentration of heavy bombers – estimates put the total at around 2,500 planes – dropped 5,000 tons of bombs, including white phosphorus and napalm, crushing their own soldiers, the enemy and the civilian population in the devastation. It has been described as 'among the greatest concentrations of killing power in the history of warfare'.[32]

The Typhoons of 266 Squadron were still gaining height as they arrived at the front line. They were greeted by puffs of anti-aircraft smoke. They were high over their target, a group of 20 or more vehicles hidden in a wood 4 miles west of Thury-Harcourt. At 10,000ft the leader called them to attack. He dived down with the first group of four aircraft and began to circle the area. Bob, leading the following flight some 200–300 yards behind, flew straight into heavy flak. Bursts of fire and smoke surrounded them. Still the formation leader continued to circle, orbiting the area looking for the target vehicles. As yet another shell exploded close to his canopy, Bob cursed quietly into his silent microphone. He wanted to call out. 'Watch out. For Christ's sake get on with it. Dive down and attack or we'll be hit.'[33] At last, with irritating deliberation, the leader peeled off and began his attack. Bob had to hold back for a few more seconds to avoid colliding. The flak got worse. Finally. He put his wing over and began to dive at 45 degrees. As he dived he spotted the target. A glint of what might be metal in some woods just where the enemy was supposed to be. He set his sights. His aircraft had accelerated fast in the steep dive. He had to wait. The correct rocket-release height was

3,000ft. Then he could press the button and climb away. Out of trouble. At around 5,000ft he was about to start firing his cannon before releasing his rockets when there was a loud thump from the tail. His plane, still diving fast, began to yaw out of control. He had been hit. He released his rockets in the general direction of the target and tried to pull the aircraft out of the dive.

Bob struggled to pull his aircraft up but it continued to plunge. Rolled on its side and dived steeper and faster. He realised he was in serious trouble. His instinct was to jettison the canopy and get out. But that would leave him in enemy territory. He tried again to control the aircraft. To fly on. The dive continued out of his control. He pulled the canopy-release lever. The Perspex bubble over his head disappeared. The windscreen remained in place. He still stood a small chance of regaining control. But the aircraft was not diving straight. It was flying out of true. A slipstream rushed through the cockpit from side to side, pinning him hard back against the seat, so he could hardly reach the control column. All hope of saving the aircraft was lost. Now a basic instinct for self-preservation kicked in. He released the pin of his safety harness so he could get free of the aircraft. He felt the harness go. The buffeting slipstream sucked him out. Out over the cockpit and over the tail of his plane. His aircraft went on crashing downwards. He felt for the ripcord on his parachute. It opened immediately. He was swaying some 800ft above the ground.

Fast approaching the fields of enemy-held Normandy, Bob looked around for somewhere to hide. Then, suddenly, he was down with a thump. Landing with some force in a cornfield that had just been cut. The breath knocked out of him. He breathed slowly to recover and released his parachute. It drifted across the field. He was standing in the stubble with bare feet. His flying boots and socks had been sucked away as he left the aircraft. His right ankle was sufficiently painful to make walking, let alone running, very difficult. That cut down his chances of escape. And now there was the sound of gunfire. Running across the field came a number of German soldiers firing at him. They looked determined to stop him evading capture. Bob reluctantly decided that he would have to surrender. He stood still. An excited posse of young Germans raced up. Surrounded him. Pistols and rifles at the ready. '*Hände hoch!*' they shouted. Bob let them take the rather large .45 Smith and Webley revolver that he always carried. The soldiers, who were obviously from the group that had just been attacked, were nervous and jumpy. Afraid of another attack. They hurried him across the field. He stumbled across the stubble in bare feet to the shelter of the wood he had attacked only moments before.

There was an unreality to these events. Bob found it hard to believe that this was happening to him. Just 30 minutes ago he had been taking off from his airfield. The front line was only 10 miles away and yet he had been unable to nurse his aircraft there or to bail out over friendly territory. Looking back, he was surprised at how little thought he gave to his narrow escape. He could have gone in with his plane. He was lucky that his parachute had opened at such a low level and at such high speed. But here he was. Uninjured except for a sprained ankle. Feeling at a distinct disadvantage at having to hobble along through the wood in bare feet.

It was 25 July. The battle for Normandy would take another month to resolve. But by then Bob was far away.

7

Behind the lines

THE WOODS WERE QUIET. Bob was urged forward by his rather nervous captors. Thankful to leave the sharp stubble of the fields, he stumbled, trying to forget the pains in his ankle and his bare feet. It was a sunny morning. The target had been close by the village of Thury-Harcourt. It had looked rather different from the air. The woods were dense. They hid tanks and armoured vehicles. Bob was amazed to see how many there were sheltering under the trees. Camouflage netting reinforced by foliage made them almost invisible. Then he saw the troops. They looked impressive. Fit, well-equipped men who wore an instantly recognisable badge on their caps, the skull and crossbones of a notorious Waffen SS Division, the Totenkopf – Death's Head.

So it was that Bob's first encounter with the Germans was with a group who had a reputation for brutality. The Waffen SS was the 'Imperial Guard of the National-socialist regime'.[1] Five years of war had turned them from fanatical ideologues into Wehrmacht legionaries[2]. The roll call of atrocities committed in Eastern Europe continued to grow. In the west the terror began in France in 1940. A group of retreating British soldiers holed up in a farmhouse called Le Paradis had surrendered. All 97 were lined up against a wall by a company of soldiers from the 3rd Panzer Division and machine-gunned down. Four years later, shortly after D-Day, the 2nd SS-Panzer Division Das Reich, in retaliation for attacks on their positions by the French

Resistance, killed 140 French people by hanging them from balconies and lamp posts in their town of Tulle. One woman described coming home from shopping to find her husband and her son hanging from the balcony of her house.[3] Days later Das Reich destroyed the entire village of Oradour-sur-Glane. Two months later the SS-Panzer Division Hitlerjugend shot 64 Canadian and British prisoners of war. It was men from the Waffen SS who led Bob deep into the woods until they reached a camouflaged caravan. He was escorted up the steps. Inside sat an immaculately uniformed SS colonel. Bob was all too aware of how vulnerable he was. These men would not hesitate to shoot an unarmed prisoner.

The SS colonel began asking questions in German. Bob had studied German at school but he hadn't used it since he left and it was now pretty rusty. He was asked if he was a fighter-bomber pilot. As he had been shot down attacking the colonel's position, Bob saw no point in denying it. His command of German came back with a rush as he realised that his life lay in the hands of his interrogator. The colonel seemed particularly agitated about a recent attack on German ambulances on the road south of Caen. There had been many casualties, he shouted. What the hell did they think they were doing? Bob knew that he was only obliged to give name, rank and number. He also instinctively knew he had to make an acceptable reply, officer to officer. He sensed that his life might depend on his answer. He knew that ambulances had been attacked by other squadrons but they had been heading towards Caen and were believed to have been carrying troop reinforcements. He was in a tense and tricky situation. He must not say anything to help the enemy. In his broken German, Bob declared quite truthfully that if ambulances with wounded men had been attacked then that was a mistake. He attempted to assure the colonel that neither he nor his squadron had been involved in any such incident. He addressed the colonel as

'Sir' in a disciplined manner. The colonel paused. He looked hard at Bob. Noted that Bob had campaign medals and a DFC (Distinguished Flying Cross). The colonel turned to his aide, remarking that with his fair hair and pale complexion, this man could be a German. Then he dismissed him. Bob hobbled down the steps of the caravan. He could hardly believe that his looks could have saved him.

An open vehicle arrived. Two men in the uniform of non-commissioned officers of the Luftwaffe got out and ordered Bob to get in the back. They bounced along forest tracks until they reached a rough road. After about 15 minutes they began to climb a small hill. Bob found himself looking up into a battle. A number of German AA guns were keeping up a constant barrage of fire against groups of British and American aircraft that were attacking a bridge over the Orne River in the valley below. It could have been him up there. Bob saw an American Lightning hit and crash in flames. His captors whooped with delight. Bob was presented to the AA battery as a prize – a tangible result of their efforts. The crews were intrigued by their captive. Bob was impressed by their proficiency. The AA crews, stripped to the waist, loaded 88mm guns. They kept up an almost constant barrage of fire at a stream of Allied aircraft passing overhead. Bob realised that it must have been one of these shells exploding near the tail of his aircraft that had damaged the elevators and controls so he had been unable to come out of the dive.

Bob watched the men as they lost interest in him and returned to becoming preoccupied with firing the battery of guns. Would there be a chance of escape? He was too well guarded. What chance would he have barefoot and lame? It was almost mid-morning. He was beginning to recover from the shock of losing his aircraft and started to feel hungry and thirsty. He had been sick the night before and had had no breakfast before taking off. He realised he was faint with hunger. He tried out his German, poor as it might be. Could he have something to eat and drink. With somewhat bad grace his captors provided a metal mug of lukewarm black ersatz coffee and a chunk of dark brown, rough bread. The bread was rather mouldy. It seemed that these were the only rations the Germans had. The ersatz coffee was made from acorns and some sort of grain. As he nibbled at the mouldy bread, Bob thought about his colleagues just a few miles away who would now be tucking into a second breakfast of bacon and eggs. He was furious with himself. He had been so close to the line. If only he had been able to pull out of the dive, he might have made it to friendly territory, however disabled his aircraft. He might have died. He might have been burnt alive. He had a lucky escape with only a swollen ankle. Now he had to get back over the line. First, he needed boots, or some form of footwear. His bare feet were pale and pathetic. He felt undignified. Even walking was painful. Here he was sitting on an empty ammunition box in a French farmyard. The chatter of his German guards was punctuated by gunfire as they shot at his allies overhead. He must try to escape. But first he needed boots.

Bob thought out a few German phrases and addressed himself to the elder of his escorts. Could they find him some shoes or boots? He hoped he had asked correctly. His request provoked a rapid exchange between the two guards. One of them left. He returned ten minutes later with a pair of very dilapidated civilian boots and threw them at Bob's feet. Bob could see at once that they were too small; he took a broad size nine. There was nothing for it but to try to get them on. With some difficulty, especially without socks, he pulled them on his feet. It was impossible to lace up over his injured and, by now, very swollen ankle. He stood up. At least he could walk, or rather hobble, without suffering the pain of sharp stones. but he gradually developed a way of walking that minimised the discomfort and avoided blistering his feet. He did think about the boots' previous owner. Most likely a Frenchman. Possibly a dead Frenchman. His boots were Bob's salvation.

That first night of captivity saw Bob under the guard of a group of Luftwaffe signals NCOs. They put him in one of their caravan-type vehicles parked under camouflage nets in the courtyard of the farmhouse. There was just one thing on Bob's mind – escape. He knew that his best chance would be now while he was guarded on an ad hoc basis, before he was handed over to more heavily organised surveillance. All aircrew had been given advice on what to do if captured. They knew it was their duty to escape. It was their responsibility to 'protect the security of the Royal Air Force by every means within their power'.[4] A directive had been issued to every squadron flying over Europe. A copy hung in the Adjutant's office. It covered interrogation procedures, tips on the sort of tricks that might be used to winkle out information and a series of Dos and Donts, which included: give nothing but name, rank and number; behave with dignity, maintain resolution and morale. It also suggested emptying pockets before going on operations and destroying aircraft maps and documents. All aircrew were supposed to carry an escape purse but these seem frequently to have been left behind or not issued. Two million miniature compasses were made and hidden in uniform buttons, penholders and smoking pipes. Magnetised needles for finding North were hidden in toothbrushes. The full contents of an escape kit included malted milk tablets, fishing line, boiled sweets, compass, water purification tables and Benzedrine tablets for energy. Another purse contained money and language cards.[5] Of all these items, Bob was carrying only a series of silk maps and some French and Spanish money sewn into his flying jacket. Would he find a chance to use them?

In the early evening he tried engaging his guard in conversation. The guard was a young corporal, an Austrian and clearly not a Nazi fanatic. He did, however, take his guard duties very seriously and kept his Schmeisser sub-machine gun cocked ready for immediate use. Bob realised that unless he was prepared to risk assaulting the young man, he had little chance of escape. Hungry and tired, he fell asleep on the hard floor of the caravan. Later, during the night, he woke several times to the sound of Morse code coming from earphones lying on the table. Each time he even stirred the watchful guard turned the loaded gun in his direction.

Bob had been shot down at 10.56 in the morning of 25 July. Forty miles away, Operation *Cobra* was finally underway. At 9.40am 600 fighter-bombers followed by 1,000 heavy bombers were engaged in 'softening up' the front line west of the Saint-Lô–Périers road. Tragically, some Allied troops were caught in the bombing, but the effect on the German troops was devastating. The German Panzer Lehr division lost 1,000 men, including an entire paratroop regiment, 25 tanks and ten assault guns. The men were traumatised; the countryside devastated.[6] They went on fighting. Saint-Lô would not be taken for another two days, by which time it was a smoking ruin. German morale began to falter. Men wondered out loud why they were fighting. The enemy had more men and better weapons. The Germans had few aeroplanes and scarce ammunition[7]. German Commander-in-Chief, FM von Kluge, wrote of the effect of such a mass of bombs raining down on them: 'The troops have the impression that they are battling against an enemy who carries all before him.'[8] German troops were being pushed back across the river Seine. They took their prisoners with them.

At home in Chichester, Alice was writing a loving letter to her absent husband. She knew or rather guessed he was somewhere in Normandy because she had the local newspaper article with his picture. She wrote to him daily. Telling him what she was doing, whom she had met, how their daughter was progressing.

Bob had asked one of his squadron to ring her and make sure she was OK as their letters were not getting through. She told him about the ceremony of 'Lighting the Lamp' for Toc H in the Lady Chapel of Chichester Cathedral. There was an informal supper afterwards. Alice was introduced to the Bishop's wife, who took her round the gardens. Alice continued her letter:

> Miss Nuthall has been in for a chat tonight, and she really is quite nice when you get to know her. Her fiancé an American Lieutenant was killed in Normandy, and she's feeling pretty cut up, but carries on pretty well. Oh darling, I do pray and keep my fingers crossed all the time for you. I only wish I could be with you sharing the same dangers. Bobbie dearest don't let's be apart after the war Darling, sometimes when I'm just sitting with you and being quiet, I am really just terribly happy and contented, and I sometimes like to absorb your nearness. I can make my mind quite blank of other things, and then fill it with an absolutely clear picture of you. Now I can see you looking at me and smiling, and you do look happy. ... Goodnight my own dearest and God bless you and keep you safe, I will always be your very own wife xxxxxx Alice xxxxx

Alice posted her letter in the afternoon. It carries the postmark of 4.45 on 25 July. Bob was already a prisoner of a retreating army.

Bob had been awake or drifting between sleep and wakefulness until at last it was daylight. He asked permission to leave the caravan to 'attend the needs of nature'. Could this be his chance to escape? No. Another guard was called and he was closely escorted to the outside privy of the farmhouse. It did give him a few minutes' privacy, enough time to extract his escape purse from where it had been sewn into the lining of his uniform. He hid it under the eaves, thinking that if he managed to escape, he could return to the farm and collect the maps and money before leaving the area. It was vital that the silk maps remained hidden as they carried coded messages showing the locations of safe houses where an evader could find food, shelter and assistance. The maps were printed on silk because the fabric was durable, could be scrunched up into tiny wads and made no noise[9]. Waddingtons, the manufacturer of popular board games including Monopoly, were the only firm who had the technology for printing on silk. The International Red Cross supplied prisoners of war with 'care packages' made by Waddingtons, in which playing tokens secreted maps, compasses, money and even a metal file.

As he left the privy Bob met a young French girl returning to the farmhouse. Suspended across her shoulders was a wooden yoke with buckets filled with milk. She gave Bob a sympathetic smile. He was quickly marched back into the signals vehicle. There was a shout from the courtyard. It seemed that someone had arrived to take charge of Bob and escort him elsewhere. There was no sign of transport. But a stout, bovine-looking German corporal, armed with a machine pistol, ordered Bob to march in front of him away from the farm. Desperate, Bob asked if he could visit the lavatory again but his new escort would have none of it. They must leave at once. Without delay. As they crossed the courtyard, the young French girl, who had been watching from a window, ran out of the house with a large mug of fresh, still warm milk and a crust of dark brown bread, which she gave to Bob. It was good to have something to eat and drink. It was even better to receive this small friendly kindness. As he handed back the mug Bob expressed his gratitude in very rusty French and received a smile and a look of sympathy, maybe even a promise of help from the young girl.

Bob and his portly escort walked through mostly open country for the next couple of hours. Just the two of them. A grumpy soldier and his charge. Bob hobbled along in front, chewing his crust of bread. His whole attention was on how to get away from his escort. It was hot and dusty. Many of the fields had recently been harvested. Stooks of wheat awaited collection. The remaining stubble looked sharp as knives. Distant contrails marked the sky. It was a lonely road. No one passed them. Bob had heard of escorts shooting their charges and leaving them in a ditch. He knew that he must give his escort no reason to shoot; there would be no witnesses. So they trudged for mile after mile, with Bob finding it more and more difficult with his tight boots and swollen ankle to keep walking. Soon after midday they arrived at a small village. Little more than a gathering of stone houses with bright summer flowers tumbling over gates and walls. A large number of Allied prisoners were corralled into an enclosure surrounded by barbed wire. There were a few huts and a guard house. Bob was delivered to the guard at the gate. His escort turned round and began to plod back the way they had come.

Bob soon realised that this was a front-line prisoner of war (POW) cage. Its occupants were mainly soldiers, all looking very scruffy and dirty. There were a few British or Commonwealth aircrew. Bob was exhausted by his forced march and took refuge in one of the huts. Quite soon he was visited by an Australian pilot bringing a can of hot, watery soup. It looked ghastly. There were strange objects floating in it. Seeing his hesitation, the Australian laughed and explained that the basic ingredient was cow's stomach. Well, Bob knew that some people considered tripe a delicacy, so he closed his eyes and spooned the contents of the can into his mouth.

That very morning Alice and Suzanne were enjoying a breakfast of scrambled egg and toast. It was made from egg powder and the toast had no butter but they were both in a merry mood and chatted about what to do that day. They had not finished their meal when there was a knock at the door. Mrs Hughes, their friendly landlady, was standing in the hall with a telegram in her hand. Alice, her heart in her mouth, opened the telegram. She saw the words but could not read them. She stared at the paper. Then she read:

```
PRIORITY MRS A B ALLEN 10 WEST PALLANT
CHICHESTER = FROM OC 266 SQUADRON STOP
REGRET TO INFORM YOU THAT YOUR HUSBAND F/
LT R N G ALLEN IS MISSING AND BELIEVED
TO HAVE LOST HIS LIFE AS THE RESULT OF
AIR OPERATIONS ON TUESDAY 25 TH JULY
STOP LETTER FOLLOWING STOP ANY FURTHER
INFORMATION RECEIVED WILL BE IMMEDIATELY
COMMUNICATED TO YOU STOP PENDING RECEIPT OF
WRITTEN NOTIFICATION FROM THE AIR MINISTRY
NO INFORMATION SHOULD BE GIVEN TO THE PRESS
STOP = RAF BRACKNELL[10]
```

Alice held out the telegram for Mrs Hughes to read. She was completely stunned. For three years she had been expecting bad news. Now the shock was absolute. She asked herself how she could not have known. She had felt so close to Bob yet she had sensed no loss. She could not believe it. She did not cry but her face was ashen grey and full of misery. Suzanne looked at her, wondering what was the matter. Alice said that Daddy had had an accident and may not come home for some time. Then she asked Mrs Hughes to take her downstairs to play with the other children. She paced to and fro, trying to get control of herself. She realised there must be people to tell, things to do. She told Mrs Hughes she was going out to send telegrams to Bob's mother and her family. Alice walked across the square to the main post office. It seemed a normal day. People were out shopping. Chatting. There was a queue in the post office. She handed the messages to the clerk, a man of about 60. He checked the contents, then looked up at her, telling her how sorry he was and how he hoped maybe there would be better news. 'That will be eight shillings and six pence to send,' he said. Alice looked at him. For a moment she didn't understand. Then she realised that she had completely forgotten to bring her handbag. He told her not to worry. He'd send them off right away and she could bring the money next time she was in. When she arrived back at the house, there was another telegram. Sent by Bob before he had set off on operations. He would be home on Thursday, weather permitting. Alice held on to it. Was this the last message from her dearest Bobbie? She spent the rest of the day tidying the flat. Going back to the post office. Taking Suzanne to play in the park. At bedtime she read Suzanne a story. Before falling asleep the child asked what had happened to Daddy. She answered with surety, 'His aeroplane fell down and he is lost somewhere, but soon he will find his way back. Don't you worry, just be a good girl for Daddy.'[11] Before going to bed she read the telegram again. They have only said 'missing', she thought. Events over the next few weeks would test her confidence.

In the POW compound, Bob and the Australian swapped stories. First and foremost in their minds was finding a means of escape. The Australian explained that aircrew were considered prize prisoners and got moved on almost at once to more secure premises, whereas soldiers sometimes stayed in the temporary camp for a week or two. It was often possible to swap uniforms and identities, giving the aircrew a better chance of escape. The soldiers were quite willing to bluff out the remainder of the war in the relative luxury of an officer prisoner of war camp. There was much talk of an American breakthrough at Saint-Lô. Bob reckoned that if only he could stay around in Normandy the chances of the camp being overrun and released by the Allies was pretty good. The Australian admitted, somewhat cautiously, that he was in the process of negotiating a swap of identity. It needed care to ensure that the intended 'partner' was not a German 'planted' in the compound. Bob felt delighted for him. He told him about his miraculous escape from being killed in his aircraft and asked him, should he be successful in escaping, to seek out his squadron and report their meeting. The Australian readily agreed.

On Thursday 28 July there was a tremendous commotion in the compound. The guards burst into the huts, shouting at their prisoners as they separated out officers from aircrew and aircrew from soldiers. With several others, Bob found himself herded into the back of a German army lorry with two armed guards. He noticed with some satisfaction that the Australian pilot was not with them. He had managed either to hide or to conceal his identity in someone else's uniform. The lorry set off in a cloud of dust down a narrow country road. From time to time Allied fighter planes appeared. The lorries would stop. The guards jumped out of the vehicles and took shelter in the ditches that lined the roads, keeping their guns trained on the prisoners in the back of the lorries. The aircrew knew only too well how effective the cannon on their aircraft could be. They agreed among themselves that if they were attacked they would jump and scatter, risking the guns of their guards rather than being shot or burned in the vehicle. Fortunate or not, they did not suffer a direct attack.

Being moved from one place to another offered opportunities for escape but it was also a more dangerous time for prisoners. It was important that they remained in uniform and kept their 'tags' for identification. The Geneva Conventions of 1906 and 1929 provided international rules for the treatment of prisoners of war. Germany and Britain were both signatories. Under pressure of possible defeat, the rules were regularly flouted.

There was no pardon for escapees who were recaptured in civilian clothes. At worst they might be shot and left on a street corner with a 'terrorist' label around their neck.[12] In another incident, two Canadian aircrew, shot down at the end of June, had succeeded in making contact with the Resistance and evaded capture for two weeks before being caught in civilian clothes. Flying Officer H.W. Birnie and Pilot Officer D.S. Jamieson were interrogated by Sturmscharführer Albert von Bertoldi in the Caen SD – the Bertin Farm at Martigny. They were driven away by Bertoldi and two Gestapo men, Staffeloberscharführer Hermann Sieff and Oberscharführer Herbert Koch. On reaching an isolated area, the airmen were ordered out of the vehicle. While Sieff turned the car round, Bertoldi and Koch led the men into the woods. They were never seen again. Investigations after the war identified Bob Allen as one of the prisoners travelling in the same convoy.[13]

In the same area, escapee Frank 'Dutch' Holland tells how he fell in with a group of refugees moving south from Norrey-en-Auge. A German lorry appeared. Stopped. Ordered the whole group to line up along the side of the road. Then the Germans pulled out an old Frenchman, of about 70 years of age, blindfolded him and tied him to a tree. A German officer speaking good French explained what was going to happen. The old man had disobeyed an order. He had been slow to evacuate his farm. The group including women and children, were now going to witness his execution. Frank Holland described it as 'murder to make a point and to spread fear'.[14]

It was afternoon when the convoy carrying Bob arrived at a largish town. The road signs indicated that it was Chartres. All the aircrew members were offloaded at a church not far from the centre. There was a sense of relief among the prisoners on arriving in the ancient city with its historic cathedral. They felt they would be safer from Allied bombing. Their confidence was misplaced, although the worst damage came after they had been moved on. Before taking the city, the Allies subjected it to heavy bombardment. The cathedral was saved by an American army officer, Colonel Welborn Barton Griffith, Jr. He was a logistics officer who heard of a plan to shell the cathedral because Germans must be using the towers as observation posts. He offered to go behind the lines. The colonel and his driver went right up into the bell tower. There were no Germans. He succeeded in getting the order rescinded.[15] The Allied prisoners in their church close to the cathedral heard and felt the shudder of bombs night and day. Their astonishment and optimism at being delivered to the church was short-lived. When they entered they found that the interior had been emptied of all artefacts and furniture. Straw pallets covered the floor, heads to the walls with a clearway between rows. Armed guards covered each end of the building. It was a grim sight.

Bob found an empty bed space and took stock of his surroundings and his companions. There were men, not seriously injured, but bearing wounds from being shot down or beaten up. A few were in civilian clothes, though they had been careful to retain some article of uniform underneath their borrowed or stolen French civvies. They had heard how the Germans dealt with men without identity disks or uniform. At five o'clock some black bread and unsweetened acorn coffee was distributed. This was their only food and the last food for the day. Weakened by lack of food, Bob's plight was made worse by an attack of dysentery, probably brought on by the terrible 'soup' he had drunk in the previous camp. Always a rather fastidious man, he was appalled to find that toilet arrangements were extremely primitive. There were no washing facilities. To defecate you had to balance your rear end over a pole suspended over a pit in the graveyard of the church. It was open to the elements, which was both good and bad. Good because the stench was somewhat dissipated. Bad because it required a fine degree of balance to avoid falling backwards into the pit. Was there any chance of escape here? Bob noted that the pits were dug in the high-walled enclosure adjacent to the church, and that the guards appeared rather casual in their observation. The trouble was that his will and ability to escape was sapped by the dysentery. He was using all his energy just to survive. After several days of successfully negotiating the 'pits' he began to feel better but he was filthy. Some of the prisoners had managed to get pieces of rough French soap and razor blades but without water everything seemed impossible. Morale was at an ebb.

Being imprisoned in a church had its curious side. One prisoner remembers a machine gun replacing the altar crucifix. As the table was swept clear, there was a metallic clatter of altar candlesticks and chalices bouncing on the stone-flagged floor.[16] Bob describes surviving several heavy daylight raids by formations of Allied bombers. The raids seemed to be directed at airfields out of town but they were close enough to cause the church to shake. While the raids were on, prisoners were forced to lie full length on their pallets, watched carefully by guards crouched at the doors, guns at the ready. Around the church were niches some 15ft above ground level. Each recess held a freestanding stone sculpture of a saint. Lying flat on his pallet, Bob watched both fascinated and apprehensive as the statue of St Peter immediately above his bed moved an inch or so each time there was an explosion. All the statues wobbled in their niches. In time, one toppled and injured an unfortunate prisoner below.

It was early August. The battle lines in Normandy had turned. With the fall of Saint-Lô, the way was clear for Avranches and then Brittany. On 3 August Bradley ordered Patton and his newly formed 3rd Army to turn east towards Paris. Hitler urged his generals to counter-attack from Mortain. At midday on 7 August, Typhoons armed with rockets swooped down in a 'shuttle service' or 'cab rank' of attacking formations. Air history was being made – this was an outstanding example of the tactical use of air power.[17] The German army retreated into a deadly trap, in retrospect called the 'Falaise Gap'. It was one of the 'killing grounds' of the war. From the hilltop castle of William the Conquerer in Falaise, all that could be seen was the utter destruction of men and machines by the rockets, the cannon and bombs delivered by fighter-bombers. It was not without cost: 289 Typhoon pilots were killed in the battle for Normandy. During August, Typhoon pilots often flew three sorties a day. Ninety aircraft were lost and 55 pilots killed in the battles around Falaise.[18] Battles were fought and won field by field. It was almost a rout – 'the Allies took 50,000 prisoners, another 10,000 Germans were killed ... of the 2,300 German tanks and assault guns committed in Normandy only 100 to 120 were brought back across the Seine'.[19] It has been said that the 'cruel martyrdom of Normandy ... saved the rest of France'.[20] The carnage was appalling. Almost 20,000 civilians killed; countryside despoiled; trees stripped bare; orchards destroyed; the corpses of livestock left to rot. 'In the *department* of Calvados 76,000 people lost their homes and virtually everything they possessed.'[21] Liberation was violent. In less than a week Patton and his men liberated Chartres but by then Bob and his fellow prisoners had once more been moved east – behind the line.

On 5 August, Alice received two letters. The first was an official notification from the Air Ministry (Casualty Branch). It read:

Madam,
    I am commanded by the Air Council to express to you their great regret on learning that your husband, Flight Lieutenant Robert Neil Greig Allen, DFC, Royal Air Force,

is missing and believed to have lost his life as the result of air operations on 25th July, 1944.

On that day your husband set out in a Typhoon with other aircraft to attack enemy transport at Hamars, Normandy. During the attack your husband's aircraft was hit by anti-aircraft fire and was seen to crash in a field west of the target.

Enquiries are being made through the International Red Cross Committee, and any further information received will be immediately conveyed to you. Should none become available the Council regret that in due course the presumption for official purposes of your husband's death will be necessary, and a further letter will then be addressed to you.

The Air Council desire me to convey to you their deep sympathy.

I am you obedient Servant,

Signature

This letter, while not destroying all hope, depressed Alice considerably. She began to think about life without Bob. Her mother-in-law had come down to Chichester for a visit. They had a somewhat abrasive relationship. But now at least Alice had had a good cry and was ready to get on with life. When she saw Bob's mother off at the station, they parted on good terms. They had looked at the various official notices that Alice had received. 'Advice to the Relative of a Man who is Missing' explained how men were sometimes found on official lists of prisoners kept by the enemy government. 'Capture cards' might be filled in by the prisoner and sent home to relatives. If she received one she must hand it in at once. Enemy broadcasts were not reliable, it warned, and often raised cruel false hopes. The notice ends: 'Even if no news is received that a missing man is a prisoner of war, endeavours to trace him do not cease. … This official service is also a very human service, which well understands the anxiety of relatives and will spare no effort to relieve it.' Another notice warned relatives against passing on any information to the press that might jeopardise a man's chances of evading capture.

The second of her two letters that day was from Squadron Leader J.D. 'Barney' Wright, who had taken command of 266 Rhodesia Squadron just ten days before Bob was shot down. The letter of condolence was one of the more onerous tasks expected of a squadron commander. Barney Wright sent handwritten letters to both Alice and Bob's mother. There are subtle differences that give clues to Bob's character and his value to the squadron. To Alice:

Dear Mrs Allen,

I wish to express my profound sympathy to you for the very sad loss of your husband.

It was a great blow to the squadron and we miss a very fine personality indeed. Bob always lead his flight and the squadron on many occasions, setting a fine example of courage and determination which all of us shall not forget. (continues…)

And to the mother who has just lost her son, he writes:

Words fail me, as they are not sufficient to express one's feelings; Mrs. Allen; Bob was a great lad and one who had a marvellous personality, which we in this squadron miss very much indeed.

He led a flight and on many occasions led the squadron with a determined will, and courage which was a grand example that was followed and looked up at by the rest of the squadron. (continues…)[22]

Alice did not know Barney Wright. She had not met him. The letter was precious to her but she could not believe that Bob was dead so she put it aside. The following day she received another handwritten note. This was from Squadron Leader J.W.E. Holmes, until 14 July commanding officer of 266 Squadron. Alice knew Joe Holmes and his wife. As soon as he heard Bob was missing, he went to find out what was known.

From: S/Ldr J.W.E.Holmes, Officers Mess, 84 G.S.U.,
RAF Thruxton, Nr. Andover

Dear Alice,

I went to get details, and here are the bare facts. Bob was last seen at 1056 hrs on the 25th July attacking enemy transports. He did not pull out of his dive, and his aircraft was seen to crash near a small village called La Ruelle. This is just off the main road leading from Aunay-sur-Odon to Thury Harcourt.

I can't give any more details. All sorts of strange things happen in wartime – but I can't commit myself to give you any good news.

You know that Bob and I were great friends, and we both relied upon each other. He had done some excellent work in the Squadron and we must all be grateful to him for that. I'm sure that all the boys will join me in sending our sympathies to you in what must be a most trying time.

If there is any news at all I shall hasten to let you know.

Best wishes Alice, I'll write again Joe

Bob had now been missing for more than a week. Alice knew that men had been found or just turned up months after being shot down. There was still hope. Was there? She just could not believe that he was dead. Her family began to worry about her. Especially after she told them she had had a message from a ghost. She had been up at dawn and was looking out of the window at the rising sun. There was an oval mirror on the wall opposite her bed. She could see a reflection of something – the head and shoulders of a person in a flying helmet. Tense with excitement, she saw movement. He was trying to make Alice understand something. The face was hidden by goggles and an oxygen mask but the meaning was clear. Bob was all right. He was not with them. A little frightened, she got up and touched the mirror. It was perfectly clear. She thought maybe she had been half asleep. But she felt so calm. She was convinced that Bob had managed to communicate with her and that he was alive. She could not wait to tell Mrs Hughes. Her landlady was a level-headed woman who admitted somewhat wistfully to believing in the supernatural. She consoled her young tenant. It could be wishful thinking and a vivid imagination. Alice's sisters hoped that she was not as delusional as their dear sister Rose, who had found it so hard to accept the death of her naval husband. Despite all the reasonable evidence to the contrary, nothing would persuade Alice that Bob was dead.

And in France, behind the lines, Bob was feeling a little better and actually looked forward to breakfast even though it was the usual ersatz black coffee and a thin slice of brown bread. Before breakfast arrived, a bossy guard called out a number of prisoners, Bob included, and lined them up outside the church. They were herded into the back of an open lorry with two armed guards seated either side next to the tailboard. There was no chance of escaping. The lorry set off at a furious pace in the general direction of Paris. Every signpost took them further into enemy territory. Always apprehensive about being attacked from their own squadrons, Bob and his fellow prisoners kept a wary lookout. Within an hour or so they began to pass through ever increasingly built-up areas. They were now in the suburbs of Paris. It was still early morning. There were long queues of depressed-looking French women and old men outside the bakeries.

The prospect of being imprisoned in Paris gave the prisoners new hope. Here, surely, there would be a chance of escape, with or without the help of the French. It was only after they crossed the Seine and drew up in the courtyard of the Gare de l'Est, the mainline railway station to the east, that their hopes were dashed. They would soon be put on a train to Germany. Now escape was paramount. Would there be a moment? They were marched, single file, under close armed guard, up the steps into the station. It was vast. With echoes from shunting trains. Belching steam. Whistles. Barked orders from the guards. They were not taken to the trains but directed up more steps towards first-floor offices. The floor was set with yellow tiles. Overhead, great arching structures supported the glass roofs. Then up again. Up narrower stairs. Past smaller rooms. They were pushed inside a room tight under the roof. It was a hot summer day. They were left alone. They continued plotting. Could they find something to use as a tool to weaken the mortar around the window? Even if they could get it open, how could anyone survive sliding down a sheer glass roof, onto another glass roof below? The prospects deterred even the most enthusiastic escapee.

By nightfall the men had fallen quiet. Their hopes faded and morale deteriorated. The only break in the monotony was the arrival of some watery soup and the inevitable ersatz coffee and bread in the early evening. Anyone who wanted to go to the lavatory had to hammer on the door. They were accompanied one at a time to a toilet down the passage by an extremely alert and well-armed guard. There were ten prisoners with barely room to lie down. There was an iron-framed bedstead without a mattress. They drew lots for it. Two men would try to sleep head to feet on the bare springs of the bed. The rest would sleep on the floor. By dawn, few had slept at all. It was a weary, scruffy, dejected-looking party that was led out down the stairs across the station concourse to a waiting passenger train. They were escorted the whole length of the platform to an empty carriage next to the engine. They passed carriage after carriage filled with wounded German soldiers, many heavily bandaged around the head and limbs. The first-class carriages were occupied by immaculately dressed Army or Luftwaffe officers. It looked as though much of the German military was being evacuated from Paris. It was galling and depressing that Bob and his companions were included. They were not to know, but within two weeks Paris would be liberated.

The prisoners were installed in the front of the train immediately behind the engine. There was a toilet close by at the end of the corridor. The windows of their compartment were barred. There was no handle to the outside door, which was locked. There were two guards in the corridor, one positioned next to the sliding door into their compartment, the other further down the corridor near the exit. Before the train moved off, a Luftwaffe NCO appeared. He seemed to be in charge of the guards and made it clear that anyone attempting to escape would be shot. They would be allowed to visit the toilet singly. If the train stopped during an air raid, the guards would leave the train and take refuge on the side of the track. The prisoners would remain locked in their compartment. In broken English, the NCO explained that guards would be posted on either side of the train and in the event of any attempted escape they had orders to shoot and kill. He left. With much huffing and puffing and escapes of steam from the engine, the train pulled out of the station. The prisoners discussed their predicament. They agreed that if they were attacked from the air they should take their chances and make a dash for it. Best to try the unlocked corridor side of the train. Being burned alive in the carriage appealed to no one.

For the first few hours the train made steady progress. There were several prolonged halts at signals. It increased speed as it ran through open country. The prisoners dozed in their seats. In mid-afternoon, they were suddenly jerked awake by the driver slamming on his brakes to bring the train to a shuddering halt. There was much shouting and confusion in the corridor. Crashing of doors as they were flung open and shut. The Germans were obviously expecting an air raid and were evacuating the train. Soon the prisoners in their carriage near the engine were the only ones left on board. Everyone else was sheltering under the trees and shrubs that covered rising ground on either side of the track. For about 20 minutes all was quiet except for the sound of steam escaping. The tension was almost unbearable. It was broken by two blasts on the engine's whistle. Everyone climbed back on the train. After a short delay it moved off and soon entered a long tunnel where it stopped and remained for over half an hour. The prisoners were resigned to spending at least one night in their cramped carriage. They discussed sleeping arrangements. If two men slept feet to feet in each of the hammock-like luggage racks, two would occupy each of the side benches and the remaining two could sleep in the floor space under the seats.

Eventually the train moved off and gathered speed until it was going so fast that it was difficult to read the unfamiliar names of stations as they passed. The sun set. Night. The group of prisoners arranged themselves according to their plan. Bob found the luggage racks were difficult to get into but quite comfortable. Certainly a better perch than the dirty floor. The jolting train prevented anyone from sleeping more than half an hour at a time. With daybreak, the train came to a halt at a large station. They gave up any pretence of sleep and took their seats, tired, hungry and dirty. Then they saw the station's signboards – Saarbrüken.

They were out of France and entering Germany. For the first time since he had been shot down, Bob lost hope. He was in despair. All the time he was in France there seemed there was always a chance of escape in a friendly country, but now it was as if they were entering a dark, unfriendly fortress from which escape or release was impossible.

Again the train moved off, making good time through picture-book farming land. At eight o'clock they arrived at the main train terminal of Frankfurt-on-Main. For the first time they saw the impact of the Allied bombing offensive against German cities and industry. Frankfurt had received 23,000 tons of bombs in a series of major attacks by the RAF. The London *Times* reporter who saw it in 1945 described it as a 'melancholy sample' of Germany's cities. The medieval city was in ruins; a sign in front of a crater read 'Here was the house where the old great poet Goethe was born'.[23] The whole medieval neighbourhood had gone. The opera house and the cathedral were roofless. Supplies of electricity, water and coal were uncertain. Food was brought in by cart. As they left the train, Bob and his small group of fellow prisoners were glad of their armed escorts as they were herded roughly through crowds of hostile civilians waiting for trains to carry them out of the city. The POWs were in uniform. The uniform of the hated RAF. It seemed that there was a common assumption that they were the captured crews of shot-down aircraft. It was an ugly scene. The guards had to keep back hostile crowds shouting abuse, spitting, aiming blows. The bedraggled prisoners were hurried on to another platform and on to a suburban train that had just arrived and was disgorging its load of commuters arriving for work in the battered city.

The prisoners, much relieved, though shaken by their experience, were locked into their compartment and tried to relax on the hard, uncomfortable seats. Their compartment had just been occupied by relatively affluent civilians on their way to work. The ashtrays were stuffed with discarded cigarette stubs. Men addicted to smoking seized the stubs and extracted the residue of tobacco. They divided it and rolled it in discarded newspaper. Rooting in the sooty ash, they found a match. Struck it on the bevelled edge of an ashtray and hungrily smoked the improvised cigarette. Bob, admittedly a steadfast non-smoker, found it incredible that otherwise clean-living chaps could be driven to smoking saliva-ridden cigarette butts collected from ashtrays. Discards from German civilians who could have been suffering diseases brought about by wartime privations. It was totally degrading and shocked Bob almost more than any of his recent experiences.

After a short journey through hilly countryside, the train came to a halt at a station named Oberursel. New guards who had joined them in Frankfurt ordered the prisoners to disembark and march down a country road. They were exhausted. Weak from hunger. In a filthy state. Progress was painfully slow. Eventually they arrived at a military camp. The sign over the main gate read *Dulag Luft*. They had arrived at the Luftwaffe's central interrogation centre.

8

A prisoner in Germany

F IRST, THERE WAS THE reception procedure. All new arrivals were ordered to strip naked. Their clothes were rigorously searched by a number of guards. Personal items, wallets, wristwatches were confiscated and put in large envelopes carrying their owner's name. They were allowed to get dressed, in their filthy old clothes. One by one they were escorted to the cells. Bob, feeling dog-tired and weak from lack of food, found himself in a small cell with high, barred windows. There was an iron bedstead covered by a thin straw mattress inside a hessian cover. A threadbare, brown, Army-type blanket and a filthy-looking striped pillow. Bob examined the bedding for bedbugs. Maybe they had been treated with some toxin for they didn't seem to be active. For the first time since his capture he felt he could relax. He stretched out full length on his bed, drew up the blanket over his filthy uniform and closed his eyes.

The prison camp, Dulag Luft, was about 4 miles north-west of Frankfurt, 300 yards from the main Frankfurt–Bad Homburg road. The camp had been built in 1939 on the site of a government poultry farm. There was a white-stone house with a steep roof, once used to accommodate agricultural students. Now it was used as a reception and interrogation centre and for holding prisoners in solitary confinement. In 1940, several purpose-built barrack blocks had been added to provide temporary housing for prisoners in transit[1] and a hospital with 50 or 60 beds for the wounded. To the north and west were woods, to the east a market garden and to the south a sports field.[2] Dulag Luft is a short form for *Durchgangslager der Luftwaffe* – transit camp for Air Force. As he passed through the heavily guarded gates Bob regained, at least inwardly, his military resolve. From time to time they had been briefed on what to expect if they found themselves taken prisoner. Physically and mentally exhausted, degraded and filthy, he felt in no state to remember, let alone follow, instructions given months before. Training and discipline stiffened his resolve. The cardinal rule was to declare only rank, name and number. These three answers would be all he would give.

Just before he was overtaken by sleep he had looked at the marks and scratches on the wall by his bed. Some were obviously a means of keeping track of time. Others were messages. There were snatches of prayers and poems, not all of them in English. Bob was dozing when he was abruptly awakened by a guard slamming open the door and placing a can of soup and some bread on the floor of the cell. Before he could rouse himself, the elderly guard had gone, slamming and locking the door behind him. That prison sound – slam, clunk, click and echoing retreating footsteps – confirmed Bob's plight. Hope of escape seemed remote. He ate. Feeling stronger, he stood on the bed and could just peer out of the small barred window. All he could see were other cells across the courtyard. There were no washing or toilet facilities in his cell so Bob banged on the door to attract the guard. After a short pause he appeared. Bob tried to ask in German to visit the lavatory and was escorted down the corridor. This was to be the pattern for the next few days. Escorted visits to the toilet. Two meagre meals. Sleep.

On the first afternoon of his imprisonment in Dulag Luft, Bob was visited in his cell by a well-dressed English-speaking civilian who said he was a member of the Swiss Red Cross. He explained that to prove his identity as a prisoner of war, Bob would need to complete certain forms. He handed them to Bob and politely enquired about his health, assuring Bob that if he filled in the 'Arrival Report Form' his family could be notified more quickly that he was safe, but a captive.[3] With that inducement he left. Bob looked at the questionnaire. Alarmed, he saw that the answers would reveal far more than the minimum requirement of name, rank and number. At the back of his mind was some vague warning of a briefing by bogus Red Cross officials. When the visitor returned the next day, Bob somewhat defiantly returned the questionnaire unanswered, save of course for his number, rank and name.

After a further two or three days the strain of solitary confinement began to tell. The guards refused to be drawn into conversation. The need to communicate with someone was overwhelming. After dark there was much tapping of pipes by other inmates but Bob could not interpret the Morse signals. He was alone. After the war, some men admitted that they had been quickly broken by solitary confinement. They answered all the questions and were transferred to a permanent camp. A bomber crew member remembered his time in Dulag Luft; 'Three days in a room by myself when I first came here. No exercise (mental or physical), no one to talk to, not good food. The relief when someone did come in was tremendous. I talked like a drain.'[4] Most prisoners were only kept here a day or two. Bob could see from the marks on his cell wall that the longest sequence amounted to three weeks. He prepared himself. On the morning of the fourth day his cell door was flung open. Bob was ordered to accompany the guard down the corridor to a small room. In it was an immaculately uniformed Luftwaffe officer seated at a plain table. He motioned Bob to be seated. The guard withdrew. In perfect English the German officer invited Bob to take a cigarette from the newly opened packet of Player's[5] cigarettes he pushed across the table. Bob refused. He was not a smoker so it didn't require much effort to say no, but he wondered about his colleagues who had fallen on slobbery stubs of tobacco rolled in newspaper. They would have found the temptation near impossible to resist.

And so the interrogation began. The Luftwaffe officer declared that he already knew much about Bob. He knew his squadron, the names of his fellow pilots, where the squadron was based, what aircraft it was equipped with and of course how Bob had been shot down. As he listened to the litany of names and places Bob realised that while some of the information was correct, there were some important inaccuracies. Names of pilots were mentioned who had already been killed or reported missing. The present location of the squadron and its role was incorrect. Bob could tell that, while his interrogator's information was impressive, it was out of date. Day after day, two or sometimes three times a day, interrogations followed the same formula. 'We know all about you but you must tell me all I want to know in order that your claim to be an RAF pilot can be corroborated, so that you can be declared an official POW and passed to an appropriate camp.' Psychologically it was a very tempting lure but one that Bob, he knew not from where, drew strength to resist. After a week or so, even Bob became bored by the monotony of his replies – rank, name and number. Name, number and rank. Number, rank and name. Just those three.

When the war was over, five German officers faced trial for war crimes committed in Dulag Luft. They were accused of breaching Articles 2 and 5 of the Geneva Convention, which declared that all prisoners should be treated humanely. Article 5 expressly forbade pressuring prisoners to reveal military information. From 1941, Dulag Luft was the Central Air Force Interrogation Centre or 'Auswertestelle West' for the whole of the western theatre of war. Its function was to obtain information about the Allied Air Forces through the interrogation of captured aircrew. It was their job. The commandant from

November 1941 was ObstLt Killinger. He had a small staff of 50, including three or four interrogators. By August 1944, when Bob was imprisoned, there were more than 500 staff and 60–65 interrogation officers,[6] chief of whom was a Maj Junge. Junge had been a POW in World War I.[7] He is reported to have emphasised the need for courtesy in dealing with detainees. His team gleaned information through 'Booty' – scraps of material recovered from aircraft and airmen. Pilot's maps, letters, newspaper cuttings, theatre tickets – anything and everything was meticulously filed. One prisoner, sitting at the entrance to the interrogation room, remembers running his fingers through the sand in a fire bucket next to him. He pulled out a complete escape kit minus its cover.[8] He hurriedly reburied it. Maj Jung believed in using 'disarming amiability' in interrogations. Bob learned to be very wary of him.

Another of the soldiers later accused, Lt Eberhardt, was almost certainly the man who presented Bob with the fake Red Cross form on his first day. Eberhardt was not an interrogator. His job was to assess the character of the prisoner and suggest what type of interrogation would be successful. Eberhardt was a young man who had been in the Hitler Youth. He was a fluent English speaker, educated at an English university, a smooth talker and courteous. However, at his trial Eberhardt was accused of colluding with the guards to subject prisoners to excessive heat to wear down their resistance under interrogation. The cells had been purpose built. The walls were thickly insulated and soundproofed, to prevent prisoners communicating with each other. Windows were tight shut. Each cell had a heater, operated from outside the door. At the trial, prisoners testified that they had suffered from intense heat for hours at a time. Sqn Ldr Cairns said that it was so hot in his cell that he could hardly breathe and that his metal bed was too hot to touch.[9] There was sufficient evidence from 11 prisoners who suffered this treatment to convict Eberhardt. The tribunal sentenced him to three years' imprisonment. Although he was interrogated by Eberhardt, Bob was not one of those subjected to the heat treatment.

Bob had been in solitary for 11 days when he was summoned earlier than usual. His interrogator was uncharacteristically brusque and frigid. He did not invite Bob to sit but slowly and deliberately closed the file in front of him. Then he declared that, as Bob had failed to co-operate, he had no alternative but to assume he was a terrorist and would be handed over to the Gestapo for questioning. With a click of his heels he gathered up his papers and left, leaving Bob still standing. After a short delay, two heavily built civilians in leather coats came into the room. This looked serious. They began their interrogation. Name: Robert Allen. Rank: flight lieutenant. Number: 63484. More and more questions followed, to which he gave no answer. Date of birth? Place of birth? Rate of pay? Where shot down? Where taken prisoner? Squadron? Group? Station? Letters and numbers on aircraft? Type of aircraft? The questions ran on. Apart from confirming that he was the holder of a Distinguished Flying Cross, the evidence being sewn on his uniform jacket, he said nothing. The interrogators shouted. If he didn't answer their questions he would be removed from the jurisdiction of the Luftwaffe and dealt with by the Gestapo using their own methods. Bob began for the first time to feel afraid. He was determined to remain calm. To appear unruffled. He repeated his name, rank and number and said that was all he was going to say, here or anywhere else. He wished he were as confident as he pretended to be.

Suddenly his interrogators got up and without a further word left the room. Bob was ordered to return to his cell, escorted by his guard. In the quiet of that small, silent space there was nothing to console his isolation. He spent a long and troubled night thinking about the change in his interrogation. For the whole of the next day, after his meeting with the Gestapo, Bob braced himself for a further interview. The morning wore on. A paltry lunch was pushed through the door with no comment. As the afternoon ended and the cell grew gloomy in the evening light, Bob became increasingly tense. Without the usual summons he found his emotions jangled. Had he been forgotten? Overlooked? Was his transfer to the Gestapo in the process of being arranged? That night, deprived of the daily jousting with his interrogators, Bob felt at his lowest ebb since arriving at Dulag Luft. He even began to speculate how much he could tell about himself to achieve POW status and be allowed to leave. Anything to be free of solitary confinement. He studied the marks on the wall. His own scratches numbered 13. Deeply depressed, filthy, hungry, despairing, he somehow, somewhere inside, found an inner resolve – the strength to hold out. At last he slept. Next morning he woke ready to face whatever the immediate future had in store for him.

It was now more than three weeks since Bob had been shot down. Back home in England, his family were getting used to the idea that he was gone. Only Alice held on to her unfounded belief that he was still alive. She kept busy. She kept hoping. One morning in early August she had a surprise visitor. David Hughes (no relation to her landlady, Mrs Hughes), one of the pilots from Bob's squadron, phoned to say he was in Chichester and would like to call on her. Alice could hardly hold down her excitement; he must be bringing news of Bob. Mrs Hughes showed him up to the flat and, although she was longing to listen in, left them to talk. David introduced himself, then closed the door carefully. He listened until Mrs Hughes' footsteps could no longer be heard on the stairs. Then he stepped forwards and grasped Alice's hand. He could hardly contain his delight. He was smiling as he told her that they had every reason to believe that Bob was alive. Alice took him by surprise. She knew it. She was ready to dance around the room. But David wanted her to realise the seriousness of his news.

An Australian navigator who had escaped from the Germans in France had come to see the squadron in Normandy. He told them that he had met Bob in an improvised POW camp near the front line. Bob was well except for a sprained ankle. He had asked the Australian, who had already laid plans for escape, to search out the squadron and tell them he was alive and well. When they showed the Australian the squadron photo he immediately identified Bob Allen as his fellow POW. Furthermore, said David, smiling, Bob told the Australian his wife's name was Alice. That clinched it. There were celebrations in the mess that night. But, David stressed, Alice must share this news with no one until it was officially announced. David had been briefed to tell Alice: it must go no further. It could even harm Bob if, for example, he was trying to escape. Alice was so excited she had to try to calm down. David told her that the Germans were being pushed back day by day so no one knew where Bob might be. But he had been seen alive. They toasted the good news with tea. As he left, David reminded her, 'Tell no one. Then we'll all get together and have a party when this lot is over.'[10]

It was mid-morning before Bob was once more summoned from his cell in Dulag Luft. He was surprised to find a new Luftwaffe interrogator seated at the table in the interrogation room. This officer was all smiles and charm as he explained that his colleague had been called away on active duty so Bob had now become his responsibility. No mention was made of the Gestapo. Showing much solicitude for Bob and his treatment to date, the new interrogator invited Bob to take lunch with him in the officers' mess. Bob could hardly believe his ears. Determined to appear unmoved, he accepted. But, he pointed out, he was hardly in a fit state, filthy and tatty, to dine in an officers' mess. The Luftwaffe officer brushed excuses aside and, without the

184

customary guard, accompanied his charge to the dining room of what appeared to be the staff officers' mess. They sat at a small table for two.

Thinking about it later, Bob realised that he hardly noticed the meal. It seemed to be slices of fried corned beef and potatoes. It took great control to resist the impulse to gulp it down quickly. It had been so long since he had eaten real food. He ate very, very slowly. To prolong the occasion, Bob accepted a cigarette from a packet of Player's and smoked awkwardly as he sipped his coffee. His host laughingly chided him for his defensive attitude. The Germans knew all about a film the RAF had made about their interrogation procedures. The various methods and tactics used to make men talk. Bob, determined not to rise to the bait, shrugged his shoulders. At least he had had a good meal.[11] He was taken aback when his host abruptly rose to his feet and announced that Bob would be escorted back to his cell to await the next phase of his interrogation. It would begin tomorrow. Bob slowly stood up, looked his host straight in the eye, thanked him for his hospitality and walked out to the corridor where a guard waited to escort him back to his cell. He kept a calm exterior. Inwardly he was dejected. In turmoil. It was so unfair suddenly to be reminded of decent surroundings and proper food. He resolved not to give in. He would be prepared for whatever they had.

Bob wasn't to know that the Luftwaffe men who ran Dulag Luft had fought off a takeover by Hitler's secret police. The Luftwaffe took some pride in playing the game of war by the rules. Commandant Killinger was not a member of the Nazi party. Towards the end of 1944, he and his deputy Maj Junge were accused by their own Reichsmarschall of fraternising with the enemy and being too lenient with prisoners. They were both acquitted. This episode was taken into consideration by the Allied War Crimes Trials at the end of hostilities and they both received relatively short, five-year sentences.

It was unusually early the next morning when Bob's cell door was flung open and the guard, who had previously refused to be drawn into any conversation, told Bob to follow him to where he could wash and shower. Bob was amazed. What luxury. Shower. Warm water. Breakfast. A chatty guard, who managed to spring a big surprise: he told Bob that he would be transferred to a proper POW camp after breakfast. Bob, still wary of the soft approach, thought he would believe this when it happened. The guard became quite talkative and friendly. They used a mixture of German and English. Bob was astonished to hear the guard's final words: that for Germany the war was nearly over and that very soon the western Allies and Germany would be united against Russia. These were almost the last words that Bob heard in Dulag Luft. Within the hour he was escorted to the camp office where his watch and wallet were restored to him. Then it was out into the courtyard to join other prisoners, mostly American flyers. Bob realised that he had spent 14 days in solitary confinement. Most of the Americans had only spent at most three or four days at the camp. The majority of them were members of large crews of Fortresses and Liberators. Unless a particular aircraft was known to carry new equipment or suspected of being on a special mission, the passage of crew survivors through the interrogation centre was routine. At this stage in the war, Dulag Luft was taking in 60–70 new arrivals a day. They needed to process their prisoners and move them on as quickly as possible.

There were two lorries in the courtyard. With much shouting and pushing by the guards, 20 prisoners were herded into the open-backed vehicles. Always alive to an opportunity for escape, Bob noted that the two guards by the tailgate were well armed and vigilant. The drivers set off with a rush. Prisoners lurched against each other, barely able to stand. In less than an hour they arrived at a barbed-wire-enclosed camp with guard towers at each corner. The barbed-wire perimeter fence was equipped with floodlights. They were at the Wetzlar camp, which had been newly built at Klosterwald, 37 miles away.

Wetzlar was a vast improvement. Apart from a nucleus of 30 RAF prisoners who were kept as permanent staff, prisoners stayed in Wetzlar a few days, a week at most, in transit to other camps across Germany. By July 1944, it housed more than 700 prisoners. All new arrivals were examined for lice and other infestations before going on to hot showers. Clothing and footwear were issued. For the first time since parachuting to earth, Bob became the possessor of a proper pair of boots. He could admit to a twinge of nostalgia when he saw his French peasant's boots thrown into a dustbin, but his feet were finally pain free. The Red Cross had been supplying clothes, blankets and food since the early days of the war four years before. Large consignments of airmen's service issue clothing included greatcoats, battledress and sets of underwear. Men who escaped burning aircraft often arrived with their clothes in tatters. Some had been captured in civilian outfits. Others, particularly Americans, wore 'fancy articles of clothing', which were confiscated[12] and replaced with standard RAF issue.

After the initial reception, Bob joined the other prisoners, several hundred RAF and Americans, for a communal meal. On the day when a Swiss delegation visited, the lunch was: soup, meat with green peas and potatoes, and a custard pudding.[13] Meat was served every other day to conform to rationing quotas. The food, mainly from Red Cross parcels, was served in reasonable quantities. Food, or the lack of it, or the quality of it, was a constant issue in POW camps. According to the Geneva Convention prisoners should be served the same food as their captors, or at the very least the same as second-line troops. However, in Germany from 1941 this was amended to a German civilian worker's standard, which was very meagre.[14]

Red Cross food parcels, two per week per prisoner, supplemented the German rations. Food was pooled and prepared by NCO prisoner cooks. After three weeks of bitter ersatz coffee and black bread, Bob was delighted with two meals a day in a friendly environment. It was prison but it was a caring environment. He began to relax.

Officers, NCOs and airmen slept in separate barracks. There was time to talk to fellow prisoners about their experiences. Bob heard of incredible escapes from burning aircraft. He heard of many crew members being captured soon after crash landing and taken back to their aircraft the next day to view the wreckage and burned bodies of their fellow crew. This practice was a prelude to interrogation in the hopes that distress might loosen lips. Many men had been ill-treated by local German civilians. There were stories of severe beatings and even lynchings. There were a few men who had been shot down several months earlier who seemed broken in mind and spirit. They had been sheltered by an underground organisation in Holland that had been infiltrated by the Gestapo. They were recaptured and, under torture, had revealed the identities of their helpers. The helpers were rounded up and shot without trial. At night, men sleeping ten to 15 to a room revealed their hidden thoughts and fears. Tortured minds screamed with dreams and nightmares, waking both themselves and others more fortunate, who had been able to sleep or rest easy.

Bob was just getting used to his new surroundings when he was called to assemble with 100 others in front of the main gate. After much counting and checking of identities they were marched off under guard to the railway station. They were loaded into two carriages standing in a siding. They were told nothing. After a short delay, the carriages were shunted off by a small engine and attached to the back of a goods train. The prisoners quizzed their guards. Where were they going? '*Nach dem Ost*' (to the east).

They learned nothing. For two days they moved slowly across Germany. As their train negotiated curves and bends they could see that the front carriages were loaded with tanks and military hardware. They were moving east, further into Germany and closer to the killing grounds of the Russian front. News had been swirling around about Marshal Zhukov's crushing defeat of the German Army in Operation *Bagration*, and that 25 German divisions – more than 350,000 men – had been obliterated since the end of June. With the defeats in Normandy and other fronts in the east and in Italy, the German Army had lost more than half a million men in three months.[15] Still they sent reinforcements, younger and younger, to fight on. When their train halted at various stations, Bob and his fellow prisoners saw wounded men returning from the front. Their morale and spirit seemed high. German Red Cross women, well dressed and good looking, distributed food, cigarettes and hot drinks to their troops. They pointedly refused to even look at the Allied prisoners of war. Yet the German troops were not hostile and exchanged smiles and waves.

After two days and nights the train stopped. The two carriages were shunted into a siding. It was unnaturally quiet. Fresh guards arrived. With the usual shouts of '*Raus, raus*' the prisoners were disembarked, counted several times and eventually marched away from the town. They saw signposts. The town was called Sagan. No one seemed to know where it was except that it was many miles east.

It was late August. As they made their way uphill along a tree-lined dusty road they annoyed their guards by searching for half-ripe apples in the verges. At the brow of the hill they looked down on an orderly barbed-wire-enclosed camp. They had reached Stalag Luft III.

Stammlager Luft, base camp for aircrew, was purpose built to house air force officers near Sagan, a small town in lower Silesia close to the Polish border. The site had been chosen carefully. It was far from a neutral country. The camp was built on the edge of a pine forest on yellow sandy soil, easy to extend. Difficult for escapees. Eventually there were 10,949 inmates: about 2,500 were RAF officers, 7,500 US Air Force and some 900 from other Allied forces. There were hundreds of guards, known as the 'goons'. Each compound was surrounded by a 9ft-high double barbed-wire fence. Watch towers, the 'goon-boxes', were set

POW CAMPS
HOLDING
BOB ALLEN
1944–45

DENMARK

SWEDEN

BALTIC SEA

NORTH SEA

Danzig

Lubeck

HOLLAND

Hamburg

Elbe

POLAND

Vistula

Berlin

Luckenwalde

Zagan

GERMANY

Torgau

Stalag Luft III

Leipzig

Dresden

Oder

Dulag Luft

Frankfurt

Prague

CZECHOSLOVAKIA

Rhine

FRANCE
Strasbourg

Danube

Vienna

Bratislava

Bern

AUSTRIA

0   100 miles

SWITZERLAND

ITALY

HUNGARY

every 100–150 yards. The guards had machine guns, searchlights and a clear view of the camp. Just inside the main wire, a trip wire ran the length of the perimeter.[16] It was a formidable sight.

On arrival, after much searching and checking of identities, the newcomers passed through reception into the main camp, where they were warmly received by the inmates. They were divided into small groups and escorted to a hut. Each hut had several rooms. A room was called a 'mess' or 'the mess'. Bob was the sole newcomer to his mess, which already had 11 occupants. The only remaining bed was at the top of a three-tiered set of wooden bunks. After a welcoming meal he clambered with some difficulty up the side of the other bunks and lowered his exhausted body on to the straw-filled mattress. He had been given two clean but thin blankets. He felt safe. He had filled in a postcard to be sent home. He could relax. He fell asleep.

Bob woke next morning to the sound of clinking mugs on a table in the centre of the room. Steaming-hot coffee was being poured. By each mug was a thin slice of German black bread. One by one, men left their bunks and sat on stools either side of the table. Bob managed to climb down from his lofty perch. He did wonder if he would make it at night in the dark. This, he was told, was breakfast. There would be a similar meal at midday and a more substantial main meal at about 6pm. Bob had just finished his coffee when 'appel', the ritual roll call, summoned them all to the parade ground – Bob noticed it had been marked out as a football pitch – to be counted. Then, Bob was told by his room leader, he must present himself at a meeting in one of the other blocks.

The 'meeting' took the form of a debriefing. Three RAF officers sat behind a table. They indicated that Bob should sit opposite. For about three-quarters of an hour they chatted informally. He noticed that every now and again a question about his background, service career and experiences as a prisoner was slipped in. He was clearly being vetted to guard against the danger of his having been infiltrated into the camp to supply inside information to the Germans. Once Bob had convinced the 'security committee' of his authenticity, they welcomed him and briefed him on the ground rules he must observe while in the camp. One rule in particular came as a surprise. Bob had understood that to escape, or at the very least to plan to escape, was a duty. Now it was made clear that, until further notice, escape attempts were forbidden by the senior British officer. Bob was shocked to learn the reason for the ban: 50 Allied airmen who had attempted to escape from the camp had been executed on recapture. This notorious episode became known as the 'Great Escape'. Escape had been in Bob's mind since he was first captured standing barefoot in a field in Normandy. Now he was being told to forget it. The game had changed completely.

In the early years of the war, Germany had a reputation for treating its prisoners in accordance with the Geneva Convention. During the first winter of 1939–40, RAF officers were fellow players in the game of war. They shared meals, drinks and even skiing excursions with their captors. As the war dragged on, however, the relationship between the players cooled. Among all military prisoners, the RAF men had a reputation for being inventive, inclined to be defiant towards authority, belligerent and alert for any opportunity to escape. They developed an esprit de corps with a humour and language all of its own. An Army lieutenant commented: 'The RAF were always a thorn in the German flesh. They had no respect for anything German and said so rudely ... Consequently they followed the sport of "goon-baiting" with joy and zeal, careless of German threats and happy over German wrath and exasperation.'[17] Stalag Luft III was built in 1942 on the express order of the commander-in-chief of the Luftwaffe, Reichsmarschall Hermann Göring, as a high-security camp for RAF prisoners of war. A camp impossible to escape from; a camp so comfortable that inmates would not find it worth their while trying to escape and one where the Luftwaffe retained control.

The first commandant of Stalag Luft III, Obst Friedrich Wilhelm von Lindeiner-Wildau, was a highly decorated professional soldier, never a member of the Nazi party, who had the respect of the prisoners in his care.[18] The camp was run by the prisoners with a senior officer in overall charge and another senior officer appointed to each hut. There were men who had spent years of their life in the camp. One of the first Americans to be taken prisoner in July 1942 was Spitfire pilot Lt Col 'Bub' Clark. He remembered having clean sheets every week. 'We were probably the best-treated POWs anywhere in the world at the time.'[19] There were activities: sports, including football and golf, education, theatre – and planning escapes. The first successful escape was in October 1943. It became known as the 'Wooden Horse'. Prisoners built a gymnastic vaulting horse from plywood taken from Red Cross parcels, put it out in full view of the guards and used it to carry away sand from their tunnelling. Three men managed to escape as a result.

The next breakout, several months later in March 1944, was the 'Great Escape'. The senior officer and the Escape Committee agreed to a plan that they thought would be a serious embarrassment to their captors and a big boost to prisoner morale. In the planning stage, they thought as many as 250 might escape. To their advantage there was a steady stream of new prisoners who brought experience and expertise. At least one-third of the prisoners in Stalag Luft III were involved in some way or another. Perhaps one-third of the others kept their heads down, content to wait out the war, but all supported the escapers' efforts. The commandant, Von Lindeiner-Wildau, could not spare scarce manpower to chase after escapees as it was needed on the battlefields. He reluctantly passed down the orders of his Nazi High Command. In future, recaptured escapees would be handed straight to the Gestapo or put in jail prior to being processed by the Gestapo. A second order decreed that all recaptured officers except British and American would be executed at Mauthausen concentration camp.[20] Von Lindeiner-Wildau, suspicious that a mass breakout was being planned, tried to persuade the senior RAF officer against it; the Luftwaffe could only guarantee the safety of prisoners if they were in their hands.

The tunnelling continued. Tons of yellow sand were dispersed about the camp. Hundreds of forged passes, travel documents and identity cards were produced. Uniforms were tailored into civilian suits. More than 600 men were involved in the preparations. On 24 March 1944, they were ready. In total, 76 men got out before the escape was discovered. One of those who escaped was Romas 'Rene' Marcinkus, Bob's Lithuanian room-mate in 1 Squadron. He stood a good chance of getting away as he had first-hand knowledge of the Baltic ports.[21]

Within hours, Hitler was informed of the breakout. He was incandescent with rage, demanding that all recaptured prisoners should be shot. His aides, including Göring and Himmler, argued that such action would provoke an international outcry. Hitler compromised: 50 prisoners would be shot as an example. On 27 March, the notorious 'Sagan order' was issued. The Gestapo carried it out. As groups of escapees were recaptured they were taken away and shot. Rene Marcinkus was caught near the Baltic port of Danzig, taken from a lorry with three others, and machine-gunned – shot in the back in a wood near the village of Gross Trampken.[22] At Stalag Luft III, the news was slow to arrive, but on 15 April a list of 47 escaped men was attached to the camp bulletin board. Another three names were added later. During his 21 months as commandant, Von Lindeiner-Wildau had witnessed 262 escape attempts, of which 100 involved tunnels.[23] Two days after the 'Great Escape' he was replaced.

The full story of the Great Escape from Stalag Luft III did not emerge until after the war was over. At the time, 14 April 1944, the British Foreign Secretary, Anthony Eden, informed the House of Commons that 47 prisoners had been found shot. Two months later, on 23 June, he was blunt: 'From these facts in His Majesty's Government's view, only one possible conclusion. These prisoners of war were murdered at some undefined place or places...'[24] The search for perpetrators to charge with war crimes began. The Great Escape made headlines in the press. Perhaps it was because the prisoners had been airmen – some had flown in the Battle of Britain, others flew the Lancasters and Blenheims carrying the battle to the enemy – it caught the public imagination. A few months later, in September, shortly after Bob Allen arrived in Stalag Luft III, a poster was distributed to all POW camps. It read: 'TO ALL PRISONERS OF WAR, THE ESCAPE FROM PRISON CAMPS IS NO LONGER A SPORT.' Nothing daunted, escapes continued to be planned. The change was that escape was no longer an officer's duty.

Bob found that he easily fell into the daily routine of the camp and his mess. Time revolved around twice-daily parades, when all prisoners had to turn out to be counted. Hours were marked by set mealtimes. In the evenings, food from Red Cross parcels provided a reasonable hot meal. Bob never got used to the long wait during the day when only coffee and a single slice of black bread spread with German margarine and sometimes a little jam or ersatz honey was available. At first he was just content to sleep a great deal, even during the day, and become part of the backdrop of the camp's activities. He marvelled at the mental and physical resilience of some of his fellow inmates who had been prisoners for up to four years. He was told that compared to the early days, when the Germans were riding the crest of their successes, it was now relatively easy to bear the monotony and routine of confinement. It would only be a matter of time, maybe only weeks, before the Germans were defeated.

They had a secret radio in the camp. The BBC's daily news bulletin was clandestinely received and distributed on handwritten sheets read after lights out. The Germans knew about the radio but, however hard they tried, making innumerable snap searches, they failed to find it. It brought the prisoners news of home. Bob had sent his official postcard and *Kriegsgefangenenpost* (POW letter) forms as soon as he had arrived in Stalag Luft III. He received his first letter from home in mid-September. Prisoners were allowed to send two letters per person per month. Each was subjected to German censorship before it left the camp. It was some sort of two-way communication and despite the inhibiting eye of the censor it was, next to the Red Cross parcels, a big factor in maintaining morale. MI9, a department in the War Office dedicated to helping British POW escapees, encouraged the use of 'dotty' codes – a row of dots in the heading or text to indicate a hidden message. Very few prisoners used the codes. News from home was not always comforting. Some wives and girlfriends abandoned their absent partners. Members of the family and friends were killed in air raids. There were anxieties.

Bob's first postcard home said:

'I AM FIT AND WELL DARLING. NO INJURIES AT ALL. MY ADRESS [sic] ON FRONT LEFT CORNER BUT WILL GIVE PERMANENT ADRESS [sic] NEXT TIME. GIVE MUM THE NEWS AND MY LOVE. RED CROSS SUPERB PLEASE GIVE DONATION. YOUR MONEY SHOULD BE STILL PAID AS BEFORE, ANY TROUBLE SHOW THIS TO BANK. GOD BLESS AND ALL MY LOVE TO YOU AND SUZANNE. BOB XXX signed F/L RNG Allen'

He sent it care of Alice's father in Chatham. The front left corner showed his name Flt Lt Robert Allen and his number 63484. The address was 'Lager-Bezeichnung: M.-Stammlager Luft 3'. Alice received this postcard in October, though it was dated 15 August. It was unusual. Cards from POWs were written in pencil. This one was written in ink. Was it authentic? Alice was sure she recognised Bob's handwriting. She had been under some financial pressure. Within a few weeks of Bob being reported missing she had received a letter from the Air Ministry. For the next 26 weeks (taking her up to January 1945) she would receive 'the married rate of allowance and two-sevenths of the pay in issue to your husband on the previous day'.[25] It amounted to £4 16s 0d a week. It would last until 'it were known that your husband had died in circumstances entitling you to a pension'. She took Bob's postcard to the bank, but they would not accept it as evidence that he was alive. Alice considered returning to teaching. There was a vacant post but it would involve leaving home at 7.30am and not returning until 6pm. Mrs Hughes offered to look after Suzanne but Alice decided it was too long a day. She would manage. At least she knew Bob was alive, even if the officials would not recognise the fact. In late August, Alice had received a letter from Scotland. It was from Mrs Beatrice Bell, 11 John Str., Penicuik, Midlothian, Scotland:

'Dear Mrs.Allan, [sic] While listening to the wireless tonight I heard your husband's name mentioned as being taken a prisoner of war in the West. They gave his name and number as:- Flight Leiut. Robert Allan no.63484 and his next of kin as on enveloppe. [sic. This was Alice's father's address in Chatham]. I don't know whether you will have had official word yet or heard the broadcast which was from a German station but I thought I would write and let you know in case you hadn't. Please write and let me know if this has helped you in your anxiety. I am Yours truly, (Mrs) Beatrice Bell'[26]

Alice cherished the letter, though she was wary. She had been advised by the Air Ministry not to make contact or discuss her husband with anybody. How would she know if Mrs Bell was genuine or a fifth columnist? What was the broadcast? Why had she not had official notification? These were anxieties that she did not share with Bob. He would want to know that everyone at home was well and managing to cope with the wartime restrictions.

In addition to rationing and issuing coupons, the Board of Trade had introduced a 'Utility' scheme for clothes. Top designers used approved fabrics to make clothes for mass production. The rules were strict, specifying the number of buttons, length of hem, number of pleats, pockets and belts. Men were not allowed trouser turn-ups, wide lapels or double-breasted suits. The Royal princesses appeared in Utility dresses. Alice was aware that women had taken many jobs that had previously been men's preserve; they were even flying Spitfires as ferry pilots. There was a shift from pre-war social attitudes. The *Beveridge Report* had been an instant bestseller. It promised a new deal for poor families and a fairer society. It was the foundation of the welfare state, promising free health care, unemployment benefits, sick pay, and old-age and widow's pensions. Alice and her sister Joan, who had managed to get a posting nearby, had many an earnest discussion about the future. In Joan's case, it would be a future in America. Her fiancé, Freddie, would arrive unexpectedly from his airfield in France bearing American food and the occasional bottle of champagne. Their visits brightened up a rather dull routine.

In September the 'blackout' was reduced to a 'dim out'. There was still no street lighting but windows could be left uncovered unless there was an air-raid warning. The V1 flying bomb and doodlebug attacks that had peppered the home counties over the summer had eased. This was largely because the Allies had overrun their launching sites in France but also because a way had been found to shoot them down. A new fighter aircraft, the Tempest – a faster version of Bob's Typhoon – had arrived. Brave men using radar to guide them could shoot the flying bombs down or tip them over by clipping their wings. Together with anti-aircraft fire and barrage balloons, they brought down 3,912 V1 flying bombs between June and September 1944.[27] A government minister spoke out: 'The battle for London is over.'[28] He was wrong. A new menace was about to arrive – the second of Hitler's secret weapons, the V2 rocket.

This was a supersonic ballistic missile. There was no chance of interception and it could carry a ton of explosives. It could be launched from a small concrete platform that was almost impossible to target. It could demolish an entire street; in September and October nearly a million homes were lost and 2,754 people were killed in London and the suburbs. The government imposed a total news blackout, so fearful were they of the effect on civilian morale. In November, the ban was lifted and the press reported: 'The V2 rocket comes to southern England ... Britain's front line home is under fire again ... There is no siren warning. No time to take shelter.'[29]

The great hope that D-Day would be followed by a quick end to the war was fast fading. The advance through Normandy had been much slower than anticipated. The Allies were in Paris but no closer to the Rhine. In September, Gen Montgomery led Operation *Market* – a plan to drop airborne troops on a series of bridges from the Dutch border to Arnhem on the lower Rhine. It would be closely followed by Operation *Garden* – armoured troop corps would drive along a 60-mile corridor through German-held territory to link the bridges.[30] Operation *Market Garden* was a costly failure dogged by bad weather and poor intelligence. The First Airborne Division lost 7,000 elite troops (1,300, or by some estimates 2,500, killed).[31] News of this setback reached Stalag Luft III. Hopes that they might be home for Christmas diminished.

Among those captured during the *Market Garden* offensive was Bob's erstwhile 266 squadron commander, Rhodesian Barney Wright. On 15 October he was ushered into Stalag Luft III where, as a squadron leader, he had rather comfortable accommodation – a room with a bed, mattress, sheets, three blankets, two chairs, a washstand and a fireplace.[32] When he had a chance, he told Bob his story. He had been leading an attack on enemy ships in the Hook of Holland. Diving through 3,000ft at 460mph, he fired when the ship's funnel was in his gunsight. He pulled out of the dive, blacked out, then heard a huge bang. The aircraft lurched and he was heading straight for the earth. Metal from the exploding ship had torn into his aircraft. He crashed, just missing some houses. Almost at once he was seized by German soldiers.

Barney Wright's experiences were similar to Bob's. Initially, he was taken to the local ak-ak HQ, where he was given tea and complimented on his shooting. Next day he was taken to a camp where about 200 airborne troops were looking miserable behind barbed wire. Later, they were all put on a train to Dulag Luft. Barney saw devastation all around. Frankfurt was like a dead city. He spent nine days in solitary. Interrogated, threatened with the Gestapo. Finally, he was moved on 'out of the cages of starvation' to the relative comforts of Stalag Luft III. Barney Wright had only taken over 266 Squadron a week before Bob was shot down. They'd had hardly any time to get to know each other. Bob had had reservations about his squadron commander. Now they were in the same prison camp but in separate compounds with few opportunities to meet. Future events would bring the two men together once more.

As the days got colder there seemed to be less food. The German economy was feeling the strain of five years of war. Disruptions to agricultural production had forced a reduction in rations – for both the German people and their prisoners. The brutalities of the Nazi regime and the full horrors of the war with Russia were revealed as territories in the east were regained. By 1944, 7 million men of working age – Jews, Poles and Russian POWs – had been killed or left to die.[33] Russia was not a signatory to the Geneva Convention. More than half the Russian POWs died of starvation. There was a group of Russians in a compound attached to Stalag Luft III who had to survive on German rations alone. The British and American prisoners had their Red Cross parcels. The distribution of food from these parcels was the highlight of the week. The contents, mostly of American origin, were designed to sustain one person for seven days. In the interest of economical living, with the exception of two chocolate bars and packets of cigarettes, all the other contents – margarine, sugar, biscuits, dried fruit, tinned spam and Nescafé – were pooled within each room and used for communal meals. The Red Cross parcels were literally life-saving.

The British Red Cross Society and the Order of St John of Jerusalem worked together for British POWs and their families. The King gave them space in St James's Palace to organise their POW department. They were, like the International Red Cross in Geneva, both neutral and independent of government control. In the first year of the war, parcels were addressed to individual prisoners but with swelling numbers this became impossible and batches were sent to the camps. It was a vast operation. By 1945, more than 19 million food parcels, packed at 23 centres in the UK, were sent. In addition there were 1,643 special parcels for sick POWs and, in the last two years of the war, 39,758 medical parcels including 12 dental units for surgery and lab work.[34] The whole operation was paid for by subscriptions and donations from the public. Workers donated into a 'Penny-a-week Fund' directly from their wages. Flag days, cinema collections, sales of produce in village halls – all raised thousands of pounds. International Committee of the Red Cross, ICRC, ships were allowed through the European blockade to offload in Lisbon, Marseilles and later Antwerp, Lübeck and other north-German ports. From there they were loaded into railway trucks. Many prisoners swore that but for the Red Cross parcels they would never have 'made it'. They would have died of starvation.[35]

In Bob's mess there was much secrecy surrounding the use of sugar and raisins from the parcels. At least half the total of each parcel was surreptitiously funnelled into a large carboy, half full of water. This was concealed in the wall of their room behind the corner stove. With the addition of some yeast stolen from the German kitchen, the hope was that the liquid would ferment and provide an alcoholic beverage in time for Christmas. Home brews were strictly forbidden by the Germans, mainly because of irrational behaviour from drunken prisoners. Otherwise careful and conscientious inmates had been known to climb the high wire fence around the compound. Unfortunately, this gave guards in the nearest sentry box a legitimate excuse to open fire. Every hut in every compound had some alcohol in production. Potatoes were a good bet. 'Potatoes put into a container with an appropriate lid which was made airtight by scraping bitumen off the roof and melting it down, opening it up after about six weeks and then taking off the scum, leaving a liquid of varying degrees of potency.'[36] The results could be devastating. One hut found a use for their brew as lighter fuel.

It was one of the wettest autumns on record and as November turned to December a bitter cold gripped Europe from east to west. The Allied armies fought in mud and water through Holland and met stiff resistance in Alsace. All the POW's hopes of being home for Christmas faded. Bob was aware that despite the escaping ban some preparations were being made. Security was tight. Only those directly involved in digging a tunnel or disposing of earth over the gardens knew the direction and location of tunnel routes. On one sombre day in early December the whole camp and a representative from the Swiss embassy attended the unveiling of a memorial to the 50 tunnellers who had been shot. The German camp commandant not only permitted it but contributed to it. The stone cairn with the names of all who were killed still stands.

As days turned to weeks, weeks to months, how were the prisoners to keep up morale and stave off despair? Many long-term prisoners had begun educational courses in the hope that they would be of use when they returned home. Books were circulated from block to block. It was claimed that at least 300,000 books had accumulated in Stalag Luft III. Much time was spent gambling. Card players had regular poker, whist and bridge nights.[37] The currency of gambling was cigarettes and chocolate or *Lagergeld,* a form of currency issued to the POWs out of their pay. Enshrined in the Geneva Conventions was an agreement that up to 20 per cent of an Allied officer's pay could be forwarded to a POW through the Red Cross. The German authorities scrupulously converted the hard currency into *Lagergeld* – a voucher or script that was used to buy toothpaste, soap, music and books and to pay off gambling debts.

There were more athletic pastimes for days when the pitches were neither too waterlogged nor too frozen for play in the rugger league or soccer league, with equipment sent in Red Cross parcels. The east compound, the first to be built at Stalag Luft III, constructed a nine-hole par three golf course running between the blocks. Golf balls were handmade out of tinfoil, rubber bands and shoe leather until a consignment arrived via the YMCA.[38] Golf clubs were made out of broken hockey sticks and melted-down metal water jugs. Over time, enough musical instruments arrived at the camp to supply a full 42-piece orchestra[39] based in the North compound. There were glee clubs, a choir, chamber-music groups and light entertainment to be had in all the compounds.

In Britain it was bitterly cold. Christmas Eve 1944 was one of the coldest for 50 years. In Chichester, Alice was determined to put on a brave face. Suzanne was three years old. Her dancing school put on a charity performance. The older girls showed off their ballet, the younger ones performed playlets and the tiniest sang nursery rhymes. Suzanne sang a little solo of *Mary, Mary Quite Contrary* followed by *Little Miss Muffet* with her best friend acting the spider. The hall was full. They raised a substantial contribution for the Red Cross. Alice and Suzanne joined the family in Kent for Christmas. There had been no news from her brother Bill (he was in the Navy) for three months, which caused some anxiety, but at least they thought 'no news is good news'. Surely they would have heard if his ship had gone down. There was bad news from the western front. After a news blackout of four days, they learned that the Germans had made a big push forwards in the Ardennes, a wooded plateau across the borders of Belgium, Luxembourg and France. They took the Allies by surprise. It was the start of what would become known as the 'Battle of the Bulge', with huge Allied casualties. As she sat in her parents' home that Christmas, Alice thought of the young men who had sat round that table laughing and joking and planning the future. Of the 27 boys in Bob's class at the Grammar School, 18 were already dead. It had been five years and still the war was not over. It seemed worse than ever.

The 12 members of Bob's mess greeted Christmas Day not for its church services and carol singing but for the moment when they could indulge in their special meal and the home brew. The camp news-sheet, called the *Log*,[40] included recipes from 'Basil Beeton', a joky reference to the book *Mrs Beeton's*

Household Management. Cakes were made from semolina, sugar, raisins and margarine available in Red Cross parcels. They had their Christmas meal at 6pm. The inevitable corned beef was turned into a 'shepherd's pie' with a topping of mashed potato. To follow, an enormous sweet bread pudding seemed to contain just about everything the duty cooks could lay hands on – crushed biscuit, stale bread, margarine, powdered milk, cocoa, sugar and raisins that had escaped being consigned to the brew. This concoction was baked in an oven in the communal kitchen at the end of the block. For once, when the meal was finished, everyone felt full. The moment had come. Excited, they held their mugs out to be filled from a jug of liquid decanted from the carboy behind their stove. First there was toasting. Forced jollity. The liquid was sipped cautiously. It was OK. Larger swigs were downed. Half an hour later they began to look at each other to see what effect it was having. Nothing. Even after consuming two whole mugsful there was no sign of anyone being inebriated. The awful truth dawned. Fermentation had not occurred. They were seriously disappointed. Resigned to yet another sober evening.

The mess settled down to the usual routine. They played cards or dominoes. Read their books. Lay on their bunks dreaming of past and future Christmases. But not for long. The effects of unfermented liquor on half-starved stomachs was dramatic. Without exception, everyone was forced into a hurried exit to the lavatory block not once but several times during the evening and night. By midnight, all were suffering from stomach pains and diarrhoea. Their discomfort was heightened by the sound of much hilarity and drunken noises coming from an adjoining room where the brewing had been successful.

So Christmas came and went with the weather remaining snowy and very cold. The temperature in the huts was bearable but well below comfortable. For once the prisoners had some sympathy for their guards, who manned the sentry boxes and patrolled the perimeter in very bitter, icy conditions. There were times when the prisoners thought they could hear the roar of Russian field guns at Poznań 50 miles to the east.[41] They noted that German planes that normally took two hours to attack the Russian front line were returning in less than half an hour. Some of the stronger, fitter guards were sent away to fight. The Red Cross parcels and mail stopped. On New Year's Day the Scottish prisoners planned some rather limited Hogmanay celebrations. However, before the evening meal, a routine BBC news-sheet arrived. It was terrible news. For weeks, even months, the POWs had fastened their minds and morale on news of German reverses and retreats in both the west and the east. Now here was news of a major German offensive in the Ardennes. News of a considerable German success, particularly by the Luftwaffe against Allied airfields in Belgium and Holland. The Luftwaffe had chosen New Year's Day for the surprise attack. They managed to assemble 750–800 fighters from their diminished resources and, in complete radio silence, with training units making up the numbers, took 16 Allied airfields.[42] Later it was calculated they had managed to destroy more than 300 aircraft and damaged a further 190.

For the men in Bob's mess, where no special celebrations had been planned for the New Year, the news was particularly depressing. Could it be that the war would continue for another year? Even the sturdiest of minds struggled to contemplate such a bleak future. Bob found it hit him hard. For the first time since his narrow escape from death, his capture and imprisonment, he felt extremely depressed. He lay on his bunk trying to put the bad news into some sort of perspective. He reminded himself that he personally had been involved in the successful invasion of Normandy. In the six months since the initial assault there had been hardly a single serious reverse.

During that time the Allies, and particularly the Americans, had been pouring men and material into Europe. He asked himself, 'How could Germany, on the point of defeat both in the East and West, mount an offensive sufficiently powerful and effective to do more than cause a momentary setback to the Allies' plans decisively to defeat Nazi Germany?'[43]

One thing was clear to the RAF POWs as they pored anxiously over the news-sheets over the next few days. The weather. It was winter fog, snow, sleet and rain that wrecked the Allies' aerial observations and allowed the German troop advance in the Battle of the Bulge. Fog and low cloud prevented any action against advancing German Panzer divisions. Operation *Ultra* had been defeated by the complete radio silence of German troops and aircraft. Operation *Bodenplatte*, the German attack on Allied airfields, had been waiting for a break in the weather. The news of the attack, especially the German broadcasts over the camp loudspeakers, was depressing, but it had been at a huge cost to the enemy. The Luftwaffe lost the best of their commanders and had 143 pilots killed or missing and 76 captured. Veteran Adolf Galland said: 'We sacrificed our last substance.'[44] The Luftwaffe had neither men nor resources to recover. The Allies had replaced their aircraft within a week. As the weather improved, the British and American tactical air forces reasserted their air supremacy over the battlefield.

To a certain extent the bad news from the west overshadowed continued successful offensives and advances by the Russians on the Eastern Front. The Eastern Front ran from the Baltic through Poland, Slovakia and Hungary to the Dalmatian coast. The German Army still used horses[45] but their mechanised forces were desperately short of fuel. The last few oilfields in German possession were in Hungary. It took the Russians weeks to take Budapest, so determined was the German resistance to losing the last of their oil. The Western media were so taken up with events in the Ardennes that the battle for Budapest received scant coverage. In deep winter snow, the Russians surrounded the city. The opera house, theatres and cinemas remained open. The sound of Russian guns inspired one Hungarian to write: 'This is the most beautiful Christmas music. Are we really to be liberated? God help us and put an end to the rule of these gangsters.'[46] It would be February before Budapest was recaptured. The Red Army had 180 divisions and 9,000 aircraft ready for a winter offensive against the Reich. The Stalag Luft III camp loudspeakers, in blatantly distorted and exaggerated German news bulletins, announced 'strategic withdrawals' and 'regrouping' of the victorious defenders of the Fatherland. Reading the truth between the lines of the official bulletins, it was obvious that the Russians were maintaining their advance across Poland and even into Germany. Place names of towns and villages being evacuated by the Germans indicated that their prison lay directly in the path of the advancing Russian armies.

9

'Raus Raus' – 'out out'

B
Y MID-JANUARY, THE PRISONERS in Stalag Luft III were faced with a new, rather frightening prospect. They had always thought they would be liberated by British or American forces as they advanced across Germany to link up with the Russians on the line of the Oder River. In that scenario, most of the Allied POW camps would be overrun and their inmates released and repatriated to the West. Now it seemed much more likely that the rapidly advancing Russian forces would be the first to reach them. The last thing the German High Command wanted was to lose several thousand Allied aircrew officer POWs to the Russians, who would immediately use them as a bargaining chip in the negotiation of surrender terms. The POWs were likely to become pawns in a very dangerous game. Rumours swept the camp. Bob Allen and his fellow inmates scanned the evening news-sheet. They listened to German radio, while official Wehrmacht communiqués shouted from camp loudspeakers twice a day. When the clandestine radio sets picked up BBC news it was quickly circulated round the compounds.

On 12 January, the BBC reported: 'Marshall Konev's army has broken out of its Vistula bridgehead south of Warsaw … it is heading for Silesia.' Meanwhile, Gen Zhukov was heading for Berlin and behind him more units of the Red Army were driving past Danzig. It was time for the prisoners to pack their bags. Some had been in Stalag Luft III for years and had accumulated precious possessions. But would they be liberated by the

209

Russians? If they were, what could they expect? Russian soldiers had a reputation for brutality. The Russian Army travelled light. It lived off the land. The Soviets did not recognise the Geneva Convention. There was small chance of food for prisoners, let alone Red Cross parcels. The senior British officer in the North compound, RCAF Gp Capt Larry Wray, urged the men not to flap but to 'be sure you have clean socks and a good pair of boots. Get exercise every day. We may soon be walking'.[1] By the time the Russians took Warsaw and Kraków, the 'kriegies', long-term prisoners, had started to pack.

As the Russians swept in from the east, the Germans were losing their battle in the Ardennes. By 16 January the German Army was back to the line from which they had set out. They had lost some 120,000 men, killed, wounded and missing, 600 tanks and assault guns, 1,600 planes and 6,000 vehicles.[2] The Americans had also lost heavily but they could make up their numbers; the Germans could not. They had already introduced conscription for boys aged 15 to 18 and men aged 50 to 60. Desperately inexperienced, but called to the front, urged on by FM von Rundstedt to 'defend Germany's sacred soil ... to the very last'. The Germans had fought their wars on other people's soil. Now, for the first time since Napoleon, the battle had come to them.[3] Their cities had been bombed. The Luftwaffe was fatally weakened. The army was short of men, tanks, artillery and fuel. Deserters were hanged from the nearest tree with a notice: 'I failed to defend the fatherland.'[4] It seemed inevitable that Germany would lose the war. Yet despite terrible losses the German Army could still claim 289 divisions, enfeebled but not ready for surrender. Some generals even toyed with the idea of persuading the Allies to join in the fight against the Russians.

The POWs noticed the change in their guards. The fitter, younger men had been sent to the front. Their replacements seemed increasingly nervous.[5] With Germany in such peril, why should looking after prisoners be a priority? Stalag Luft III had 10,000 prisoners. It seemed beyond possibility that they would be massacred but there were rumours. The Allies were insisting on unconditional surrender. Might Hitler threaten to shoot the prisoners to enforce better terms? The execution of the 50 escapees was proof of the scant regard for prisoner rights. When it came to the crunch, the German High Command decided to hold on to their prisoners. They might be more valuable alive.

Bob and his mess mates had had their evening meal and were settling down to an evening of cards when the order came. It was dark. Bitterly cold. The roads hard packed with snow and ice. Without any warning, armed guards entered the camp and gave notice that by midnight all the inmates were to assemble outside the barrack blocks, ready to march to a new camp 'somewhere to the west'.[6] The effect of this order was devastating. Despite the rumours and the preparations for a possible takeover by the Russians, most of the men had prepared themselves to sit out the war until liberated by one or other of the advancing Allied armies. Since the 'no escaping' directive, men for whom escaping had become a way of life kept morale high by considering what might happen if their Red Cross parcels were cut off. They channelled their ingenuity into squirrelling their scarce resources of food. Their huts were relatively comfortable. They were prepared to wait. Now they were faced with leaving it all behind. They were dismayed to be faced with a long march in severe mid-European winter weather. They didn't have suitable clothing or footwear and would only be able to take what food and belongings they could carry. No one in the camps or in command back home had even remotely considered this scenario.

At first the reaction of the prisoners was sheer disbelief that the Germans were serious and in general the response was to ignore the orders. However, they soon realised that their German guards were in an ugly mood. Machine guns were cocked. Orders had to be seen to be obeyed. The senior British officer confirmed the order: they must be ready to evacuate by midnight. That was in three hours' time. Other compounds had already begun to move. The British prisoners in the North compound had to abruptly interrupt a camp theatre performance of *The Wind and the Rain* and hurry back to their huts.[7] It was Saturday 27 January. American prisoners in the South compound were out of the camp by 9pm. By 11pm they were joined by Americans from West compound. Some 2,000 men were out and on the road in the bitterly cold, dark night. In the early hours of 28 January, British prisoners from North compound left. At 6am, some time before light, the East compound was cleared. That day, 28 January, the day of mass evacuations, was also the day the German Army admitted retreat from the Ardennes. The Battle of the Bulge was over. One consequence of the failure of the German Army was that it enabled the Waffen-SS to gain control. The Allied airmen who had been to some extent protected by the Luftwaffe were now being force-marched into a volatile and dangerous situation.

There was an unexplained delay in evacuating the last 2,000 men from Belaria compound.[8] They had a day in which to plan what to take and what to leave. For Bob, a recently arrived inmate, the decision was simple. He had nothing but his somewhat inadequate clothes and two German Army blankets. Others, who had been prisoners for three years or more, had carefully hoarded stocks of cigarettes, books and other possessions acquired through parcels from home. Possessions became a liability. For these prisoners it was like packing and leaving home. The most pressing and immediate problem was not so much what to take but how it was to be carried. No one had a rucksack, bag or rope. Without some means of transporting things, even essentials were at risk of being abandoned. They were quick to get organised. Within half an hour of accepting that they would have to leave, all available food supplies had been divided up and handed out. Meanwhile, small teams of two or three began to make wooden sledges from anything handy, such as their three-tier wooden bunks, which were quickly demolished. The sides were cut up into lengths to make runners and sides. Bed boards made ideal cross-beams for sledge floors. A few saws and other tools had mysteriously appeared from the Escape Committee's resources to make these modifications. The sledges looked quite robust. With the aid of improvised straps, Red Cross parcels were turned into rucksacks for those who could manage to carry them.

After two or three hours of hectic efforts, they were ready to move out of the camp and on to the roads. Something close to 300 sledges were constructed in less than an hour.[9] These were loaded, often overloaded, with whatever each small team considered that they needed. They practised pulling, or in some cases pushing, the unwieldy vehicles. As for warm clothes, a lucky few had overcoats while the rest tried to make coats and cloaks from blankets. Thick, warm socks were an obvious necessity. The woollen socks they used for exercise around the camp perimeter might be adequate if doubled up. One man wore three jerseys, one pair of long underpants, pyjamas, long trousers, a battledress overcoat, a balaclava, shoes and mittens and he was still cold.[10] Bob had boots but many prisoners only had lightweight shoes quite unsuitable for a march, let alone a march over ice and snow.

Then came news that the evacuation of their compound had been put off until morning. The senior British officer had persuaded the German camp commandant to refer to a higher authority for confirmation. The American prisoners had already been on the road for 24 hours. Most of the British had left the main compound. Only a small group of prisoners too weak to travel and those in Belaria remained. Now what to do? It was in the middle of the night. They had destroyed all their bunks to make sledges so they lay around on their mattresses on the floor. Whatever the outcome, the thought of trying to reconstruct the bunks or sort out the chaos was too much. They would think about it in the morning. Few slept. Most dozed fitfully, fully clothed, by their sledges.

Promptly at first light the guards returned and, barking '*raus raus*', ordered the prisoners out. A motley parade, belongings precariously packed on sledges, gathered outside the huts they had called home. For more than an hour they waited in the bitter cold while the guards conducted a hut-by-hut search for hidden prisoners. Bob and his cohort stamped and hugged their arms to keep some movement in their freezing bodies. At last the main gate swung open and the head of the column began slowly to move off down the country road leading past the camp. On either side, at intervals of 50–100 yards, were German guards dressed in regulation ankle-length greatcoats and special cold-resistant boots. The British prisoners were about to experience a march that would have tested the endurance of fully trained infantry soldiers, let alone ill-equipped, half-starved aircrew POWs, many of whom had had little exercise for months, if not years, other than a brisk daily walk around the camp perimeter path. The open road was covered with frozen snow and ice.

They had left the camp at 6am. Progress was slow, mainly because of the improvised sledges. Bob helped a colleague. Their sledge stood up to the rough road conditions but several others began to break up over the uneven surface. Emergency repairs were attempted. Sledges were abandoned. Loads were transferred to more robust vehicles. It was not just the sledges that made progress slow. The prisoners were encouraged to 'go slow' by the senior British officer. He assured them that he had only agreed to the evacuation after a vigorous protest that it

266 Squadron pictured in 1944. Bob is in the second row at third right.

Typhoons of 266 Squadron lined up on an airfield in 1944.

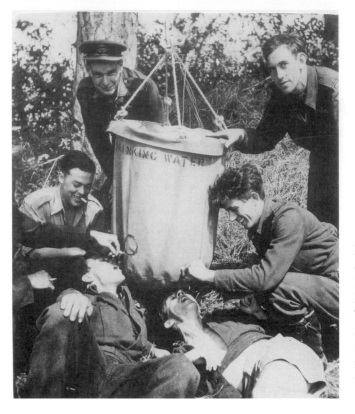

Bob (top left) and other members of 266 Squadron relaxing in Normandy in 1944. They are drinking from a 'water-cow' which had six taps at its base which flowed when a button was pressed.

Men of an RAF Repair and Salvage Unit working on a damaged Supermarine Spitfire Mk IX of No 403 Squadron, Royal Canadian Air Force, at a forward airstrip in Normandy, 19 June 1944.

The ruined city of Caen in June 1944, following the Allied invasion of Normandy.

German military vehicles destroyed by rocket-firing Typhoons on a country road in Normandy.

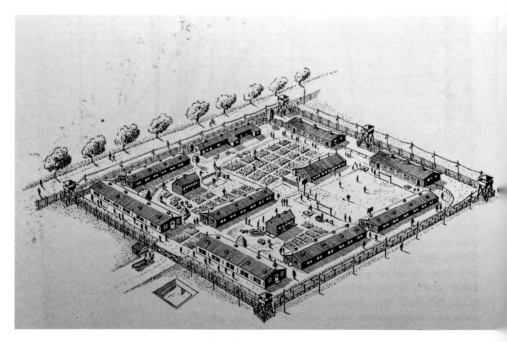

landed at B8 near Bayeux.
landed at B3 but moved on to B8.
Attacked with R.P. traffic (?) on roads 1·10
19th. We lose Maps, McElroy, Harrold –25

— KILLED WHILST ON OPERATIONS.— 55

JULY 25th 1944

TOTAL TYPHOON HRS :— 141
TOTAL 'OPS' HRS :— 66
TOTAL 'OPS' HRS JULY:— 2

The page from Bob's flying logbook with the line 'KILLED WHILST ON OPERATIONS, JULY 25TH 1944.

A POW sketch of the Belaria compound in Stalag Luft 3.

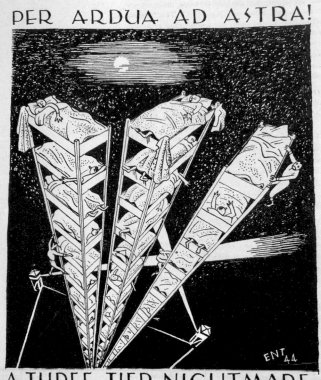

PER ARDUA AD ASTRA!

A THREE TIER NIGHTMARE

ENT 44

A cartoon ridiculing the many-tiered bunks in the Belaria compound.

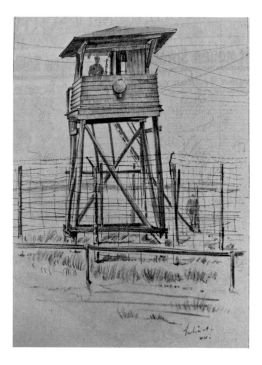

The guard house in the Belaria compound.

A POW shelter in a barn at Birkenstadt during the first week of the winter march from Zagan.

Prisoners drag their sledges in the early days of the march, February 1944.

Soldiers of the Red Army and the US army meet on the banks of the Elbe River at Torgau in Germany on 25 April, 1945.

Bob with Suzanne in 1945.

Bob Allen at the end of the war.

contravened the Geneva Convention. The German commandant had agreed that, in accordance with the Convention, only 25km (15 miles) a day would be marched. The prisoners should not be too enthusiastic or co-operative in making more than minimum progress. Also, any prisoners unable to continue through injury or exhaustion would be carried in lorries following the column. Soon after leaving the camp, their column of several hundred prisoners converged with another, making its way from the main camp. They headed roughly westwards. As they walked up a small hill, Bob looked back. As far as he could see the road was filled with prisoners and their sledges, looking like a dark river flowing through a white landscape.[11]

All that day the column shuffled onwards. There were occasional pauses for rest. Prisoners were advised not to sit in the snow or on milestones. 'This leads to rheumatism, piles and other frightful trouble which will aggravate the difficulty of walking … don't let it get you down – all you have to do is to keep your bowels, ears and mind open.'[12] Bob Allen found that despite the rigours of the march, there were compensations. They were no longer confined under close guard. They were moving westwards, if slowly. They could see and experience the countryside, small villages and hamlets with neat vegetable patches and well-maintained houses. The roads were full of German refugees, their family possessions piled high on carts pulled by bullocks. They were mostly old men, women and children under ten. Many were bandaged or walked with a stick. There were wounded German troops making their way back from the front. 'They begged cigarettes from the prisoners and called them *Kameraden*.'[13] All were moving west in flight from the Russians. The POWs were urged onwards, the guards relentless in their determination to maintain progress. Perhaps, Bob realised, they thought that their own freedom depended on speeding west. Both guards and prisoners had lost the sense of security that prevailed in the camp. The feeling that it would only be necessary to sit out the remaining months of the war had been replaced by a mood of unease and uncertainty as they stumbled and shuffled their way along the road.

Soon after midday, the guards called a general halt. Improvised meals were made. Every sledge was festooned with packets and tins, drinking mugs and tin plates. As they left the camp they had not been issued with rations but had been given a Red Cross parcel each. Left in the camp were at least 23,000 Red Cross food parcels. Some prisoners reported seeing German guards helping themselves, including the commandant, who was seen stashing four big boxes each containing 20 parcels into his car. Also left in the camp were 100,000 books, thousands of pounds worth of prisoners' belongings and, in the British North and East compounds, at least 2 million cigarettes.[14] They had to make do with a cold meal. Not even a hot drink. As the bitter weather chilled bones and cramped muscles, they remembered the relative luxury of camp life – the warmth, regular hot food and drinks. In the camp there had been nothing to prepare them for the exertion of pulling sledges in freezing conditions. Their feet were blistered. Spirits and morale buoyed up by the excitement of the evacuation quickly evaporated and conversation ceased as the column dragged itself slowly westwards.

By 3pm the already dim daylight began to grow darker and snow started falling from a leaden sky. They were out in the countryside in sub-zero temperatures. Where would they be spending the night? A German staff car with an officer on board sped past, overtaking the column and going on ahead. His purpose was soon clear. Just as darkness began to fall, the head of the shuffling column arrived at a large farm with a group of barns surrounding a not very prosperous-looking farmhouse.[15] The staff car stood in the farm courtyard. As the column of prisoners arrived they were directed to the various barns.

By the time Bob's group arrived, all the barns were occupied and they realised they would be sharing their barn with the cows. Some prisoners had already found a ladder in the cowshed and managed to find a place among fresh straw in the loft. As one of the last to arrive, Bob found he must make a bed on the floor of the barn in straw already trampled and soiled by the cattle. Too weary and dispirited to care, Bob and his fellow aviators burrowed into the piles of straw to escape the bitterly cold air that filled the barn. Too tired to do more than eat a few biscuits from their reserves of food, they tried to make themselves comfortable. In fact, the straw insulated them from the worst of the cold and Bob discovered that by moving as close as possible to the cows on the barn floor he gained warmth from the animals' bodies. He marvelled at how philosophically the cattle accepted the situation. After some initial noise they settled to sharing their barn with several hundred human beings.

Before going to sleep, Bob thought he should attempt to ease his sore feet by removing his boots. It was bliss to relieve the pressure. A few prisoners lit cigarettes, which immediately silenced all conversation in the barn. The barn was locked. It was full of straw. The chance of a carelessly discarded match or cigarette setting it ablaze was quickly appreciated. In an instant a complete ban on smoking or lights of any kind was imposed, and accepted by all. Bob woke several times during the night, feeling cold despite the animals, the straw and his thin blanket. He woke, finally, as the guards noisily opened the sliding doors of the barn. It was still dark. He reached out for his boots. They were not there. Devastated at the prospect of marching without them, he searched frantically in the straw. With great relief he found them a short distance away from his bed in the straw. Unfortunately, unlike Bob, they had not had the body heat from the cattle and were frozen hard and rigid. Too late, he realised he should have just loosened the laces and not removed his boots altogether in such cold. It was impossible to soften the boots but somehow he managed to wriggle his still-sore feet into the frozen leather and tied the laces loosely.

Walking in frozen boots was like trying to walk with one's feet encased in blocks of concrete. It was some time before the warmth of Bob's body restored the boots to some level of flexibility. There were others in the same plight. Until the leather of their boots softened, they presented a painful spectacle as they hobbled along. It was hard to know what was best: take off the boots and have trouble getting them back on or, as some found to their cost, keep the boots on and wake in agony as the leather froze and contracted overnight.[16] They queued in the farmyard in the dark waiting for a mugful of hot water from the farmhouse kitchen. Hot porridge for breakfast – made from rolled oats and a little sugar from the Red Cross parcels – was a meagre meal, but gave sufficient warmth and strength to sustain body and spirit for the second day's march. It was dawn when the guards shepherded the prisoners out of the barns and into their column on the roads. Any attempt to escape by hiding in the straw was deterred by the guards vigorously forking through the ruffled straw with vicious-looking pitchforks. Would-be escapees were told they would be shot as deserters.

The overnight stay gave the prisoners a chance to reappraise their situation. All but essential loads were jettisoned. Only food requiring a minimum of preparation would be carried on. Some tins of food were opened and hurriedly consumed. Much was left behind. At least the icy conditions made it possible to pull sledges. The second morning of the march was sunny and still bitterly cold. The events of that day were just a blur to Bob. It took all his willpower and determination not to drop out. He just plodded on mechanically, absolutely oblivious to hardship. They passed through several villages. Women came out and stared at the column of ill-kempt, disreputably dressed men shuffling past. In one village they were abused and subjected to hostile gestures. They had been taken for Russians captured in the east. When the villagers realised that they were mostly British aircrew their attitude changed dramatically. They produced jugs of water, pails of hot water and bread. The prisoners gratefully accepted these simple gifts despite the guards' efforts to keep the column moving.

Almost every account of the march comments on the kindness of German civilians. Freiwalden villagers opened the doors of their church and its church hall and encouraged prisoners to take shelter. A carload of SS troops soon put an end to that.[17] Prisoners and guards trudged onward. Many of the guards were Volksturmers. Many were elderly, frail and unfit for such a march. They were anxious about leaving their families in the path of the advancing Russians. Their prisoners even felt sorry for them and helped carry their packs. In return, the guards tended to turn a blind eye to transactions, usually involving cigarettes, between villagers and prisoners. However, the Luftwaffe officers accompanying the column were infuriated. They reminded the villagers that these men had been bombing their country. They were the gangsters and child murderers that Dr Goebbels had warned them about. The villagers took little notice. Bartering for cigarettes continued.[18]

It was 4pm when the column arrived at a large group of farm buildings. It was still light. They had a better chance of making an evening meal from their stores of food. And, surprisingly, they were issued with some warm barley soup from a German field kitchen in one of the barns. The kitchen had been set up to feed German Army units moving westwards. Bob recognised their insignia. These soldiers were members of the same Death's Head Panzer-SS division that had first taken him prisoner in Normandy. He was astonished. They were almost unrecognisable. In Normandy they were smart, well-fed and arrogant; the officers in particular had been immaculately dressed and, although well camouflaged, their tanks and vehicles were in first-class condition. Now, six months later, after retreating from the Russian onslaught, both men and officers looked gaunt and dishevelled. They had obviously suffered. There were no tanks, only travel-worn half-tracks, lorries and a few staff cars. But they were still dangerous. Each man carried a gun. The unit behaved like a disciplined force capable of offering local resistance.

In one of the barns, the prisoners switched on an electric light. The farmer was furious at first but was bought off with a few cigarettes. The next day they rested. There was plenty of scrap wood. The farmyard was soon peppered with small fires to heat up cans of stew or hot water. Bed was still among the straw but at least it was clean straw. Quick to spot an opportunity to supplement their rations, one group managed to trade cigarettes for a chicken. It was boiled and shared between 21 men.[19]

Their spirits lifted when they heard Germans say the war would be over within days. 'The war is lost,' Albert Speer attempted to tell Hitler. Göring still thought the Allies might join the German cause against Russia. It was all rumour and hearsay. Bob's column had by now lost contact with the one clandestine radio the prisoners had managed to carry out of Sagan. After one more night at the farm they were ordered back on the road. The presence of the SS division had the effect of hardening the attitude of the guards. They showed no sympathy to their already weakened prisoners. Many, including Bob, were sick with a mild form of dysentery. They were finding it difficult to face another day's marching. The guards announced that anyone unable to march would be left to the SS. Anyone found hiding or malingering would be treated as if they were attempting to escape and would be shot. There was nothing for it but to keep going. All but those unable to stand assembled outside the barns with their sledges. There was a new problem. Overnight it had become noticeably warmer. As the column moved off, light snow was falling. It soon became slush.

As the morning wore on, keeping the sledges moving became more and more difficult. One by one they were abandoned as the rough surface of the country road broke through melting snow and ice. Those who persisted in dragging their vehicles hit ruts and potholes that damaged the runners beyond repair. Long-term prisoners especially were desperate at having to leave their improvised conveyances by the roadside with the few meagre possessions that had helped them survive. For the rest of the day they could take only what they could carry, which, in their weakened state, was not much more than the food they had left. They trudged on, covering some 20 miles before reaching their next overnight resting place, a farm in Birkenstadt. This time the barns were unlit and unheated. Even in daylight, they were dark and gloomy. The farmer's cattle, it was noticed, had running water and heat and light. The prisoners were locked in at 5pm without water or sanitation. Even though the weather was warmer the men still felt chilled to the bone. Many felt that they would not survive much more. There was talk of escape. The general consensus favoured sticking together. Late at night there were sounds of drunken revelry and singing coming from German soldiers in a nearby farmhouse. The British POWs felt nervous and vulnerable locked in their stinking dark barn while demoralised German troops made their desperate retreat through the countryside around them.

The prisoners spent another day at the farm. Apparently there was no room on the roads for more columns of men. Reports from Sagan prisoners ahead of them were dire. The group of 2,000 prisoners from North compound marched 21 miles on their first day, reaching Leippa after dark, where 60 officers had to spend the night outside in the lee of a barn. By morning, many were suffering frostbite and vomiting. Inside the barns, conditions were so cramped that men were forced to urinate where they lay. Several officers collapsed. They were found lying in a ditch by a search party organised by the prisoners themselves. Complaints were made to the Luftwaffe officer, Maj Rostek, in charge of the column.[20] There were clear breaches of the Geneva Convention, which entitled POWs to the same rations, shelter and medical attention as local garrison troops. Before marching the prisoners off, the guards attempted a headcount. 'All present.' No one had escaped. No one died. One prisoner too sick to continue was left at the farmhouse.

After another long day's march, the column from North compound reached Muskau, where the German military had made arrangements to billet their prisoners about the town. Bad Muskau is an historic spa town close to the Polish border. It has a castle and a lake and all that might be expected from the seat of Saxon nobility. So it was that 300 prisoners spent the night in a cinema, another 600 in a glass factory, 400 in a riding school, 150 in a stable, 80 in a laundry, 100 in a pottery and about 300 in a French POW camp.[21] The French medical officer treated British prisoners and shared rations. German civilians were helpful and did their best. The local mayor arranged for the furnaces in the glass factory to be lit. Spades and pickaxes were provided to dig latrines.[22] In quarters with no sanitary arrangements, dysentery was inevitable. Before they left Muskau for Spremberg, some Red Cross parcels arrived from Sagan and were distributed. Each man got one-third of a loaf of white bread. Only once they reached Spremberg, a military depot, did they get hot soup and hot water. It was there that they were given their destination – Milag und Marlag Nord camp, 20 miles from Bremen in the north of Germany. It would be five more days' travelling before they got there, by which time more than 70 per cent were sick with exhaustion or dysentery, vomiting and frostbite. However, their plight was not the worst suffered by POWs in what became known as the Long March. Some were kept on the road for weeks. Luckily for Bob and his cohort their march, desperate as it was, lasted only days.

1 February. In the four days since Bob left Sagan they had been issued with no rations. Apart from the barley broth, they had lived off the stocks of food they had been able to carry but these were exhausted. The Germans produced one-fifth of a loaf of black bread per man. It was a grim day. Raining. The countryside sodden and miserable under a dark, overcast sky. As the prisoners lined up to be counted they all looked and felt appalling. Several days without washing or access to toilet facilities, months of poor food followed by days of marching on almost no food at all had weakened their bodies. They were relieved to hear that they were to have another rest day and that the following day they would only march a short distance, no more than 5 or 6 miles to a railhead where they would be taken by train to their next POW camp. That was cheerful news. The prospect of returning to some form of organised, sheltered life, albeit in a prison camp, was positively attractive. There would be warm food, shelter and washing facilities. This could be the last lap of their nightmare journey. The next day, Friday 2 February, it was two painful hours before the bedraggled column reached the outskirts of a large town – the first their column had encountered since leaving Sagan. The signpost announced that it was Cottbus. Unlike the neat village cottages they had passed, the houses in Cottbus were drab, ugly and unpainted. Bombed and derelict factories added to the general gloom. Cottbus was a major railway junction with extensive sidings and depots – all targets for Allied bombers. The POWs were marched down the centre of the main road. Sullen, openly hostile civilians glared at them from the pavements. Journey's end, at least that part that

had to be walked, was the marshalling yards. They waited for the whole column to arrive, including the lorries carrying those who could not walk. While they waited a train passed, loaded with tanks and recently wounded German soldiers heading west on retreat from the advancing Russians.

The Sagan evacuees waited. Eventually, several uniformed railway officials arrived and slid open the doors of a line of wagons. Armed guards ordered the prisoners forward. Each wagon carried a notice '40 hommes ou 10 chevaux'. These limits were ignored by the guards, who prodded the prisoners with their guns. The wagons were filled until the men stood shoulder to shoulder. Each wagon eventually contained at least 90 and in some cases 100 standing men. While the doors remained open they tried to find out their destination from the railway officials. To their dismay, it sounded like Buchenwald, the notorious Nazi concentration camp. They could not be sure. The immediate problem was how to cope with their overcrowded conditions. Discussion in Bob's wagon resulted in them deciding that half the occupants would lie on the floor while the rest stood. Every two hours the positions would be reversed. They didn't wait long before, with much crashing of buffers, a locomotive was coupled to the lead wagon. The doors were rolled closed and the train began to move.

It was the beginning of a nightmarish 24-hour journey. Bob and his colleagues were all exhausted by the march and by lack of food. Everyone wanted to sleep. To preserve some semblance of order they insisted on changing over every two hours. But this was to prove more and more difficult to enforce. There were of course no toilet facilities. Many of the men, including Bob, had dysentery. The train made frequent halts during its erratic journey westwards. The armed guards, who travelled in a van at the rear of the train, rolled the doors open and allowed the men to disembark. Thoughts of escape were tempered by fatigue, the loaded guns of their guards and the threat of being shot. Bob's wagon was equipped with a boiler of water. It was impossible to light a fire but at least they had drinking water available. It seemed an endless uncomfortable night until at last daylight began to filter through the boards. The routine of two hours standing followed by two hours lying down had begun to break down as more and more men found it difficult to stand. If anything, the light made conditions look worse. Hope failed. Despondency set in. Self-preservation was all that was left. It was evening when the train finally stopped.

The doors rolled open. The prisoners looked out on a dimly lit platform in an orderly station. Signboards announced Luckenwalde. Word was quickly passed down the wagons. Their destination was not the infamous concentration camp but a town just south of Berlin. Bob climbed out of the stinking wagon. Guards urged the men into a now-familiar column. They could not march. They shuffled out of the station and through a darkened and deserted town. It was still quite dark when, after about an hour, they saw perimeter lights above a barbed-wire enclosure. The camp was on a hill above them. As they reached the gate they could see that it was a major POW camp. Passing down a main road between wired enclosures, they were greeted by prisoners on either side. They shouted out in French, Flemish, Dutch and Polish, encouraging them to find the strength to move on. They reached gates to an enclosure of several large huts. One by one they went through. One by one they were thoroughly searched. Anything that might help in an escape was taken from them. It was very late when the last of the men stumbled into the huts.

Bob was one of the last to reach the huts. He was thoroughly depressed by what he saw. At Sagan they had had rooms housing a maximum of 12. Here, he looked into an enormous hall with rows and rows of four-tiered bunks. His heart fell to his boots, but at least it was journey's end of a sort. He looked for an unoccupied bunk. Nobody spoke much. The weary travellers fell exhausted to sleep. Bob lay awake in the dark listening to their coughs and snores. Contemplating a bleak future.

Back home in Britain and America, newspapers carried stories about forced marches. Alice had had little news of Bob. There would be no letters for weeks, then three all at once – all of them heavily redacted. Her sister Joan's American fiancé, Freddie, arrived home one weekend looking dishevelled and despondent. His squadron had been caught on the ground in the last Luftwaffe assault on Allied airfields and his plane had been destroyed. They began to realise that the war could last much longer. Freddie's plane was quickly replaced. By mid-January, the fight was once again going in the Allies' favour, especially for the Russians. Almost every day there would be a map in the newspaper. Alice could see that Bob's camp might have been liberated by Russians. His letters had been reassuring but now pictures came from Poland of liberated POWs looking starved and bewildered. Alice kept newspaper clippings of skeletal British soldiers. Men who were too weak and emaciated to smile. She held back her fears. There was little or no official reassurance. Communications had ceased. Wives and families had little information on the health or whereabouts of their loved ones.

At first, the official line, issued as a press release from the Prime Minister's office, was that there was no information about 'the release of British and Commonwealth prisoners-of-war by the advancing Red Army'.[23] An announcement would be made as soon as reliable information was available. A top-secret message arrived at the Foreign Office from the British ambassador in Switzerland. It seemed that the prisoners would be moved. The Swiss had inspectors in Upper Silesia. They reported that the Germans were moving prisoners out on foot – but would observe the Geneva Convention. Confirmation of the marches came, in the end, from German propaganda. On 31 January, four days after the first prisoners were marched out from Sagan, an English-language radio service based in Berlin announced that they had left Stalag Luft III at their own request.[24] The report also suggested that Allied prisoners might join the Germans in their fight against the 'Bolshevik' Russians. This was repeated by a Norwegian newspaper a few weeks later. The prisoners who had just been force-marched out of their secure camps at gunpoint found these reports laughable. Information from the War Office in London eventually came three weeks later. It was out of date and unhelpful. Prisoners had been 'transferred westwards, destination unknown'. In Britain, there had been speculation about the possible fate of POWs. In November 1944 there had been questions and a debate in the House of Commons. The War Office was accused of complacency. Nothing changed. Families were left to worry. Be stoic.

On the home front, the Home Guard had been stood down. V1 and V2 rockets continued to hit London and the South East but Chichester was safe. Alice continued her work with the Toc H. She met others whose men were missing or imprisoned. For all of them, the lack of information was the greatest worry, though for some, including Alice, there were also financial worries. She had become caught in a bureaucratic hoop that held up her receiving a proper allowance for a POW wife. From the moment Bob was declared 'missing believed killed', she began to receive a widow's pension. When he was found in the POW camp, that allowance should have been revised. It was not until five months later, however, that she eventually received an additional £5 a month. Remarkably, even while he was a prisoner in Germany, Bob had been able to instruct his bank to transfer money to her accounts. The bureaucrats seem to have been overwhelmed by the sheer scale of demand.

'Nobody would tell you anything'[25] was the most common complaint. Families began to feel that everyday inconveniences, rationing and making do could be borne if only the conflict would end and their men could come home. They had five more months to wait.

In the early morning of 4 February, the day that Churchill and Roosevelt met Stalin at Yalta, Bob and his cohort took stock of their surroundings. They found themselves in a separate self-contained compound within a much larger camp. Luckenwalde, 32 miles south of Berlin, was built in 1939, just prior to the invasion of Poland. It was designed to hold 10,000 men. Six years later some 200,000 prisoners had passed through the gates. They came from all over Europe. By mid-1940, Poles and Norwegians were joined by 43,000 French POWs, including 4,000 French colonial troops from Africa.[26] Five years later, Bob met Dutch, Belgian, Romanian, Yugoslav and, for the first time, Russian POWs. The first concern of the newly arrived prisoners was to get clean. They were appalled by conditions at the camp. It stank. Latrines were deep pits with boards stretched over them. Not emptied. No paper. No water. Boards often covered in excrement. Men weakened by dysentery and lack of food were terrified of falling in. The Germans used Russians prisoners for all menial tasks, perhaps the worst of which was pumping out the latrines into '*scheiss* carts'[27]. The Russians had inadequate clothing and footwear. They were existing on the barest of rations in dreadful quarters. Bob discovered that one of the men operating the *Scheisse* cart was a colonel in the Russian Guards' regiment. He explained, through an interpreter, that he had taken the role of Russian private when he was captured and preferred to remain incognito. It avoided, he explained, the likelihood of being executed, which was the fate of officers from either side of the campaign on the Eastern Front.

The high-level meeting at Yalta scotched any lingering idea the Germans might have had of linking up with Britain and America against Russia. The Yalta agreement settled the post-war carve-up of Germany. It also made arrangements for the repatriation of prisoners. They were to be returned to their country of origin. Churchill appealed to Stalin: 'Every mother in England is anxious about the fate of her prisoner sons.'[28] Stalin replied that 'very few' British prisoners had been liberated by his men. There was a nervous trade-off going on. Both sides wanted reassurances that their men would be treated well and repatriated. The prisoners in Luckenwalde could do nothing but wait. Some men, debilitated by sickness and malnutrition, turned their faces to the wall. It was known as pit-bashing. Staying in their bunks, which they called 'pits', and missing roll call. Bob's 266 Squadron leader, Barney Wright, arrived in Luckenwalde the day after Bob. He describes staying in his pit for a fortnight, too weak to do anything except attend roll call. Coal was rationed. Fires didn't last. There was a cold snap. Snow settled on the ground. Norwegians gave them some food parcels, which they shared out with each man getting a one-seventh share. Barney Wright says his body looked like 'a skeleton that had swallowed a watermelon'.[29]

It was weeks before the first Red Cross parcels arrived. German rations were twice-daily issues of barley soup, some stale black bread and black ersatz coffee. They did nothing to improve the POWs' health or their morale. Bob took heart on days when the weather was fine and he could see large formations of American B17 bombers flying at altitude to and from Berlin to the north. At night, the sky was lit by gunfire and searchlights as night raids hit the capital and its suburbs. One night, there was no air raid and he could hear a new sound like distant thunder. The wind was from the east. Next morning there was speculation that this was gunfire from the Russian armies advancing into Germany.

Handwritten news bulletins, received from a clandestine radio, were passed around after lights out. They confirmed the approach of the Red Army.

Once again speculation was rife. Would the Germans move their prisoners again to avoid them falling into the hands of the Russians? Bob recalls the day when, completely without warning, the British and American aircrew officers were paraded and told they were to be moved to the south of Germany, which was being fortified as a redoubt against the invading Russians.[30] There was much scepticism about this move. The concept of a National Redoubt whereby Hitler and crack troops could make a last stand in the mountains of Bavaria and western Austria seems to have been more of a Goebbels propaganda bluff than a realistic strategic move.[31] It was highly improbable that such a large number of prisoners could be moved such a distance when both road and rail systems were under tremendous strain from Allied air attacks. Intact railways were in constant use as troops and equipment were evacuated from the east. To the west, the Allies had increased their bombing offensive. Dresden was flattened in three days between 13 and 15 February. On 7 March, the US 9th Armored Division reached Remagen. They found the Ludendorff Bridge intact and raced across. The Allies were east of the Rhine and began their advance into the Ruhr and southern Germany.

Two days later, on 9 March, Bob and the rest of the British officers were marched out of camp in a column down the road to the railway station. Nobody really believed they would be made to leave the camp. Even as they marched, they expected to be returned to Luckenwalde soon. However, when they reached the station there were a large number of goods wagons waiting for them. The senior British officer passed down an order: without offering dangerous resistance they must try to delay embarkation for as long as possible. The order was passed by word of mouth.

It was pantomime time. As fast as the guards got a wagon loaded it emptied as those first in jumped out. All too soon the guards lost their tempers and withdrew to the side of the tracks with machine guns cocked ready to fire. The delaying tactic worked because they gave up trying to load the wagons. The prisoners were left to idle away the rest of the morning sitting on the track beside the train.

In mid-afternoon, a railway official arrived and spoke to the officer in charge of the guards. A heated argument took place, the gist of which was that there was no locomotive. There was nothing to pull the train away. Not today. Not tomorrow. To the delight of the prisoners, and to the relief of some of the guards, they were ordered to form a column and return to the camp. Back at camp there were cheers and catcalls as they marched past the compounds. The officers in charge of the guards looked annoyed. The prisoners reached their barrack rooms without serious incident. Camp routine resumed. Nobody thought there would be any further attempt at evacuation. Rather, it was time to make contingency plans for whatever situation might arise should the Germans defend the camp against liberators, be they Allies or Russians.

For the whole of March and the beginning of April the Luckenwalde prisoners waited. There was little for them to do. No books to read. No activities. They spent hours discussing food. It was a form of self-torture in which everyone indulged. Some took advantage of their proximity to Polish, Russian, Italian or Spanish officers to learn their language. Bob practised his schoolboy German. There were no letters. No news from home. He would not hear that Alice's sister Joan had married her American pilot and was now on the Atlantic on her way to the USA as a GI bride. He did learn that the last of the V2 rockets hit London on 27 March. The last civilian in Britain to die in the five-year-long conflict was killed in her garden.

The rockets had a limited range of 200 miles. With the Allied advances, all usable launch sites were overrun. The end of the war was in sight and with it plans for bringing POWs back home were reassessed.

The evacuations of the eastern camps had taken the military planners by surprise. They had presumed that Germany would surrender and send their prisoners home. Why were they hanging on to them? Would they continue to feed them? The overall plan for repatriating prisoners, Operation *Eclipse,* assumed that there would be a functioning government, adequate transportation and that the prisoners would 'stay put' until ordered otherwise. Meanwhile, rumours surfaced that Himmler had a plan for 'N-Day', *Niederlagstag* – the Day of Defeat.[32] Himmler suggested that all prisoners, including POWs and foreign workers, should be liquidated. It was time for reprisals, for revenge – for Dresden and for losing. The rumours were enough to convince the Allies to set up a war room at Supreme Headquarters Allied Expeditionary Force (SHAEF) dedicated to prisoner repatriation.

Not a moment too soon. The senior British officer at Oflag 79 near Brunswick requested troops to protect the camp against hostile Germans. The 'special' prisoners at Colditz were thought to be in particular danger. There was talk of parachute drops. It rapidly became clear that some sort of military operation might be necessary if the prisoners were to be safe. In March 1945, there were something close to 257,000 American and British POWs in Germany.[33] Of these, 90,000 could be expected to be liberated by the Soviets. Meanwhile, Allied fighter planes were ordered to fly over the camps to boost the morale of the prisoners and catch the attention of their guards and the local civilian population.

On 14 April, a group of RAF officer prisoners from Luckenwalde were once again marched to the local railway station. They saw many RAF and American aircraft overhead. Feeling vulnerable, they persuaded their guards to let them paint 'RAF – POW' on the tops of the carriages in yellow paint.[34] The guards were unusually friendly. To anyone who would listen they denounced Hitler as a *Schweinhund* and protested that they themselves were anti-Nazi. The next day, the prisoners were marched back to camp where they were met by increasingly polite and obsequious German staff who asked for 'good conduct notes' to show the victors.[35] At night, the sound of gunfire could be distinctly heard. Clandestine news bulletins confirmed that it could only be a matter of days before the Russians arrived. Secret plans for taking over the camp had been agreed by senior representatives of each nationality. They would put pickets on the perimeter to prevent prisoners wandering off. They would share out whatever provisions were available. Try to maintain law and order until arrangements for repatriation were in place. In the event, liberation was quite unlike anything anyone had imagined.

On a dull rainy Saturday morning, 21 April, the early risers noticed that the sentry boxes overlooking the compounds were no longer manned.[36] In fact, not a single guard could be seen anywhere. At about midday, the remaining Germans were paraded outside the main gate. The senior officer, Norwegian Gen Otto Ruge, was sent for. When he could not be found, the Germans rapidly made a formal handover to an American officer and they marched out. The camp was officially evacuated but, surrounded by German forces, it was left in a sort of No Man's Land. Water and lighting had been turned off at the mains in the town. A small group set out to find out what was going on. It looked as though the town was being evacuated. There were SS troops and soldiers in the woods around the camp who warned that anyone found outside the wire would be shot. The rest of the day was taken up with distributing food and cooking for the 25,000 inmates. Order was maintained. When some Russian prisoners broke into a potato store, they looked so starved they were allowed to keep their haul.[37] White flags were hoisted on watch towers. At intervals, refugees from outside working parties arrived and were accommodated. A total of 80 German soldiers surrendered and were taken prisoner.[38] The mayor of Luckenwalde was so fearful of the Russians he tried to hand over his town to the senior camp officer. He was politely turned down. That night a German aircraft strafed the camp. No one was hurt. The night was eerily quiet.

Bob missed the first Russians to appear. All the reports tell of one small and rather dirty Russian in a fur hat who arrived at speed. Leaping out of his armoured car, he hugged and kissed everyone in sight. Then, taking General Ruge with him, he drove out of the gates and straight into a German ambush. Shots were exchanged but the Russian sped safely away. Three Russians on horseback were spotted in the woods. All went quiet again.

Bob saw his Russian liberators arrive at about 9am. A roar of tanks, armoured cars and a large troop carrier appeared on the main road from town. To get a better view, a number of prisoners climbed their barbed-wire enclosure. They cheered as tanks with Russian infantry riding on them began to enter the camp. They were amazed to see women soldiers, each armed to the teeth with rifle, pistol and machine gun. One tank driver left the road and put his tracks in line with the barbed-wire fencing. He demolished it at speed, oblivious to the inmates clinging on. Prisoners jumped down and fled. One man, wearing clogs, abandoned them because they slowed him down. When he went back for them the tank had smashed them into splinters.

The Russians' first objective was to liberate their countrymen. Within half an hour all those Russians who could walk were armed with weapons and formed into a loose column ready to march out. About 4,000 men, weak with malnutrition and illness, marched, hammer and sickle flying, to join their country's troops encircling Berlin. The offensive into Germany had been hugely costly in lives. Replacements were urgent. A vast Russian officer invited prisoners of any nationality to join them to capture Berlin. On behalf of the British, the senior RAF officer declined the offer as gracefully as possible. The Russians shook their heads in disbelief at the lack of enthusiasm, fired their machine guns in the air and left as quickly as they had arrived.

The camp was quiet again. After the excitement and euphoria of the Russian arrival came an anticlimax. There was nothing to stop prisoners wandering about the camp. Instead, they shouted greetings, barely appreciating that they could walk across and mingle with prisoners from other nations. They were free. There were dangers, not just from the enemy encircling their camp, but from a possible breakdown in behaviour, looting, theft, disobeying orders to stay put. Compound by compound, a chain of command was re-established based on rank. Senior officers in the RAF compound organised small groups of men to find out what was happening in other parts of the camp and, if possible, what the situation was outside.

Bob was detailed to be a member of a small party sent to explore the vacated Russian compound. He found it very strange, even unreal, to pass through gates that had previously been barred and padlocked. He instinctively looked up at the guard towers. Deserted. Would a guard return to menace them with rifle and machine guns? The watch towers remained deserted. Silent. The small party of young RAF officers entered the first Russian compound in silence. Appalled, they looked around them, scarcely believing what they saw. The living accommodation was squalid beyond belief. In one building apparently dedicated to sick prisoners, single bunks lay in cells just large enough to crawl into. The general barrack room had not even bare necessities such as stoves for heating and cooking. What bedding or clothing remained was threadbare and filthy. They found six bodies in one of the huts. It was suggested they had been hidden so that the others could continue to claim their rations. As the Russians were not signatories to the Geneva Convention, the Germans had no reason to observe common principles of care with Russian prisoners.

The next building Bob entered was an amazing contrast. From the outside it was like any other but the inside was unbelievable. It was a church, decorated and furnished in the Russian Orthodox style. The altar dominated by a seemingly gold cross, ornaments and richly embroidered cloths. As he got closer he could see that ingenious improvisation, including scrap metal, blankets and bits of clothing, had been used to create this centre of worship. The walls were richly decorated with tapestries, icons and pictures designed from memory with such skill and ingenuity that the overall effect was not only breathtakingly beautiful but humbling. Comfort from blankets and clothing had been sacrificed to produce materials for the artists and workmen to beautify their church. It was a symbol of hope and inspiration[39] for the Russian prisoners, who were without the protection of the international Red Cross. It was with mixed feelings that Bob and his party returned to their own barrack block.

Other parties had gone as far as the local town without encountering local troops. Accounts of what they found there differ. Some said that the Russians looted shops and molested women, others that the Russians behaved properly and that it was German civilians who looted shops, taking linen goods and footwear and all the flour from the town bakery.[40] Whatever the cause, they concluded that there were no stores to boost the camp supplies. Finding daily rations to feed the remaining 15,000 men was the most pressing problem. There were no reserves. The departing Germans had taken what remained and there seemed little likelihood of Red Cross parcels. Parties were sent into the countryside to glean what they could from farms and villages. They returned empty-handed but with tales of skirmishes between Russian and German troops. That day, no rations were issued from the kitchens.

Late at night a large party of Russian troops arrived. They were the advance guard for a force that would occupy and administer all areas captured by the front-line troops. Arrangements were being made to secure the camp under Russian control. There was confusion and at times hostility between the Russians and Allied officers representing the prisoners. The Russians had drawn a cordon of troops around the camp under the guise of protecting the prisoners. The watch towers were once again manned by men with machine guns. No one was allowed to leave the perimeter. On the other hand, they promised to provide sufficient daily rations of fresh meat, bread and flour to maintain a reasonable standard. It was good, but a great disappointment to the camp's occupants who had expected an immediate release with transport to the West.

Over the next few days, supplies picked up. The bakery in Luckenwalde delivered 9,015 loaves of bread. The Russians supported foraging parties, who came up with sugar, jam, barley, oatmeal, potatoes and canned meat, as well as 15 cows and 50 pigs, which were driven into a holding pen. The supplies kept coming. It seemed that every man in the camp would get two good meals a day and new blankets, sheets and even tobacco, most of which were identified as German. The Russian garrison commander Capt Medvedev quickly earned the respect and gratitude of his charges. He was appalled by the conditions in the camp. He referred to the aircrew barracks as 'the place where the eagles live'[41] and provided brooms and cleaning equipment so they could be cleaned out. He promised films in Russian, English and American, and concert parties to improve morale. Life in the camp certainly improved but it was still desperately overcrowded and they still felt like prisoners. They began to wonder if there was not another agenda that might affect their repatriation west.

The Germans had been gone three days when Bob bumped into Barney Wright, his Rhodesian squadron commander. Barney was quartered in another compound so they hadn't met since their time in Stalag Luft III. They exchanged stories of the march and train journeys. Barney agreed that he had never felt so cold as he did on the march. He had found shelter in a pigsty, which he had filled with hay. It was one of the worst nights of his life. Luckenwalde was not much but at least there was shelter and some hot food. He had been one of the second group to be marched off to the train and back. On that occasion he had managed to exchange 60 cigarettes for a loaf of bread. He had heard rumours that put the Americans just 10 miles away and was very excited. 'But', he wrote in his diary, 'this was not to be. Bombing all around us … in a week we will be free men again and on our way home. Please hurry up. It can be quite agonising at times. The Russians have liberated us, but nothing has turned up to take us home … my patience is at an end.'[42] Bob felt the same. Although the Russians were not as rigorous as the Germans in confining the prisoners within camp boundaries, it was as if one oppressor had been substituted for another. So Barney and Bob decided to explore.

They opted for a daylight walkabout and managed to elude the patrolling perimeter guards without too much difficulty. They walked through the woods and out on to a main road into Luckenwalde without meeting anyone. The sense of freedom was intoxicating. The outing was uneventful. The town was quiet except for small bands of Russian troops, most of whom appeared to have been drinking. They saw very few Germans. A few old men. Very few women. The town felt deserted. Bob and Barney decided to return to the relative safety of the camp well before dark. Their sortie had proved that it was quite easy to leave the camp and walk about without being questioned either by Russians or Germans. The question was, would they be able to make it to the Allied lines?

They got back to the camp safely, only to be disconcerted by a new order from the senior British officer. On no account was anyone to attempt to leave and make their own way west. They were warned that units of the German Army were still hiding in the nearby woods. The Russians knew they were there but had bypassed them. Anyone attempting to go through was at considerable risk. But events were moving fast. The Russians arrived in Luckenwalde at 4.40pm on Wednesday 25 April. Four days later, members of the forward Russian 58th Guards Division met patrols of the US 69th Infantry Division at Torgau on the Elbe.[43] The British press carried photos of the historic moment. Hitler was trapped in Berlin. Germany split in two. It had to be the end of the Reich. There were reports of atrocities committed by all sides in this brutal conflict. The Russians had liberated concentration camps in Poland and Hungary and the true horrors of the Nazi 'final solution' for the Jews were revealed. The mood turned against Germany and the German people. The Russian Army had itself earned a reputation for reprisals and mass rape in payback for the treatment meted out during the invasion of their country. As the Allies and Russians swept across Germany, they liberated more than a million slave labourers who had been working in mines, factories and farms. They joined other displaced persons, DPs, on the roads. SHAEF and the Allied Military government were finding it hard to cope.[44] Towns already hit hard by Allied bombers now submitted to 'looting, fighting, rape and murder'. It was dangerous outside the camp.

The next day, as if to add to the inmates' fears, the Russians made an announcement. There would be no evacuation to the west. Instead, the whole camp would be transported eastwards towards Russia and be repatriated by ships from Odessa. Russian Gen Famin[45] was put in charge of the repatriation of POWs in the area. When he saw conditions at Luckenwalde he suggested moving all prisoners except the Poles and Italians to the Adolf Hitler Lager at Jüterbog, approximately 6 miles away. It had been built as a training camp and officer rest camp for elite pilots. There was a sports field, swimming pool, warm showers and baths and an officers' club and canteen. Unfortunately, this luxurious accommodation had been looted and then overrun by refugees and some 15,000 French civilians.[46] It would be some days before they could be transferred. In any case, the senior British officer refused the offer. His orders from London were to stay put. In Luckenwalde, food was running low again. Local supplies were almost exhausted. More POWs from all nationalities were leaving to try to make their own way west. Gen Eisenhower broadcast an order – prisoners were to stay put.

Bob and Barney made their decision the following day. A convoy of 50 American trucks arrived at Luckenwalde to begin evacuation. They were stopped by armed Russian soldiers. The Russians refused to recognise the American drivers. The movement of prisoners was a diplomatic not a military matter. The Americans should get back to the River Elbe where they belonged. The Russians were still two or three days from taking Berlin. They were determined to keep the territory they had liberated so far. Despite long arguments and negotiation, the vehicles eventually left without any passengers. It was a bitter blow. Now there could be no pretence. They felt as if they were prisoners of the Russians. That night there was much gloom and despondency among the disappointed, angry inmates at the camp. After supper, Bob and Barney found a quiet corner. They were faced with disobeying a direct order or staying in worsening

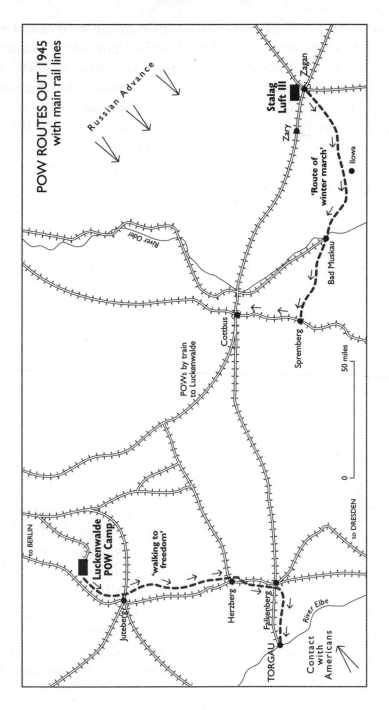

POW ROUTES OUT 1945
with main rail lines

Russian Advance

Stalag
Luft III

Zagan

Zary

Ilowa

'Route of
winter march'

River Oder

Bad Muskau

Cortbus

Spremberg

50 miles

0

POWs by train
to Luckenwalde

to DRESDEN

to BERLIN

Luckenwalde
POW Camp

'walking to
freedom'

Juteberg

Herzberg

Falkenberg

River Elbe

TORGAU

Contact
with
Americans

conditions in a camp under Russian control. Barney declared: 'My patience is at an end.'[47] Bob was ready to leave. They could make their way westwards towards the American front line on the River Elbe and reach England by the most direct route. It sounded easy but the countryside around the camp was still a battlefield and they would be men on the run.

10

Last lap to freedom

L UCKENWALDE POW CAMP. MONDAY 30 April 1945.
Two young men sat on a grassy mound in bright spring
sunshine. They had strolled nonchalantly through the
main gate. Now, outside the prison perimeter fence, they kept an
eye on the surrounding woods. Russian guards patrolling the camp
noticed them and kept them under some sort of observation.
Bob and Barney had left all their possessions in the camp. They
had stuffed their pockets with bread. To all appearances they
were just taking a little exercise. It was mid-morning before they
felt confident to slip away unseen.[1] So began a week on the run.
A week of momentous events that would end with a declaration
of peace in Europe and, Bob hoped, his return home. But first
he had to reach the American front line, which was still some
distance away through lawless and war-damaged country. It
could take a week. Bob and Barney counted it day by day. Night
by night.

Once in the woods they knew they had to distance themselves
from the camp as quickly as possible. Sunlight through the trees
cast dappled shadows to create perfect camouflage. They were
wearing RAF blue battledress and grey shirts. They just hoped
there were no remnants of the German Army hiding in the area.
They came across a single-track railway leading, Bob's compass
told him, directly westwards. They followed it. Curiously, no
trains passed. Many lines had been fractured by bombing and
it seemed this one was leading nowhere. Bob and Barney made

fast progress. Barney later noted in his diary: 'We were following the railway line and not daring to look back.'[2] By nightfall they were several miles from the camp. Seeking somewhere to spend the night, they came across an empty woodcutter's lodge. There was fresh water. No food. Before falling asleep they made a plan for the next day. There had been reports of the Russians and Americans meeting at Torgau on the Elbe River. It would be slightly further, south-west rather than due west, but a more likely place to find a river crossing. It would probably take three or four days. They would need to find food.

Next morning, they headed south on the first main road they found. They were prepared to find Russians troops and possibly a few Germans. Russian trucks rumbled past. They didn't stop. The two men were ignored. All day they walked through rolling, wooded country bathed in sunlight. Their newly acquired freedom was a tonic to them both. The only signs of war were the occasional bloated bodies of dead livestock, horses and cows, casualties of battle. Villages seemed deserted. If there were people about they were keeping well hidden. At the end of the afternoon, Bob knew they would have to risk stopping at one of the village houses. They needed food, shelter and rest for the night. They tried a house close to the road. After much knocking the door eventually opened a crack. A woman looked out cautiously. As soon as she saw they were not Russians her apprehension and fear passed. She opened the door and let them in. It was an extraordinary moment for both men. This was the first house either of them had entered since being captured and taken prisoner. It was clean. Homely. While their welcome was reserved and cautious, the woman, aged about 30, was willing to help. Bob explained that they needed to wash, to have somewhere to sleep and some food. She indicated that they could sleep in the spare room and what little food she had would be shared with them.

After washing, the two young men returned to the kitchen. Supper was soup, black bread and the inevitable ersatz black coffee. It was warm, cosy and comfortable. Bob did his best to hold a conversation with their hostess. She revealed that she was married but had heard no news of her husband since he returned to the Eastern Front after leave some two months ago. Bob understood enough to gather that she was pleased to give them shelter and that she wanted them to stay longer. They would give her some protection from marauding Russian soldiers. Every historian who writes about the final months of the war mentions the brutality of the Russian Army and the occurrence of 'rape on a collective basis'.[3] As Berlin fell to the conquering Red Army, more than 90,000 women were raped. Rape was seen as a reward of war. No woman was safe. The Russians were not the only liberating army to abuse their power. Belgian villagers pleaded: 'Deliver us from our liberators.'[4] No army was free of guilt. Bob told Barney, who did not speak German, what he had understood of their hostess's fears and request for protection. Bob wanted to avoid any confrontation with either Russians or Germans. Barney agreed. He was keen to continue his journey without delay. After months of inactivity, tired by their long walk, they were soon fast asleep. At daybreak, they crept downstairs, put on their boots, let themselves out of the house without disturbing their hostess and made their way on the road south.

They had been walking for about an hour when they were overtaken by a Russian soldier on a bicycle. His machine pistol was slung across his back. His bicycle riding was very erratic. He stopped and got off, so drunk he could hardly stand. Bob tried to be friendly. Using sign language – neither of them spoke Russian – they worked out that he was asking for cigarettes. Bob had none but Barney had an almost full packet tucked in his chest pocket. He'd hoarded it from the supplies they carried on the long winter march. He offered the open packet to the Russian, expecting him to take one or two. But he snatched the whole packet, clumsily lit one and put the packet in his pocket. Now what? Could be tricky. Bob and Barney began to edge away from him. The Russian dropped his bike. It fell with a clatter. Stepping forwards, he pointed to Bob's wristwatch. No way. It was the watch he had been given by Alice. After he was shot down and imprisoned in Dulag Luft, the Germans had returned it to him. He certainly was not giving it up to a drunken Russian. Shaking his head vigorously, he began to walk away. The Russian pulled his machine pistol round to a firing position and cocked it ready to fire. Bob froze. He realised that the soldier was in no mood to be argued with and that he held all the cards in the shape of his vicious-looking machine gun. Bob took off his watch and handed it over. The Russian immediately added it to a number of others he had strapped to his wrist.

While the Russian was engaged arranging his looted watches, Bob and Barney turned and slowly and deliberately continued down the road. After a few minutes they heard the bicycle. As he overtook them, the smiling Russian waved cheerily and continued his erratic progress. They guessed he was probably on his way back to barracks after spending the night with a woman in the village where he had stolen the bicycle. Bob was furious about his watch. It was a lesson learned. Russian troops are dangerous, drunk and without regard for anyone's possessions or even life. The sooner they could get to Torgau and the Americans the better. But that was probably another three or four days. They asked the few Germans they met on the road or in the fields if they were going in the right direction. Otherwise they relied on signposts. At about midday, they found themselves in the outskirts of Jüterbog. It had obviously been an attractive, rather picturesque town with castle walls, gates and towers, many churches and a town hall dating back to the 15th century. However, in recent years it had become an important German military base. Fighting had left it badly damaged. Most of the houses were in ruins. There was little sign of life, mainly dogs scavenging for food. The streets were partly blocked by debris or burned-out vehicles.

With some trepidation the two men made their way towards the town centre. Cautiously they rounded a bend. At a crossroads some 180 yards ahead was a Russian tank surrounded by infantry soldiers. Feeling very exposed, they tried to look nonchalant and continued down the road towards the tank. Its turret swivelled. The gun lowered. They were looking straight up the barrel. The troops on either side snapped their rifles. Machine guns at the ready. A dangerous moment. As one, Bob and Barney stopped and stood quite still. What next? No shots were fired. A small group of soldiers came forwards and Bob and Barney used the only words in Russian they knew: '*Anglivskiy lotsen*' (a mixture of Russian and German)– English pilots. Adding in simplified English, 'Go to Elbe'. That seemed to satisfy the Russians. They were allowed to pass. They decided that the Russians must be patrolling the deserted town to prevent German troops from entering or passing through to the west. It was not to be the British men's last confrontation with the Russians that day.

Ten minutes' brisk walking took them out of town. The countryside was quiet. Wide fields and thick hedgerows stretched either side of their tree-lined road. It was early evening before they decided to stop at a small farm. They needed food and shelter. They turned into the farmyard and to their surprise found it full of Russian soldiers. They had walked in on a briefing. About 30 Russian infantrymen were seated on the ground before a young officer standing in front of a map hanging on the wall. It was obvious that he was giving them orders for their next objective. They totally ignored the intruders. Bob and Barney stood still until the briefing was over. The troops formed up in loose order and headed off into the countryside. Not a word was exchanged. As soon as they left, Bob and Barney ransacked the farmhouse. There was nothing except some stale bread and evidence that the Russians had slaughtered, cooked and eaten whatever livestock had been around when they arrived. Maybe the Russians would return after their sortie. Reluctantly, the two tired and hungry men decided to continue walking until nightfall.

The light was beginning to fail when they entered the small town of Herzberg. The town seemed relatively undamaged, though there were signs that the Allies had recently bombed the area around a huge radio transmitter. The Deutschlandsender III was the tallest man-made construction in Europe at the time. It transmitted radio broadcasts on long wave. Now it was silenced. As was the town. White cloths hung from buildings. The Russians had been through. Bob and Barney knocked on one or two doors but received no answer. They reached the main square. It was clearly an old town with a history. The streets were cobbled. There was a town hall and an imposing church. Bob knocked loudly on the front door of a large terraced house. Quiet. He knocked again. After some delay he heard bolts being drawn and the door was opened a crack by a middle-aged woman. He explained who they were. The woman listened then told them to wait and closed the door. After about five minutes, which seemed an eternity, the door reopened and they were asked to enter. The hall and front rooms were dark as they followed the woman through to the back of the house into a large, candlelit kitchen. A tempting aroma of soup came from a cauldron hanging over a hot coal fire. They were soon sitting down with a bowl of soup and some rough brown bread, surrounded by women.

There were eight women aged between 14 and 50 years old living in the house. They were friendly, talkative and anxious to hear what was going on outside in the surrounding countryside. They were not locals but refugees who had fled from the Russians as they advanced westwards. The house had been abandoned by its owners, who had left when the Russians occupied the town. The women were afraid of the Russians. Bob did his best with his small knowledge of German. They told horrifying stories of callous behaviour. Men strung from lamp posts. Women and girls raped. Churches vandalised. Houses ransacked. By about 9pm Bob and Barney were nearly asleep in their chairs. It was time to bid the ladies goodnight and retire to their rooms to sleep. When Bob asked if they could be excused, there was consternation. It transpired that the women never went upstairs but slept on rolled-out mattresses on the kitchen floor. It kept them warm, secure and unlikely to attract attention from passers-by. When Bob insisted that the two men would sleep upstairs there was further consternation. It took persistence and persuasion before one of the older women reluctantly agreed, on the promise that they would not use any lights or show themselves at the windows, no matter what happened outside.

Bob and Barney felt their way up the dark staircase. There seemed to be only one room with a bed. Luckily, it was a large double bed with a mattress and a cover. Keeping all their clothes on, the two pilots lay down and soon fell asleep. It must have been midnight when they were awakened by a disturbance outside in the square. Much shouting was followed by sporadic small-arms gunfire. Bob tried to see what was going on. Some drunken Russian soldiers were trying to get into the houses. Frustrated by the heavily locked doors they had taken to firing indiscriminately at the houses, particularly at the upper floors. After the yelling and confusion the noise gradually subsided and all was quiet, but Bob slept fitfully for the rest of the night.

They were in a tricky situation. The women who had taken them in seemed to be genuine refugees but they were Germans. Every British serviceman had been given a booklet that stressed that there should be no fraternisation. Keep Germans at a distance. It warned against feeling sympathy for people who had started two wars in the space of 30 years. They had brought their troubles on themselves and the war was not over.[5] Yet it was hard not to feel sympathy for women who had lost everything in the course of the fighting. It was still dark when he woke to the sound of a noisy vehicle entering the square. Shouting. Heavy footsteps. Loud banging on the door of one of the neighbouring houses. Bob hid by the window, trying to see what was going on. The door opened. Loud voices. Banging and crashing in the house. More shouting, then after a few minutes a crash, as if someone had fallen or been thrown downstairs. The light from the armoured car revealed a man being half carried and half pushed down the steps and into the back of a lorry. A number of troops got into the cab or into the back. The vehicles moved off. Once more the square was left in brooding darkness.

Next morning when Bob and Barney went downstairs to the kitchen it was obvious that the women were even more apprehensive. They thought that a German soldier who had been hiding with their neighbour had been arrested and taken away in the night. Almost certainly someone would have informed on him. Maybe Bob and Barney would be safer if they went to the Kommandatura (an inter-Allied or Russian military government council) and obtained passes. At least it would protect them from being arrested on suspicion of being Germans. One of the younger women offered to help. She said she was working in the Kommandatura as an interpreter. Should they trust her?

After some debate they agreed and accompanied her to the town hall. Like the other occupying forces, British and American, the Russians immediately replaced Nazi administrators with their own people or 'friendly' untainted Germans. They had to keep society functioning in every town and village, city, county or province. That meant finding replacements in the police force, fire services, postal and telephone operations, water supplies and railways. In Herzberg, the first thing the occupying Russians did was to shoot the burgomaster (mayor) and appoint in his place the only black citizen of the town.[6] All the other officials administering the town and local district were newly appointed Germans. The two pilots were treated courteously and with the help of their housemate eventually emerged with what they understood to be safe-conduct passes in both Russian and German.

By the last weeks of April 1945, Germany had lost any semblance of central government. When the Americans met the Russians at Torgau, the Reich was cut in two. Berlin was surrounded. Banks were likely to run out of money within days. Wages went unpaid. German soldiers went on looting frenzies. In some areas, the Nazi terror apparatus still functioned.[7] Anyone even suspected of lack of enthusiasm for National Socialism was liable to be hanged from the nearest lamp post.[8] The situation in Berlin was particularly desperate. At least 10,000 Berliners were accused of being traitors. Regular soldiers, Waffen SS, Gestapo and foreign volunteer forces including French fascists[9] fought the Red Army block by block, street by street. Hitler's order to destroy infrastructure badly affected railways and canals already hit by Allied bombing. Food was in desperately short supply. People were hungry, without coal, gas or electricity, and had to stand in long queues for water. 'No orders any more, no news, nothing.'[10] Without electricity there was no radio, no newspaper. In mid-afternoon on 30 April Hitler shot himself, but it wasn't until late in the evening of the next day, 1 May, that an announcement was made: Hitler had fallen 'at the head of the heroic defenders of the Reich'. The roads out of Berlin were clogged with fleeing families getting out of the way. Few mourned Hitler. It seemed that overnight, praise for the Führer turned to demonisation. He could be blamed for all that had gone wrong.[11] On 2 May, the German troops in Berlin were ordered to stop fighting. The Red flag flew from the Reichstag.

Back at the house in Herzberg, Bob found a welcome sight. Two of the older women had been foraging in the local marshalling yard, which had been bombed before the Russians arrived. Finding a number of overturned, locked goods wagons, they managed to force one open and discovered a consignment of German Army rations. Among them there was something they had not seen since before the war: bags of real, green coffee beans. There were also tins of meat and preserved fruit and vegetables. A great meal was being prepared in a kitchen suffused with an aroma of roasting coffee beans. There was proper strong black coffee after supper that night. As always both before and since, Bob reckoned the smell of the roasting coffee was far superior to the taste of the resulting liquid. After the meal, Bob explained that they would be continuing their journey to the American zone. The women asked if they could accompany them. Bob struggled to express in German, as tactfully as possible, that his only chance of getting a quick, uneventful passage through the recently occupied countryside was to have no possessions and no companions, particularly women. He tried to reassure them that they would do better to stay in the relative security and anonymity of their present refuge until order was restored to the undisciplined chaos outside.

When Bob and Barney left the house in Herzberg, just one of the women was awake. They thanked her and slipped out. Bob felt bad as he plodded southwards out of town. His conscience was troubled by his refusal of the women's request to accompany them. It was probably the right decision. There were more Russian troops than ever before. They ignored the two uniformed men. At about midday, they passed through a small village. A group of smartly dressed Russian officers were seated at tables in an erstwhile restaurant, eating, drinking and making a lot of noise. Not for the first time, Bob and Barney noted the difference in standards of dress between Russian officers and the other ranks. The officers were resplendent in well-cut, tailored uniforms with ample gold braid and medals. The soldiers were mainly of Eastern, even Asiatic origin and wore coarse blouse-like uniforms. As they passed, one of the Russian officers left the restaurant to relieve himself by the roadside. On impulse, Bob decided to approach him when he had finished urinating. He tried to explain in German that they were British RAF officers. He pointed to the badges of rank on their shoulders. Bob hoped to establish some sort of camaraderie with a man who was, after all, one of their allies and who might be prepared to share his food and drink. But no. Saying something like the Russian equivalent of 'b… off', the man turned his back on them. Feeling more than a little huffed[12] at his lack of friendship, the airmen continued their journey more than ever determined to avoid contact with Russians.

It was of course not only the two fleeing pilots who were having to deal with the Russians. Hitler's nominated successor, Grand Admiral Dönitz, was determined to buy time by prolonging the war on all fronts in order to get German troops back from the east and out of the clutches of the Russians. He even hoped to persuade the Western powers to join him in a continued war against Bolshevism. There would be another week of fighting, rape, retribution, pillage and misery before the final capitulation. On the day, 2 May, that German forces in Italy capitulated, code breakers at Bletchley Park in England had broken a message from Dönitz that stated that the fight would go on unrestricted.[13]

Dönitz had been in charge of Germany's successful U-boat fleet. While not a member of the Nazi party, he had been a committed National Socialist and loyal to the state. He is reported to have been stunned to be given control but 'did not for a moment doubt that it was my duty to accept the task', which was 'to save

German men and women from destruction by the advancing Bolshevik enemy'. He left Berlin and went north, back to his naval headquarters in Plön, a small town on a lake in Schleswig-Holstein, close to the huge naval base at Kiel. He established his new German government in the naval barracks that had been built for training U-boat crews.[14] Within a few days even Plön seemed vulnerable. Files and documents were trucked north on roads already choked with refugees and military convoys. Dönitz in his armoured car was strafed by RAF fighter planes as he fled north to his intended destination, Flensburg, close by the Danish border. Denmark and Norway were still in German control. To the south, the British had taken Lüneburg and the Americans had Wismar. On 3 May, Hamburg capitulated. Dönitz dispatched a negotiator to FM Montgomery at his HQ in the Lüneburg Heath, east of Hamburg. Early in the morning of 4 May, at 6.25am, in Montgomery's little dun-coloured tent, he signed a partial capitulation. Fighting ceased in the north-west. Within three days the British had 3 million German prisoners in their hands. The Russians consolidated their positions around Berlin, Mecklenburg and Brandenburg. The situation was changing almost hourly.

The two RAF pilots continued to walk west in the hope of reaching the American lines at Torgau. By early afternoon on Friday 4 May they arrived at Falkenberg. It was eerily quiet. They walked down wide streets of large brick houses built in the times of great railway expansion at the end of the 19th century. A big station accommodated four lines criss-crossing at different levels. Now it was flattened. Barely one train a day passed down the lines. The houses, built for multiple occupancy for railwaymen's families, bore the marks of rifle fire. There were a few shell holes but otherwise the buildings seemed undamaged. Undamaged but deserted. The doors of most of the houses were either open or had been forced off their hinges. Bob and Barney stepped inside and started looking for food, but every house had been systematically looted of everything that could be easily carried. Empty bottles of spirits and wines cluttered the floors. In one flat they found an empty bottle of eau de cologne on the floor of the bathroom. They guessed that some Asiatic infantryman had either not noticed or not cared about whether it was schnapps or perfume alcohol.[15]

Invading troops of every nationality, not just the Russians, took to wholesale looting. It was forbidden under army regulations, but whether under the guise of 'souvenir hunting'[16] or a desperate search for food and shelter, every town and city suffered looting within a few hours of capture. British, American and Canadian troops were fond of Nazi memorabilia, Luger pistols, flags and medals. The SS were frequently considered legitimate targets and had their wallets emptied. No sooner had the troops left than the civilian population took to looting their own neighbourhoods. Housewives in Berlin, like the villagers around Warsaw, found it easy to enter abandoned, or apparently abandoned, property whose doors and windows were broken.[17] War brings with it a form of destruction of morality. Even countries not directly affected, such as Sweden, saw a quadrupling in prosecutions for theft. In France, theft tripled. In occupied Europe, stealing and profiteering was justified to keep food and supplies out of the hands of the Germans. Of the millions of displaced persons, some 8 million slave labourers joined 4 million Germans from the east and almost 5 million in the west, and hundreds of thousands sought a route home through a devastated land.[18] They fed themselves by looting and robbing. There was no system for distributing food and shelter. The best they could hope for was to be scooped up by Allied soldiers and transported to displacement centres in the west. Across Germany the rule of law was patchy or virtually non-existent. The empty streets and desolate homes of the once-thriving railway town of Falkenberg were testament to fear not just of marauding Russians but also of their own countrymen.

The two British men decided to look for a flat or a house that they could use as a base. The Elbe River was about 15 miles away. They had no way of knowing where the Americans might be. It could take days to get across the river. After some searching, they found a suitable flat in a quiet out-of-the way road. They had settled for a house divided into two flats. Despite evidence of looting, it was comfortable and well appointed. The furniture and fittings were luxurious. They took the upper flat. A brief search of drawers and cupboards revealed that the previous occupants had been a Germany Army doctor and either his wife or his mistress. They had left in some hurry and disarray. Bob and Barney put the furniture and bedding back into order and checked out the bathroom. To their amazement, both hot and cold taps worked. The electric stove in the kitchen worked. The only problem was lack of food and soap. They went out again and searched other houses to see if the Russians had left anything. After several fruitless recces they found, much to their delight, a cellar crammed not only with jars of preserved food, mainly chicken and vegetables, but also stocks of wine. They determined to keep their treasure-trove secret and waited until after dark to fill a container with enough food and drink to keep them going for several days. They also found soap. That evening they luxuriated in a hot bath. They washed their clothes. And they cooked themselves an improvised but thoroughly enjoyable meal. It was the end of their fifth day on the run.

The next morning they left for Torgau. But first they decided to investigate more of the town. Save for two old women, they saw no one on the streets. At the back of one of the houses was a garage whose doors had not been forced. With the aid of a crowbar they prised open the door and, to their amazement, found a small German saloon car. Behind the car, at the back of the garage, were two bicycles. The car was too great a risk and anyway where would they get fuel? But the bicycles were treasure indeed. They had seen many Russians riding bicycles. They would hide these two until they were ready to use them. They wheeled them into the garden of the flat and hid them behind some bushes. The tyres were a bit flat but luckily one bike had a hand pump. Finding the bicycles transformed their plans. Soon after midday they set out on what they were sure would be their last lap to freedom.

The ride to Torgau was uneventful. The two young men might have been on a country cycle ride, enjoying gently undulating fields, stands of mature trees, orchards and quiet farmsteads. They would have seen evidence of recent events – overturned vehicles, dead farm animals, heaps of discarded loot. They passed by groups of Russian infantrymen. Russian cavalrymen were silhouetted against the skyline. It was 15 miles from Falkenberg to Torgau. The sun was still high when they arrived at the top of a rise overlooking the town. In the distance glinted the Elbe River. They cycled faster. Looking for the bridge to take them across to the Americans. At Torgau, the Elbe is wide, flanked on either side by floodplain. The steel-girder bridge built to carry road and railway was missing its central span. Closer examination revealed two breaks that made the bridge impassable for all save the most intrepid pedestrian. However, to their sheer relief and excitement a temporary bridge made up of a line of floating pontoons had been erected alongside it. Approaching from the east, Bob and Barney set off through the town in the direction of the bridge. There were large numbers of Russians who took no notice of two men on bicycles. On the east bank lay Fort Zinna prison, a notorious German Army concentration camp that had been rapidly emptied just days before the Russians arrived. It lay abandoned. Its blocks bleak and grey with horror. Close by was the entrance to the pontoon bridge. It was empty.

No traffic. A solitary armed Russian guard stood in their way. With sign language they made it clear that they wanted to cross over. The guard refused to allow them through. Bob showed him their recently acquired safe-conduct pass. To no avail. The Russian studied their passes upside down. It was clear he could not read. His job was to keep the bridge closed and that was it. There was nothing they could do about it. Tantalisingly close, on the west bank, Hartenstein Castle dominated the scene. Its medieval walls spoke of the safety of true allies, shelter and a likely passage home.

Deeply disappointed to be turned away, they cycled back into town where they found what looked like an official building, maybe a temporary town hall. Leaving Barney to guard the bicycles, Bob went inside to ask when the bridge would be open. He approached a good-looking blonde German girl who was working for the Russians. He enquired in his fractured German. She replied in good English. She told him that after the initial, much-publicised fraternisation between the Russians and Americans some two weeks previously, they had withdrawn to their respective sides of the river. There had been no contact between them since. Bob asked if she knew when the bridge would be reopened. She told him of a rumour that the Russians were waiting for the Americans to withdraw from the west bank of the Elbe to allow the Russian Army to advance further into Germany. This was devastating news. Bob went back outside to discuss it with Barney. After much deliberation they agreed to return to Falkenberg where at least they had a safe shelter and food and water. They could return to Torgau daily to find out what was happening.

Bob and Barney had unwittingly been misled by the Allied publicity machine. The Russians and Americans did meet at Torgau. They did pose on the broken bridge for a series of iconic photos, but that was later. In fact, the first meeting was just before midday on 25 April at Lorenzkirch near Strehla, a small town on the Elbe some 20 miles south of Torgau. When Lt Albert 'Buck' Kotzebue and his patrol from the US 1st Army met Lt Grigori Goloborodko and his men from the 1st Ukrainian Army,[19] they met among the carnage of a German retreat. Both banks of the Elbe were littered with the corpses of civilians. Retreating German soldiers had blown up a pontoon bridge crowded with fleeing men, women and children. Some 400 drowned.[20] Later in the day, at 4.40pm, in Torgau, the official handshake took place between representatives of the two armies. Torgau was a fitting place for marking the historic moment. The town lay between the baroque splendour of Dresden to the south and the birthplace of Lutheranism at Wittenberg to the north. Just further north was Dessau, home of Bauhaus modernism and the Junkers bomber factories.

The following day, 26 April, the world's press, packed into 15 jeeps, were invited to a photo shoot. Gen Russakov waited on the east bank to meet Maj Gen Emil Reinhardt. BBC correspondent Edward Ward told his audience: 'I saw soldiers of the First American and the Red Armies throw their arms around each other's necks and kiss each other on the cheeks.'[21] The Russians had broken into the local Hohner accordion and harmonica factory. It seems that many of them knew how to play. Americans were ferried across the river, in boats from the Torgau Racing Club, to get bread, apples and vodka.[22] Russian women soldiers danced with their allies beneath a huge portrait of Stalin. In Churchill's broadcast recognising this historic moment, he said: 'The Armies of the great Allies have traversed Germany and have joined hands together.' He talked of destroying the German military, the power of the Nazis and the 'subjugation of Hitler's Reich'. There was dancing in New York's Times Square, a 300-gun salute in Moscow and expectation everywhere that the war was over. But it was not.

Not yet. The Red Army was ordered to keep to itself, not to arrange 'friendly meetings' and to 'give no information about operational plans or unit objectives'.[23]

Ten days after the historic handshakes, the ambivalence of their Russian allies was only too apparent to Bob and Barney. Experience had taught them to be cautious. They returned to Falkenberg without being stopped or searched. The flat, they were relieved to find, was untouched. Nothing had been disturbed. They hid their bicycles and, once it got dark, returned to the cellars where they had found the food. They gathered up as much as they could carry, hoping it would sustain them for a rather longer stay than they had previously anticipated. It was now Saturday 5 May; the war was effectively over in North West Germany, the Netherlands and Denmark. The 'Heil Hitler' salute was prohibited. Pictures of Hitler were taken down from government offices. The 'scorched earth' policy, which saw much of Germany's infrastructure, canals, railways and communications destroyed, was halted. Only Norway held out for a few more days. Dönitz and his generals were still hoping to retrieve some 2 million Wehrmacht soldiers from the Soviets.[24] They clung to the possibility of a partial rather than a total capitulation. To make the situation even more unstable, there was a popular uprising in Prague against the German occupation. This triggered a rapid advance by Soviet troops into Bohemia and Moravia. The two British pilots hiding in their flat were caught in the flux of these last days of the European war without any understanding of the overall picture.

Back home, their families were waiting expectantly to hear that the war was over. It seemed to be dragging on for months. The uncertainty made many families fearful for the future. What plans had been made for the return of their menfolk? After six years of 'keeping the home fires burning', would there be a home, a job? Or would they be sent back out to the Far East, where tales of Japanese atrocities filled the news? Alice had heard that her brother, Bill, was no longer in the North Atlantic but in hospital in Canada. He would be home soon. As a regular Royal Navy officer, he might well be sent out to fight. Alice read the papers and listened avidly to every news bulletin on the radio. There were horrifying pictures of people being released from German concentration camps. She remembered her college days and thought of her Jewish tutor's family. She read that the Germans had very little food. Nothing to spare. Prisoners were surviving on Red Cross parcels. She had not heard from Bob for two months. In that time the Russians, notorious for disregarding the Geneva Convention, had taken over the POW camps in the east. She began to imagine Bob arriving home emaciated and ill. Her friend in Scotland wrote to say that as soon as Bob arrived home they should all go to Scotland, where they and their farmer friends would feed him up.

Bob and his companion despaired of finding the bridge at Torgau open. They spent most of the next day exploring locally. The town seemed absolutely deserted. They went into the unoccupied houses and found many valuable items that the marauding Russians had either missed or ignored. Thinking they might come in useful, now that neither of them had any possessions of their own, they took a few valuable ornaments and silver cutlery and put them into bags that they could strap to their bikes. The following day was bright and sunny. Before setting out for Torgau to see what was happening, they hid their loot in the bushes where they had hidden their bikes. They expected to be back. However, after just a few miles on the road they realised there had been some new developments.

The road to Torgau was filled with Russian vehicles laden with guns and troops. There seemed to be no convoy discipline and the driving was dangerous and indiscriminate. A lorry loaded with troops overtook another towing an anti-tank gun, forcing the lorry with the gun trailer into the ditch, where it turned over on its side. Instead of stopping, the lorry full of troops continued its headlong rush, leaving the driver of the overturned vehicle standing by the roadside shaking his fist in fury. The closer they got to Torgau, the more congested the traffic became. It was an amazing sight. Lorries were piled high with troops, both men and women, stores and equipment. Everything had been thrown on without any sense of order or priority: furniture, rugs, household goods, all obviously looted. Cases of ammunition and military equipment shared space with cooking pots. As they drew closer to the bridge, the lines of vehicles slowed to walking pace.

The moment Bob and Barney crossed over was almost an anticlimax. The bridge was so crowded that they dismounted and wheeled their bicycles slowly behind one of the overcrowded trucks. They were tense. Poised for the moment someone questioned their presence. No one paid any attention. The Russian Army was clearly crossing the Elbe and advancing further into Germany. Bob looked around as he reached the centre of the bridge. It was, he thought, a scene worthy of Cecil B. DeMille, though no film had created as dramatic and chaotic a sight as this. They were within reach of their goal. As they arrived at the far side of the bridge, the convoy started to accelerate. Bob and Barney had to jump clear of the headlong, undisciplined advance. They spotted an American jeep near the exit with two white-helmeted military policemen standing watching the spectacle.

They approached the Americans and explained who they were. To their intense relief they were welcomed without question, and immediately helped into the back of the jeep. As they drove through the old part of Torgau, past the castle and the town square, the Americans explained that the move was in accordance with the Yalta agreement that shared out German territory between the Allies. The local German population had fled because, as one of the Americans put it laconically, 'the Krauts are shit scared of what's going to happen to them now the Ruskies are taking over'.[25] When Stalin, Roosevelt and Churchill met in Yalta in February 1945 they had agreed to accept nothing less than unconditional surrender from Germany, after which the country would be divided into three, with France taking responsibility for a portion of the American and British territory. Berlin would be divided into four. With surrender anticipated within days, the Russians were making sure they were in place with no encroachment from the Americans.

Bob and Barney had been propelled from Russian-occupied Germany to American HQ in Torgau in the space of half an hour. They were taken to see an officer, who questioned them briefly to confirm who they were. Next they were given a meal including white bread, which neither pilot had seen since being shot down, as well as doughnuts and real coffee. The food and friendly English voices convinced Bob that his days of captivity were really over. He could look forward to returning to England. He sent Alice a message on an official form:

> **'Germany:**
> **Date** 5th May 1945[26]
> **Dear** Alice
> 1. **I am free and in safe hands.**
> 2. **Will write to you again as early as possible.**
> 3. **I hope to be with you soon.**
> 4. **Personal message (not more than 15 words).**
> Am quite well and in good hands
> will get home as soon as possible
> **LOVE AND BEST WISHES,** Bob x'

After the meal, an officer came over to Bob and Barney and explained that many ex-POWs had made journeys like theirs. On the day the American transport arrived at Luckenwalde and was turned away by the Russians, at least 200 men left the compound to head west. Arrangements had been made to take all ex-POWs to a barracks near Leipzig before being repatriated. It seemed logical, if disappointing. They sat and read some American forces' newspapers. Suddenly Barney stood up. He was not going to be taken to some American barracks. He believed he would get back to England much faster if they continued westwards to the Channel coast, thumbing lifts as they went. Bob was taken by surprise. He was not convinced and said so, whereupon Barney turned and departed without another word.

Before leaving the POW camp together, Bob had had little contact with Barney. Bob confesses that he even felt some resentment towards him because he had been formation leader in the attack that resulted in Bob and his flight bearing the brunt of the AA fire that shot him down.[27] Their 'escape' partnership was a matter of mutual convenience, yet they had worked well together. It was a shame to end it so abruptly. Theirs was not the only partnership to terminate unexpectedly. Time and again accounts tell of 'buddies' who had trained together, flown together and been prisoners of war together walking out on each other without a backward glance and never meeting again.[28] To make sure that Barney had indeed gone Bob went outside, but there was no sign of him. He told the Americans but they just shrugged their shoulders as though one or more less to look after meant nothing to them. Bob thought Barney was wrong about getting home quicker, though he never heard what happened to him. (It took Barney three months to hitch-hike his way back to England.[29]) Bob was soon back in a jeep travelling along an autobahn to an American barracks on the outskirts of Leipzig. It was pretty much like any other camp he had experienced as a POW except that food was unlimited and proper beds and blankets were provided. After the initial pleasure, even the

American food lost its attraction. It was all very disappointing. There was little to do except wait.

After signing the capitulation with Montgomery, Dönitz played for time as he tried to bring German troops back out of Russian-occupied territory. The capitulation would go into force at one minute past midnight on 8/9 May. Dönitz had sent Gen Alfred Jodl to Rheims, where Eisenhower had his HQ in a small red schoolhouse. After hours of negotiations and phone calls to and fro, the Act of Military Surrender was signed at 2.41am on 7 May. They arranged that an official announcement would be made at 9am. However, the Russians continued to act according to their own agenda. Stalin complained about the text of the surrender document and insisted on a slightly longer version being signed at Gen Georgy Zhukov's HQ in Berlin. In the end the surrender was not signed until 12.45am on 9 May and was backdated to the previous day to comply with the signing in Rheims.[30] After the signing, the Russians broke out the caviar and champagne and Gen Zhukov is reported to have joined in the dancing. He might well dance. No fewer than six European capital cities were now in Russian hands: Berlin, Vienna, Prague, Budapest, Bucharest and Sofia. News of these momentous events began to emerge. The British people were told by a public announcement on BBC Radio at 9pm on 7 May. The next day, 8 May, was declared VE day, Victory in Europe Day. It would be a national holiday.

Bob was lying on his bed in a large barrack room surrounded by ex-POWs. Most of the men were too exhausted and debilitated to do anything but sleep, albeit fitfully. Late at night on 7 May there was a tannoy announcement. The war in Europe was over. It came as a great anticlimax. There was nothing to do except reflect on the past and think about the future. Their sleep was disturbed by sounds of drunken revelry coming from a nearby American canteen. Nobody bothered to bring over even a carton of beer to those who had experienced so much captivity. The next two days passed very slowly. There was little to do except eat, sleep and read the few books provided.

The radio told them something of the celebrations in Britain. For several weeks provisions had been stockpiled and flags purchased ready for street parties. VE day was celebrated all over the country. Alice found herself shaking hands with everyone she met in the street.[31] Others danced and sang and hugged any serviceman they saw. Central London seemed full to overflowing as thousands of people sang and danced. The King and Queen appeared on the balcony at Buckingham Palace no fewer than eight times between 6pm and midnight. Prime Minister Winston Churchill gave three stirring speeches. He warned that World War II was not yet over. The Japanese still occupied large portions of the British Empire. Nevertheless, he gave victory to the people and rejoiced that they could all take a night off to celebrate. Alice was invited to a party at the town hall for all those who had helped in the Voluntary Services in Chichester. Mrs Hughes looked after three-year-old Suzanne for a couple of hours so that Alice could join in the celebrations. A friend was planning a party for the following Saturday to welcome home her husband on leave from the Royal Navy. Alice had accepted because she would be able to take Suzanne with her and stay in their spare room. She had no idea where Bob was or how he was. No message had reached her.

On VE day, 200 Lancaster bombers were redeployed to fly back more than 13,000 prisoners of war from Italy and Germany.[32] It was early in the evening the next day that Bob heard a tannoy announcement. All British POWs should be ready the following morning to be taken to a nearby airfield and flown to Brussels. This was welcome but unexpected and a little disappointing since Bob had hoped to be airlifted direct to England. After a substantial American breakfast, a convoy of buses, for once not lorries, took around 100 British soldiers and airmen from the barracks to an airfield about 20 miles away. Two camouflaged Dakotas were standing waiting for them. After a flight of two or so hours they arrived at one of Brussels' airfields. After their stay with the Americans, the British reception and accommodation was a bit of a let-down. The food was terrible. They were accommodated in an erstwhile police barracks. It was grim but the discomfort was offset by the news that they were to be flown to England the next day. It left them with a long evening with nothing to do. Some of the more adventurous exited the barracks and set out for town. None of them had any money, yet they managed to travel into the centre of Brussels, have a good time and return in the early hours of the morning very much the worse for wear.

After breakfast, buses arrived as promised to take Bob and his fellow ex-POWs to the airfield. As they arrived at the perimeter road they were amazed to see not transport aircraft but lines and lines of heavy bombers – Stirlings, Lancasters and Halifaxes. The buses stopped on the main tarmac area. As passengers disembarked they were directed in single file to the waiting aircraft. It was very controlled and orderly. As each aircraft took its complement of about ten passengers, the line was directed on to the next one. Bob found himself climbing up some steps into a Stirling that had been stripped of all equipment except what was necessary to fly and navigate back to England. Only the crew had seats. The passengers just made themselves as comfortable as possible in whatever space or corner was available.

All the men were RAF aircrew – pilots, navigators, bomb aimers or air gunners. Several were NCOs. Some had been ferried to Brussels by Dakota but, for most, this flight back home was their first since being shot down. Many had had terrifying experiences; some, including Bob, had escaped from burning aircraft. Looking around, Bob saw strained looks and clenched fists as they relived those moments. Take-off was bumpy but they were soon over the Channel. As the white cliffs of the south coast came into view they took it in turns to look over the pilot's shoulder to catch their first glimpse of England. Men who had been through hell without crying once now had tears in their eyes.[33] Bob comments with typical British understatement that it was a nostalgic moment for them all.[34]

They landed at Dunsfold and tumbled out of the aircraft's door and down some steps while the engines were kept running for a return journey to Belgium. A fleet of buses waited near the control tower to take them to the local railway station. Cheerful ladies from the Women's Voluntary Services (WVS) and Red Cross served them tea, sandwiches and biscuits from vans and trolleys before they embarked on a special train to an RAF camp at Cosford in Cheshire. As Bob was just 20 miles from his home in Chichester, he was terribly frustrated to be transported almost 200 miles in the opposite direction. There was nothing to be done. He was part of a huge project. There were 250,000 British and American servicemen to be repatriated. The plan was that men would be 'brought back under military discipline, deloused, debriefed, given their back pay, and transported home in an orderly and fair manner'.[35] Some men had been prisoners for four or even five years. Some for just months. All had been through some sort of hell. For Bob and his cohort, the journey through the English countryside had the effect of a tonic. It was a bright summer's day. Their train had been routed non-stop to Cosford, bypassing London.

On arrival, the task of receiving the returning aircrew POWs really began in earnest with forms to be filled in, replacement uniforms and medical examinations. Those requiring medical treatment or more detailed examination were transferred to a local RAF hospital. Bob mentions being identified and being equipped with fresh underwear, shirt, tie, socks and shoes and a forage cap. He was provided with a rather ill-fitting battledress in khaki, not RAF blue, but with blue braid for shoulder badges of rank for officers and chevrons for NCOs. A team of WAAFs (Women's Auxiliary Air Force) sewed on the appropriate medal ribbons.

Military Intelligence MI9 had made plans for debriefing the POWs that involved three different questionnaires: a general one, one for specific contacts or escape leaders and a third for reporting atrocities. In reality, fewer than one in three returning prisoners filled out forms. A possible 100,000 'liberation reports' are missing from the record.[36] There is none for Bob Allen. He says that after the interviewing, examining and kitting out was over he was given a new identity card and railway warrants to travel home. In addition, he received an advance of pay, real money, drawn from wages accumulated during his many months of captivity.

The matter of pay for POWs took more than 50 years to resolve. American servicemen found that despite doing their duty to escape from camp, the days they were out were deducted from their pay when they got home. The British had an issue with 'Lagergeld'. This was the special currency paid to prisoners by their German captors under the Geneva Convention. It was virtually useless outside the camp. What enraged the returnees was finding that 10 per cent of their wages in real money had been deducted from their back pay in lieu of the Lagergeld they received.[37] Furthermore, they were taxed on it. In the decades following the end of World War II these penny-pinching injustices rankled and became the focus of demands for proper compensation.

With money in his pocket at last Bob could make a call home. At this point Bob and Alice's memories differ. Bob says that he called his wife and said he would be home in the afternoon of the following day. He arranged to ring again from London to give the time of arrival in Chichester. Then he went back to his enormous barrack room to while away the last evening of separation from his family. His thoughts were interrupted by a chap arriving with an invitation from the nearby Air Transport Auxiliary (ATA) mess. Bob joined a party of about ten who walked a quarter of a mile to the airfield. When they arrived the party was in full swing. They were immediately plied with drinks and shouted conversation. The sudden change of lifestyle, the noise and excitement, was almost unbearable. After an hour or so Bob quietly left and found his way back to his bed. He was grateful for the kindness of the ATA ferry pilots, men and women, who had generously invited them to their party. It was a positive step on the way to rehabilitation. The next step would be arriving home.

Alice remembers a normal Saturday morning and being called downstairs by Mrs Hughes to take a reverse-charge telephone call. She gave her name. The man on the other end of the line said, 'You've been a long time coming.'[38] She asked who was speaking. Bob said, 'Who do you think it is, Alice; don't you recognise my voice?' At that point Alice realised it really was her husband. After months of separation they would be together again. She hugged her child and told her Daddy would be home in the afternoon. Her next thought was that she must go shopping for a meal. Mrs Hughes looked after Suzanne while Alice went out. Her first call was the butchers. She told him her Bob was coming home and he found her some off-ration sausages and liver. She used her meat ration coupons for bacon. Bob would have a proper mixed grill. Bob's mother had sent her a tin of tomato soup and a tin of peaches, which were luxury items. Five years of scarcity had denuded the nation's larders. Imported fruit had been the first to go. Eggs were inevitably powdered to preserve them. Milk was reserved for young children. Traditional meats such as lamb, beef or pork were replaced by rabbits reared in back gardens.[39] Bob's mother's chickens and eggs were in great demand.

Alice, her family and friends expected Bob to be malnourished and in need of feeding up. Alice therefore prepared herself to meet a very thin, much older-looking man. Maybe even skeletal, like the photos of prison-camp inmates. As soon as possible they would go to their friends in Scotland for good food and fresh air.

It was Saturday 12 May, just under two weeks since he left Luckenwalde and ten months after being shot down, 'missing believed killed in action', that Bob was finally reunited with his family. Feeling a little conspicuous in their improvised uniforms, Bob and his cohort were taken to the railway station near Cosford where they joined others for the journey to London. After arrival at King's Cross, Bob found himself travelling alone on the Underground to Victoria station. He felt rather self-conscious. Fellow passengers, many of them officers and airmen in uniform, gave him strange looks. Soon word must have got around and he was identified as a returning POW because without exception all were courteous and helpful. Once at Victoria, he phoned to tell his wife the time of his train's arrival in Chichester.

He saw them, waiting on the platform. Alice and his young daughter, Suzanne. She ran towards him. He dropped his small canvas holdall and hugged her. Alice put her arms round him. He was pale, rather grey-looking, rather pudgy. Strangers, recognising a family reunion, smiled and one man said 'Welcome home son'. They took a taxi to the flat. Alice was shy and flustered as she made her husband tea. Young Suzanne had noticed that he left his bag in the hall. Tugging at his trousers, she offered to help him get it. When they returned, Suzanne was clutching an enormous bar of chocolate and an orange that an American had given Bob in Germany. Alice explained that they had been invited to a party. 'Yes, let's go.' Bob would not hear of missing it. He had a bath and then fell asleep on the bed.

Alice and Suzanne changed into their party clothes. Bob slept on. Eventually, at about 8.30pm, Alice tentatively woke him. He was immediately alert and insisted they go to the party. Alice had kept his best uniform ready. They set out looking very smart. Bob soon had a whisky in his hand. One whisky led to another and with a group of cherished friends around him he began to tell them his story. It would be the only time he talked about it.

Postscript

What happened next

SOME 40 YEARS PASSED before Bob Allen was ready to describe his experiences as a fighter pilot in World War II. Even then he would not speak of them. He set down a written record of events as he saw them. He left little or no room for personal feelings. He changed names and disguised events and places. He wrote in the third person as if it were someone else who had lived through those terrible years. He suffered from nightmares to the end of his life. A life spent in the service of his country. Life as a pilot, flying fast and high.

Bob spent the summer of 1945 enjoying his freedom. He relaxed with his family in Sussex, spending longer with his wife and child than at any other time in their first six years of marriage. They visited friends and relations, went up to Scotland to be spoilt with nourishing meals and clear air. After about three months, he began to think about getting back into work. Experts agreed that three months was the optimum time for prisoners to recuperate. Psychological problems needing treatment were invariably revealed after three months at home.[1] Bob had coped really well.

Prison life made many men bitter and unsure of themselves. Some of them tried to explain. 'The mental marks left on me by prison days made me a difficult person to live with for a time. It was many years before I fully regained my confidence and could offer my family a normal, happy life.'[2] For the rest there was silence. The unwillingness to speak of their experiences hid them from view. There were 250,000 British and American servicemen repatriated. There are no statistics for prisoners who died in the last months of the war. Historians guess that between 2,500 and 3,500 died on the winter marches.[3] The majority got home and tried to take up their old lives in a country bleached by austerity. Men with jobs were on strike. Churchill was out of office. A new Labour government had plans for a 'new deal'. Bob Allen had to decide on his future and that of his family.

One day, an official-looking envelope arrived in the post. It was a certificate from the Secretary of State for Air announcing that Bob had been 'Mentioned in Despatches' for his distinguished service on 8 June 1944. That was D-Day. Less than a year before. Now the enemy was defeated and the Allies were realigning. The war with Japan was still being fought in the Far East. The draw of service life, of being able to fly again, was irresistible. Bob had applied for a permanent commission just before he was posted to France. He remembered being interviewed, but neither he nor any of his contemporaries in the RAFVR (the volunteer reserve) had heard whether they had been taken on. With the end of the war in Europe, large parts of the British military were rapidly disbanded. Within two years, the numbers of men and women under arms was reduced from 5.5 million to 1.1 million.[4] Many POWs who hoped to return to their old units were disappointed. Bob knew that to achieve a successful career in the RAF he must return to where he was known best – to the squadrons of the 2nd Tactical Air Force, and they were now part of the British Occupation Forces in Germany. The commanding officer of 266 Squadron when Bob first joined was a wing commander on the staff of 84 Group. It consisted of a number of fighter and fighter-bomber squadrons based on airfields in Northern Germany. Bob wrote to him.

It was a week or so before he got his reply. Would he like to join the staff of 84 Group? It went on to say that they had had some difficulty in arranging a posting because, all the way up to the Air Ministry, his records were marked 'Killed in Action'. It was a bureaucratic tangle. Very much alive, Bob replied immediately, accepting the invitation. Within two weeks he received a formal notification and was on his way to Germany. For the rest of the winter he held a staff job at the RAF Headquarters in Bad Eilsen in North Rhine, Westphalia. He managed to get a few flights piloting an Auster – a small, high-wing aircraft used for short trips.

In early spring 1946, just under nine months after his return from the POW camp, he was called to take command of 33 Squadron, a fighter-bomber squadron based at Gatow in Berlin. He got to Gatow as a passenger in a Dakota. The next day he was sitting in a Tempest, successor to the Typhoon with which he was so familiar. A short briefing, a check on the layout of cockpit controls and he was ready to taxi out – his first flight on operations for 21 months. The Tempest was faster, more powerful but otherwise very similar to the Typhoon. He flew for 30 minutes and made a good landing. As he taxied back to the squadron dispersal, he felt elated. He was back flying. He had made it back after being shot down without the slightest fear or trepidation. He was starting again from where he had been temporarily stopped in Normandy.

The squadron was to spend three more weeks in Berlin before returning to base a few miles inside the border separating British and Russian forces. Bob flew daily to improve his knowledge and skill with the new aircraft. When the day came to fly out of Berlin, he had to admit, it was a proud moment. He was leading 12 aircraft in formation westwards down the air corridor over Russian-occupied territory. He was just a few miles north of where he and Barney had made their way on foot during the last days of the war in Europe.

Bob Allen retired from the RAF in 1970 after 37 years of service. He continued to fly small aircraft whenever he could. In his last year, he was presented with a high honour, a CBE, by the Queen at Buckingham Palace. Official photos show Alice beside him with their two daughters, Suzanne and Elizabeth. It was not to be the end of his service to his country. He joined the Civil Service in the Ministry of Agriculture. After Britain joined the European Common Market in 1973, he frequently found himself arguing on behalf of British farmers in Brussels.

It was only when he finally retired in 1980 that Bob was persuaded by Alice to set down an account of his experiences. He agreed to put them on record for family and historical reasons. Whether he wrote in longhand or dictated to Alice we do not know. Only the typescript survives.

Bob Allen's story is a reminder of how extraordinary times divert and entangle ordinary men. In wartime, there is no such person as an ordinary pilot.

Notes

PROLOGUE

1 The Pilot's Flying Logbook is an official record kept by a pilot of all flights undertaken. It includes date, time, type of aircraft, duty, length of time in the air and, where appropriate, a note of outcome and whether or not the target was hit. It usually includes a monthly and annual survey and names the unit to which the pilot is attached for flying duties.

2 For example, the National Archives at Kew, London, hold an almost complete set of operational squadron records, which makes it possible to cross-check events in an individual pilot's log with the squadron record.

CHAPTER 1

1 Allingham, Margery, *The Oaken Heart*, Michael Joseph (1941), new edition Golden Duck (2011), p.77

2 Allingham, *ibid*, p.84

3 Bailey, M., *Evolution of Aptitude Testing in the RAF*, Cranwell papers

4 This figure is an estimated total of evacuated men, of which 225,000 were British. See Lynn, Vera, with Cross, Robin & de Grex, Jenny, *We'll Meet Again*, Sidgwick & Jackson (1989, reprinted 2005), p.35

5 Terraine, John, *The Right of the Line*, Hodder & Stoughton (1985), new edition Pen & Sword (2010), p.4

6 Terraine, *ibid*, p.4

7 Barclay, George, *Fighter Pilot – A Self-portrait*, ed. Wynn, Humphrey, William Kimber (1976), p.26

8 Thomas, Hugh, *Spirit of the Blue*, Sutton Publishing (2004), p.25

9 Gardiner, Juliet, *Wartime Britain 1939–1945*, Headline (2004), p.367

10 Wellum, Geoffrey, *First Flight*, Viking (2002), p.63

11 Wellum, *ibid*, p.63

12   Milton, Brian, *The Last Witnesses*, André Deutsch (2010), p.36
13   Gardiner, Juliet, *ibid*, p.264
14   Mackenzie, K.W., DFC, AFC, *Hurricane Combat*, William Kimber (1987), p.31
15   Deere, Alan, *Nine Lives*, Wingham Press (1959), p.184
16   Franks, Norman & O'Connor, Mike, *Number One in War and Peace*, Grub Street (2000), p.102
17   Franks & O'Connor, *ibid*, p.105
18   Milton, *ibid*, p.237
19   Allen, R. N. G., unpublished memoir, p.5
20   Wellum, *ibid*, p.95
21   Allen, R. N. G., *ibid*, p.3
22   Allen, R. N. G., *ibid*, p.4
23   Allen, Bob, personal correspondence (17.6.1941)
24   Grazina, Sviderskyte, *Uragano Kapitonas*, Vilnius: Artesia, p.327 (internet)
25   Wellum, *ibid*, p.165
26   Johnson, J. E. 'Johnnie', *The Story of Air Fighting*, Hutchinson (1985), p.112
27   Allen, R. N. G., *ibid*, p.4

CHAPTER 2

1   'Great Scot' a passenger express on the West Coast line as distinct from the more famous 'Flying Scotsman', which left from King's Cross on the East Coast line.
2   Monks, Noel, *Fighter Squadrons*, Angus & Robertson, Australia (1941)
3   43 Squadron history IWM
4   Drake, Billy, *Fighter Leader: The Autobiography of Group Captain B. Drake DSO, DFC & Bar, US DFC*, with contribution from Christopher Shores, Grub Street, London (2001)
5   Longmate, Norman, *How We lived Then: A History of Everyday Life During the Second World War*, Arrow Books (1973), p.296
6   Gardiner, Juliet, *ibid*, p.358
7   Gardiner, Juliet, *ibid*, p.359
8   Allen, R. N. G., *ibid*, Chapter 2, p.7
9   Allen, R. N. G., *ibid*, Chapter 2, p.7
10   Barnett, Corelli, *Engage the Enemy more Closely – the Royal Navy in the Second World War*, Hodder and Stoughton (1991), Penguin (2000), p.66

11 Gilbert, Martin, *Second World War*, Weidenfeld (1989), p.157

12 Allen, R. N. G., *ibid*, Chapter 2, p.8

13 In fact the details of what happened did not emerge until after the war was over.

14 Hague, Arnold, 'Military Convoy WS39', Don Kindle Convoy Web re Wikipedia

15 Bill Watt quoting Blair 1996 re troopship *Anselm* from Old Forum – www.warsailors/Siri Holmes Lawson

16 Helgason, Guðmundor, 'Anselm', www.uboat.net

17 Greene, Graham, *The Heart of the Matter*, Heinemann (1948), Penguin (1962), p.97

18 Clifford, Mary Louise, *The Land and People of Sierra Leone*, Philadelphia (1974), p.48

19 Allen, R. N. G., *ibid*

20 Allen, R. N. G., *ibid*

21 Allen, R. N. G., personal letter

22 Barnett, Corelli, *ibid*, p.264

23 Wartime Memories, www.thegazette.co.uk/supplement/37920/issue/1489

24 Cecil Pugh's George Cross citation says: 'Within a few minutes the ship plunged and sank and Mr. Pugh was never seen again. He had every opportunity of saving his own life but, without regard for his own safety and in the best tradition of the Service and of a Christian minister, he gave up his life for others', Central Chancery of the Orders of Knighthood www.londongazette.co.uk/issues/37920/supplements/1489

25 Allen, R. N. G., *ibid* This naval tradition – whereby everyone over the age of 20 was given a tot of rum (a tot measures ⅛th of a pint) – began in 1655, and was discontinued in 1970.

26 Allen, Alice, *ibid*

CHAPTER 3

1 Barnham, Denis, *Malta Spitfire Pilot*, Frontline Books (2011), p.169

2 Allen, Alice, *ibid*

3 Allen, R. N. G., *ibid*

4 Martin, Thomas, *The French Empire at War 1940–1945*, Manchester University Press (1998), p.1

5 Martin, *ibid*, p.3

6   Martin, *ibid*, p.84

7   Sutherland, Jonathan & Caudwell, Diane, *Vichy at War: The French Air Force That Fought the Allies in WWII*, Pen & Sword Aviation (2011), p.23

8   Sutherland & Caudwell, *ibid* p.23

9   Sutherland & Caudwell, *ibid*, p.28

10 Clarke, Peter B., *West Africa at War 1914–18, 1939–45: Colonial Propaganda and its Cultural Aftermath*, Ethnographia London (1986), p.21

11 Mason, Francis K., *The Hawker Hurricane*, RAF Museum edition (1962), p.133

12 Air Historical Branch (IWM), *The Middle East Campaigns Vol. X: The West Africa Reinforcement Route*

13 Mason, *ibid*, p.144

14 Air Historical Branch, *ibid*, p.88

15 Sherry, Norman, *The Life of Graham Greene: Volume II: 1939–1955*, Jonathan Cape, London (1994), p.119

16 Sherry, *ibid*, p.121

17 Mason, *ibid*, p.144

18 Shores, *ibid*, p.26

19 Shores, *ibid*, p.10

20 Shores, *ibid*, p.37

21 Thomas, Andrew & Weal, John, *Hurricane Aces 1941–45*, Osprey Aircraft (2013), p.64

22 Shores, *ibid*, p.38

23 Darlow, Michael & Hodson, Gillian, *Terence Rattigan – The Man and His Work*, Quartet Books (1979), p.102

24 Darlow & Hodson, *ibid*, quoting BBC radio interview with Rattigan 4.7.1977

25 Leeks, Stuart, programme note Theatre Royal Haymarket 2011

26 Darlow & Hodson, *ibid*, p.117

27 AIR 27/933 128 Squadron Intelligence Report 22/8/41–31/10/41

28 Killingray, David & Rathbone, Richard (Eds.), *Africa and the Second World War*, Macmillan (1986), p.10

29 Killingray & Rathbone, *ibid*/Sekgoma, Gilbert A., p.242

30 Killingray & Rathbone, *ibid*, quoting PRO CO968/132/1 C&CS Atlantic to CO 4 Jan 42

31 Killingray & Rathbone, *ibid*, p.77 quoting Shuckburgh, *Colonial Civil History Vol 1*, Rhodes Livingstone Library, Oxford (1986) p.43

32 Wansell, Geoffrey, *Terence Rattigan*, Fourth Estate, London (1995), p.116

33 Wansell, *ibid*, p.117

34 Singer, Caroline & Le Roy Baldridge, Cyrus, *White Africans and Black*, Methodist Book Depot, Cape Coast, Gold Coast (no date but approx. 1930)

35 Buckle, N. & Murray, C., *I Think I Prefer the Tinned Variety: The Diary of a Petty Officer in the Fleet Air Arm During World War II*, Spurwing (2012)

CHAPTER 4

1   Conyers Nesbit, Roy, *Eyes of the RAF – A History of Photo-Reconnaissance*, Alan Sutton Publishing (1996), p.79

2   Conyers Nesbit, *ibid*, p.93

3   Conyers Nesbit, *ibid*, p.87

4   Kosta, Del C., *Air Reconnaissance in the Second World War*, webzine *Military History*, online

5   Rowley, Clive, MBE RAF (Retd), 'The Photographic Reconnaissance Spitfire PR MK X1X and Ray Holmes', www.raf.mod.uk/bbmf/theaircraft/recspitrayholmes.cfm

6   Conyers Nesbit, *ibid*, p.129

7   Conyers Nesbit, *ibid*, p.140

8   Haley, Alex, *Roots – the Saga of an American Family*, Doubleday (1976)

9   Werner, H. A., *Iron Coffins: A U-boat Commander's War 1939–45*, London Cassells (1999) p.105, quoted in Wikipedia online

10 Bowyer, Chaz, *Sunderland at War*, Ian Allan Ltd (1976), p.74

11 Bowyer, Chaz, *The Short Sunderland*, Aston Publishing (1989), p.95

12 Bowyer, Chaz, *Sunderland at War*, *ibid*, p.49

13 Hendrie, Andrew, *The Cinderella Service: RAF Coastal Command 1939–1945*, Pen & Sword Aviation (2006), p.39

14 Allen, R. N. G., logbook

15 Allen, A., *ibid*

16 Braham, J. R. D., DSO, DFC, AFC, *Scramble!*, Frederick Muller, London (1961), p.3

17 Allen, R. N. G., *ibid*, Chapter 3, p.26

18 Hastings, Max, *All Hell Let Loose – The World at War 1939–1945*, Harper Press (2011), p.249

19 Roberts, Andrew, *The Storm of War*, Allen Lane (2009), p.301

20   Corrigan, Gordon, *The Second World War: A Military History*, Atlantic Books (2010)

21   Roberts, *ibid*, p.304, quoting from Atkinson, Rick, *An Army at Dawn – The War in North Africa 1942–43*, USA Henry Holt & Co (2004), pp.33–4

22   Roberts, *ibid*, p.305

23   Hastings, *ibid*, p.376

24   Corrigan, *ibid*, p.298

25   Hastings, *ibid*, p.377

26   Roberts, *ibid*, p.307

27   Brookes, Andrew J., *Photo Reconnaissance*, Ian Allan Ltd (1975), p.154

28   Roberts, *ibid*, p.307

29   Quoted in West, Richard, *Back to Africa – A History of Sierra Leone and Liberia*, Holt, Rinehart & Winston (1970), p.294

CHAPTER 5

1   Braham, *ibid*, p.107

2   Newspaper clipping in Alice Allen's effects, most likely from *Kent Messenger* January 1943

3   Lynn, Vera, with Cross, Robin & de Grex, Jenny, *We'll Meet Again*, Sidgwick & Jackson (1989, reprinted 2005), p.108

4   Longmate, Norman, *How We lived Then: A History of Everyday Life During the Second World War*, Arrow Books (1973), p.335

5   Longmate, *ibid*, p.337

6   Sheppard, Mark, 'RAF Hurricanes in Russia' – a comprehensive account of 151 Wing available on a Russian Airforce internet site. His figures are confirmed by Paul Dean for *Russia Now*.

7   This is Bob Allen's retelling of the event. In Leo McKinstry's *Hurricane! Victor of the Battle of Britain* (Hachette, 2010), another pilot, Ray Holms, reports two airmen involved in the accident both losing their lives. There is no 'official' account.

8   Briggs, Asa, *Go To It! Working for Victory on the Home Front 1939–1945*, London: Mitchell Beazley (2000), p.43

9   Mason, Francis K., *The Hawker Typhoon and Tempest*, Aston Publications (1988), p.7

10   Quoted in Franks, Norman, *Typhoon Attack: The Legendary British Fighter in Combat in World War II*, William Kimber & Co (1984), p.16

11   Allen, R. N. G., *ibid*, p.46

12 Mason, *ibid*, p.78

13 Braham, *ibid*, p.197

14 Gardiner, *ibid*, p.470

15 Gardiner, *ibid*, p.479

16 Terraine, John, *The Right of the Line: The Role of the RAF in World War Two*, Hodder (1985), Wordsworth (1997), p.600

17 Terraine, *ibid*, p.601

18 MacDonald, J. F., *The War History of Southern Rhodesia 1939–45: Volume II*, Naval & Military Press (2014), pp.546–7

19 Fellow pilot David Hughes was to be Godfather to Bob's second child.

20 Mason, *ibid*, p.78

21 Allen, R. N. G., *ibid*, p.50

22 Braham, *ibid*, p.169

23 Roberts, Andrew, *ibid*, p.465

24 Scott, Desmond, *Typhoon Pilot*, Leo Cooper (1982), p.99

25 Franks, *ibid*, p.114

CHAPTER 6

1 FM Montgomery's personal message to 21 Army Group on the eve of Operation *Overlord*. Wikiquotes Creative Commons

2 Eisenhower archives note from Supreme HQ Allied Expeditionary Force

3 Rommel is reported to have said this to author Cornelius Ryan, who subsequently used the title *The Longest Day* for his best-selling account of D-Day.

4 Roberts, Andrew, *ibid*, p.465

5 Beevor, *ibid*, 2010 edition, p.50

6 Bowen, Dick & Burkett, Molly, *Once upon a Wartime – D-Day the Battle for Europe*, Barn Books (2004), p.70

7 'Toc H' is an abbreviation of Talbot House, which aimed to offer soldiers on leave an alternative to the debauched recreational life of the town.

8 Alice's brother-in-law, Ted Tappenden, was one of the first paratroopers to land, secure the bridgehead and send the iconic signal 'Ham and Jam'.

9 Terraine, *ibid*, p.632

10 Terraine, *ibid*, p.636

11 Mason, *ibid*, p.85
12 Keitel was Oberkommando der Wehrmacht (Chief of the Armed Forces), Hitler's leading military advisor.
13 Terraine, *ibid*, p.637
14 Hitchens, F. H., 'History of 443 Squadron', www.mcmanus.ca/02CofC/443history_files/history1.htm
15 Hitchcock, William I., *Liberation: The Bitter Road to Freedom, Europe 1944–1945*, Faber (2008), p.29
16 Beevor, *ibid*, p.144
17 Hitchcock, *ibid*, p.39
18 Beevor, *ibid*, p.216
19 Beevor, *ibid*, p.229
20 Allen, R. N. G., *ibid*, p.59
21 Salt, Beryl, *A Pride of Eagles. A History of the Rhodesian Air Force*, Covoc Books (2000), reprinted Helion & Co (2015), p.118
22 Heraldic terms echoing Rhodesian themes. The bataleur eagle is Rhodesia/Zimbabwe's national bird. 'Volant' means wings out-stretched. This bird is renowned for its distinctive aerial acrobatics. Squadron emblems were worn with great pride. Readers of Capt W. E. Johns' 'Biggles' stories will remember that his first squadron was 266.
23 Allen, R. N. G., *ibid*, p.61
24 These figures are taken from Terraine, *ibid*, p.648, and represent the total number of sorties flown, including against Germany proper.
25 Terraine, *ibid*, p.649
26 Atkinson, Rick, *The Guns at Last Light – the War in Western Europe, 1944–1945*, Little & Brown (2013), p.110
27 Atkinson, *ibid*, p.112
28 *Daily Mail* late war news 19.7.44
29 Hastings, *ibid*, p.554
30 Atkinson, *ibid*, p.138
31 Atkinson, *ibid*, p.143
32 Atkinson, *ibid*, p.144
33 Allen, R. N. G., *ibid*

Chapter 7

1 Höhne, Heinz, translated by Barry, Richard, *The Order of the Death's Head: The Story of Hitler's SS*, Pan Books (1969), p.402

2   The Nuremberg Court would condemn them as outlaws and strip them of military designation and protection.

3   Beevor, *ibid*, p.479

4   Air Publication 1548: 'The Responsibilities of a Prisoner of War – European Theatre of Operations Only'

5   Renière, Edouard, 2011 web-article, RAF Museum, www.rafmuseum.org.uk https://prologue.blogs.archives.gov/.../escape-and-evasion-files-at-the-national-archive

6   Beevor, *ibid*, p.348

7   Beevor, *ibid*, p.353

8   Terraine, *ibid*, p.658

9   Davies, Stephen R., *RAF Police: The 'Great Escape' Murders*, Woodfield Publishing (2009)

10   Allen archive

11   Allen, Alice, *ibid*

12   Clutton-Brock, Oliver, *Footprints on the Sands of Time: Bomber Command Prisoners-of-war in Germany 1939–1945*, Grub Street Publishing (2003), p.204

13   Clutton-Brock, *ibid*, footnote 20, p.207

14   Holland, Frank 'Dutch' & Wilkins, Adam, *D-Day Plus One: Shot Down and on the Run in France*, Grub Street Publishing (2007), pp.174–5

15   Nordlinger, Jay, 'A Colonel at Chartres', *National Review* 10.5.2011

16   Rolf, David, *Prisoners of the Reich: Germany's Captives 1939–45*, Pen & Sword Books (1988), p.20

17   Terraine, *ibid*, p.661

18   Holland, *ibid*, p.198

19   Terraine, *ibid*, p.662

20   Beevor, *ibid*, p.519

21   Beevor, *ibid*, p520

22   The letters are quoted as written.

23   Hitchcock, *ibid*, p.191

CHAPTER 8

1   National Archives WO208/3269, Camp History – Dulag Luft (Oberursel)

2   Pearson, Simon, *The Great Escape*, Hodder & Stoughton (2013), p.119

3   Cuddon, Eric (Ed.), *War Crimes Trials Vol 1X – Dulag Luft Trials*, London (1952), p.22

4   National Archives WO591/2/AIR, letter on file, 14 October 1942
5   Player's cigarettes were the most popular brand of cigarettes in the 30s and 40s.
6   Cuddon, *ibid*, p.2
7   Rolfe, *ibid*, p.22
8   Cuddon, *ibid*, p.23
9   Cuddon, *ibid*, p.9
10 Allen, Alice, *ibid*, p.124
11 Allen, R. N. G., *ibid*, p.82
12 National Archives WO224/67
13 National Archives WO224/67
14 National Archives WO208/3269, Camp History – Dulag Luft (Oberursel)
15 Terraine, *ibid*, p.662
16 Pearson, *ibid*, p.252
17 Rolfe, *ibid*, p.82
18 Davies, Stephen R., *ibid*, p.11
19 Carroll, Tim, *The Great Escapers*, Mainstream Publishing (2004), p.58
20 Carroll, *ibid*, p.149
21 Carroll, *ibid*, p.214
22 Pearson, *ibid*, p.344
23 Carroll, *ibid*, p.210
24 Hansard, HC Deb 23 June 1944, Vol 401, ic 481
25 Allen, Alice, *ibid*,
26 The letter is quoted uncorrected.
27 Roberts, Andrew, *ibid*, p.516
28 Gardiner, *ibid*, p.559
29 Gardiner, *ibid*, p.561
30 Corrigan, *ibid*, p.487
31 Terraine, *ibid*, p.668
32 Letter home quoted in Salt, *ibid*, p.235
33 Hastings, *ibid*, p.504
34 Rolf, *ibid*, p.109
35 Rolf *ibid*, p.50
36 Rold, *ibid*, p.101
37 LaGrandeur, Philip, *We Flew, We Fell, We Lived: The Remarkable Reminiscences of Second World War Evaders and Prisoners of War*, Grub Street (2007), p.36

38 LaGrandeur, *ibid*, p.203

39 LaGrandeur, *ibid*, p.237

40 Cousens, Bryce (Ed.) et al., *The Log. Stalag Luft 3, Belaria Sagan*, private publication (1947), p.34

41 Philip LaGrandeur, *ibid*, p.369

42 Terraine, *ibid*, p.675

43 Allen, R. N. G., *ibid*, p.91

44 Wikipedia quote from Parker, Danny, *To Win the Winter Sky: The Air War over the Ardennes 1944–45*, Da Capo Press (1998)

45 Germany used horses – the Army had over a million – throughout World War II.

46 Hastings, *ibid*, p.599

CHAPTER 9

1 Ray Silver, L., *Last of the Gladiators: A World War II Bomber Navigator's Story*, Airlife Publishing (1995), p.165

2 Shirer, William L., *The Rise and Fall of the Third Reich*, Arrow (1998), p.1,096

3 Shirer, *ibid*, p.1,087

4 Hastings, *ibid*, p.608

5 Nichol, John & Rennell, Tony, *The Last Escape: The Untold story of Allied Prisoners of War in Germany 1944–1945*, Viking (2002), p.66

6 Allen, R. N. G., *ibid*, p.93

7 Sniders, Edward, *Flying In Walking Out: Memories of War and Escape 1939–1945*, Leo Cooper (1999), p.181

8 Bob Allen does not say which compound he was in. He had a Belaria log and his timing coincides with the Belaria evacuation. Bob describes Stalag Luft III as one camp with several compounds and does not distinguish between them.

9 Cousens, *ibid*. p.144

10 Goodrum, Alastair, *They Spread Their Wings: Six Courageous Airmen in Combat in the Second World War*, History Press (2013), p.152

11 Allen, R. N. G., *ibid*, p.97

12 Cousens, *ibid*, p.145

13 Nichol & Rennell, *ibid*, p.70

14 National Archives AIR 40/269 account of the march by Gp Capt D. E. I. Wilson – Senior British Officer.

15　This is likely to have been with the Belaria prisoners' first night at Kunau.

16　Cousens, *ibid*, p.148

17　Rae, J. D., *Kiwi Spitfire Ace: A Gripping World War Two Story of Action, Captivity and Freedom*, Grub Street (2001), p.152

18　Cousens, *ibid*, p.149

19　Cousens, *ibid*, p.155

20　National Archives AIR 40/269, *ibid*

21　LaGrandeur, *ibid*, p.372

22　Rae, *ibid*, p.152

23　Nichol & Rennell, *ibid*, p.84

24　Nichol & Rennell, *ibid*, p.85

25　Hately-Broad, Barbara, *War and Welfare: British POW Families, 1939–45*, Manchester University Press (2009), p.142

26　Schmidt, Roman, *Stalag 111-A 1939-1945*, quoted in Wikipedia

27　Bob Allen refers to 'scheiss cart' in his memoir, thus mixing German and English. The German would be 'scheiss karten'.

28　Churchill quote in Gilbert, Martin, *Winston S. Churchill: Road to Victory, 1941–1945 (Volume VII)*, Heinemann (1985), p.1,204

29　Barney Wright letters home quoted in Salt, *ibid*, p.255

30　Allen, R. N. G., *ibid*, p.107

31　Shirer, *ibid*, p.1,106

32　Nichol & Rennell, *ibid*, p.175

33　Nichol & Rennell, *ibid*, p.178

34　Cousens, *ibid*, p.158

35　Cousens, *ibid*, p.160

36　Allen, R. N. G., *ibid*, p.109

37　Nichol & Rennell, *ibid*, p.198

38　Nichol & Rennel, *ibid*, p.199

39　Allen, R. N. G., *ibid*, p.111

40　Cousens, *ibid*, p.164

41　Cousens, *ibid*, p.179

42　Barney Wright diary quoted in Salt, *ibid*, p.266

43　Shirer, *ibid*, p.1,106

44　Shephard, Ben, *The Long Road Home: The Aftermath of the Second World War*, Bodley Head (2010), p.62

45　*The Log ibid*, p.199

46　Cousens, *ibid*, p.182

47　Salt, *ibid*, p.266

CHAPTER 10

1   Allen, R. N. G., *ibid*, p.114
2   Barney Wright diary quoted in Salt, *ibid*, p.266
3   Roberts, Andrew, *ibid*, p.554
4   Hitchcock, *ibid*, p.3
5   Stafford, David, *Endgame 1945*, Abacus (2008), p.129
6   Allen, R. N. G., *ibid*, p.120
7   Kershaw, Ian, *The End – Hitler's Germany 1944–45*, Allen Lane History (2011), p.342
8   Roberts, Andrew, *ibid*, p.554
9   Roberts, Andrew, *ibid*, p.554
10 Kershaw, *ibid*, p.345
11 Kershaw, *ibid*, p.350
12 Allen, R. N. G., *ibid*, p.122
13 Stafford, *ibid*, p.283
14 Plön barracks was later transformed into a school for the children of occupying forces of the British Army on the Rhine.
15 Allen, R. N. G., *ibid*, p.122
16 Stafford, *ibid*, p.127
17 Lowe, Keith, *Savage Continent – Europe in the Aftermath of World War II*, Viking Penguin (2012), p.44
18 Lowe, *ibid*, p.27
19 Signage at Strehla erected by Texas A&M University, 1990
20 Tooze, Adam, T*he Wages of Destruction – the Making and Breaking of the Nazi Economy*, Allen Lane History (2006), p.656
21 Stafford, *ibid*, p.150
22 Atkinson, Rick, *The Guns at Last Light – the War in Western Europe 1944–1945*, Little Brown USA (2013), p.608
23 Stafford, *ibid*, p.151
24 Kershaw, *ibid*, p.368
25 Allen, R. N. G., *ibid*, p.127
26 The note says 5 May but is more likely to have been written on 6 May.
27 Allen, R. N. G., *ibid*, p.128
28 Nichol & Rennell, *ibid*, p.340
29 Letter from Sqn Ldr J. D. (Barney) Wright quoted in Salt, *ibid*, p.266
30 Kershaw, *ibid*, p.372
31 Allen, Alice, *ibid*, p.233

32 Stafford, *ibid*, p.364
33 Nichol & Rennell, *ibid*, p.356
34 Allen, R. N. G., *ibid*, p.130
35 Nichol & Rennell, *ibid*, p.340
36 Nichol & Rennell, *ibid*, p.357
37 Nichol & Rennell, *ibid*, p.397
38 Allen, Alice, *ibid*, p.234
39 Lowe, *ibid*, p.34

Postscript

1 Nichol & Rennell, *ibid*, p.368
2 Braham, *ibid*, p.187
3 Nichol & Rennell, *ibid*, p.403
4 Judt, Tony, *Postwar: A History of Europe Since 1945*, Vintage Books (2010), p.111

Select Bibliography

Ade Ajayi, J.F. & Crowder (Eds.), Michael, *History of West Africa Vol 2*, Longmans (1974)

Allingham, Margery, *The Oaken Heart*, Michael Joseph (1941), Golden Duck (2011)

Air Force Personnel, *Camp History of Stalag III (Sagan) April 1942–1945*, BL

Atkinson, Rick, *The Guns at Last Light – the War in Western Europe 1944–1945*, Little Brown USA (2013)

Atkinson, Rick, *An Army at Dawn – The War in North Africa 1942–43*, USA Henry Holt & Co (2004)

Austin, A. B., *Fighter Command*, London Gollancz (1942)

Bailey, M., 'Evolution of Aptitude Testing in the RAF', Cranwell papers

Barclay, George & Wynn, Humphrey (Ed.), *Fighter Pilot – A Self-portrait*, William Kimber (1976)

Barnett, Corelli, *Engage the Enemy more Closely – the Royal Navy in the Second World War*, Hodder and Stoughton (1991), Penguin (2000)

Barnham, Denis, *Malta Spitfire Pilot*, Frontline Books (2011)

Beevor, Antony, *D-Day: The Battle for Normandy*, Penguin (2009)

Beevor, Antony, *Ardennes 1944: Hitler's Last Gamble*, Penguin Random House UK (2015)

Bickers, Richard Townshend, *Air War Normandy*, London Leo Cooper (1994)

Briggs, Asa, *Go To It! Working for Victory on the Home Front 1939–1945*, London: Mitchell Beazley (2000)

Bourret, F. M., *The Gold Coast – A Survey of the Gold Coast and British Togoland 1919–1946*, Stanford University Press (1949)

Bowen, Dick & Burkett, Molly, *Once upon a Wartime – D-Day the Battle for Europe*, Barn Books (2004)

Bowyer, Chaz, *Sunderland at War*, Ian Allan Ltd (1976)

Bowyer, Chaz, *Men of the Desert Air Force 1940–42*, London William Kimber 1984

Bowyer, Chaz, *The Short Sunderland*, Aston Publishing (1989)

Braham, J. R. D., DSO, DFC, AFC, *Scramble!*, Frederick Muller, London (1961)

Brookes, Andrew J., *Photo Reconnaissance*, Ian Allan Ltd (1975)

Buckle, N. & Murray, C., *I Think I Prefer the Tinned Variety: The Diary of a Petty Officer in the Fleet Air Arm During World War II*, Spurwing (2012)

Buckle, N. & Murray, C., *The Tribal Headmen of Freetown from A Diary of a Petty Officer in the Fleet Air Arm During WW2* – internet blog

Bungay, Stephen, *The Most Dangerous Enemy: A History of the Battle of Britain*, Arum Press (2001)

Burgess, Alan, *The Longest Tunnel: True Story of the Great Escape*, Bloomsbury (1990)

Campbell, John, *RAF Coastal Command: A Short History*, Memoirs Publishing (2013)

Carroll, Tim, *The Great Escapers*, Mainstream Publishing (2004)

Cayhill, Peter, *No.1 Squadron at War 1939–45*, Pen & Sword Aviation (2009)

Clarke, Peter B., *West Africa at War 1914–18, 1939–45: Colonial Propaganda and its Cultural Aftermath*, Ethnographia London (1986)

Clifford, Mary Louise, *The Land and People of Sierra Leone*, Philadelphia (1974)

Clutton-Brock, Oliver, *Footprints on the Sands of Time: Bomber Command Prisoners-of-war in Germany 1939–1945*, Grub Street Publishing (2003)

Conyers Nesbit, Roy, *Eyes of the RAF – A History of Photo-Reconnaissance*, Alan Sutton Publishing (1996)

Corbin, Jimmy (Foreword), *Ten Fighter Boys*, Collins First Thus (2008) (originally published 1942)

Corrigan, Gordon, *The Second World War: A Military History*, Atlantic Books (2010)

Cuddon, Eric (Ed.), *War Crimes Trials Vol 1X – Dulag Luft Trials*, London (1952)

Cousens, Bryce (Ed.) et al., *The Log. Stalag Luft 3, Belaria Sagan*, private publication (1947)

Darlow, Michael & Hodson, Gillian, *Terence Rattigan – The Man and His Work*, Quartet Books (1979)

Darlow, Stephen, *Victory Fighters: The Veteran's Story*, Grub Street (2005)

Davies, Stephen R., *RAF Police: The 'Great Escape' Murders*, Woodfield Publishing (2009)

Shores, Christopher F., *Billy Drake, Fighter Leader: The Autobiography of Group Captain B. Drake DSO, DFC & Bar, US DFC*, Grub Street, London (2001)

Deere, Alan, *Nine Lives*, Wingham Press (1959)

Durand, Arthur A., Stalag Luft III: *The Secret Story*, US (1988), UK Patrick Stephens (1989)

Eckhertz, Holger, *D Day Through German Eyes*, DTZ History Publications 2015

Falconer, Jonathan, *RAF Airfields of World War 2*, Midland Publishing (2012), Carey Publishing (2015)

Franks, Norman, *Typhoon Attack*, William Kimber & Co (1984)

Franks, Norman & O'Connor, Mike, *Number One in War and Peace*, Grub Street (2000)

Feigel, Lara, *The Bitter Taste of Victory – In the Ruins of the Reich*, Bloomsbury (2016)

Fyfe, Christopher, *A Short History of Sierre Leone*, Longmans (1962)

Gardiner, Juliet, *Wartime Britain 1939–1945*, Headline (2004)

Gretzyngier, Robert, *Poles in Defence of Britain July 1940–41*, London Grub Street (2001)

Gifford, Mary Louise, *The Land and People of Sierra Leone*, Portraits of the Nations (1974)

Gilbert, Martin, *Winston S. Churchill: Road to Victory, 1941–1945 (Volume VII)*, Heinemann (1985)

Gilbert, Martin, *Second World War*, Weidenfeld (1989)

Ginio, Ruth, *French Colonialism Unmasked: The Vichy Years in French West Africa*, Lincoln University of Nebraska (2008)

Golley, John, *The Day of the Typhoon*, UK (1986), Airlife Publishing (2000)

Goodall, Felicity, *The People's War*, David & Charles (2008)

Goodrum, Alastair, *They Spread Their Wings: Six Courageous Airmen in Combat in the Second World War*, History Press (2013)

Greene, Graham, *The Heart of the Matter*, Heinemann (1948), Penguin (1962)

Guehenno, Jean & Ball, David (trans.), *Diary of the Dark Years 1940–1944*, Gallimard (1947), Oxford University Press (2016)

Haley, Alex, *Roots – the Saga of an American Family*, Doubleday (1976)

Hastings, Max, *All Hell Let Loose – The World at War 1939–1945*, Harper Press (2011)

Hately-Broad, Barbara, *War and Welfare: British POW Families, 1939–45*, Manchester University Press (2009)

Haywood, A. & Clarke, F. A. S., *History of the Royal West African Frontier Force*, Gale & Polden (1964)

Hendrie, Andrew, *The Cinderella Service: RAF Coastal Command 1939–1945*, Pen & Sword Aviation (2006)

Hitchcock, William I., *Liberation: The Bitter Road to Freedom, Europe 1944–1945*, Faber (2008)

Höhne, Heinz, translated by Barry, Richard, *The Order of the Death's Head: The Story of Hitler's SS*, Pan Books (1969)

Holbrook, Wendell Patrick, *The Impact of the Second World War on the Gold Coast 1939–1945*, Princeton University Press (1978)

Holland, Frank 'Dutch' & Wilkins, Adam, *D-Day Plus One: Shot Down and on the Run in France*, Grub Street Publishing (2007)

Johnson, J. E. 'Johnnie', *The Story of Air Fighting*, Hutchinson (1985)

Johnson, J. E. 'Johnnie', *Wing Leader*, London, Chatto & Windus (1956)

Jones, R. V., *Most Secret War*, London, Hamish Hamilton (1978), Wordsworth Editions (1998)

Judt, Tony, *Postwar: A History of Europe Since 1945*, Vintage Books (2010)

Kaplan, Philip & Collier, Richard, *The Few – Summer of 1940, The Battle of Britain*, *UK* Blandford Press (1989)

Kee, Robert, *A Crowd is not Company*, Eyre & Spottiswoode (1947), Phoenix (2000)

Kershaw, Ian, *The End – Hitler's Germany 1944–45*, Allen Lane History (2011)

Kempowski, Walter, *Swansong 1945*, London, Granta (2014)

Killingray, David & Rathbone, Richard (Eds.), *Africa and the Second World War*, Macmillan (1986)

Killingray, David, *African Civilians in the Era of the Second World War 1935–1950*, 1986

Killingray, David, 'Military and Labour Recruitment in the Gold Coast During the Second World War', *Journal of African History Volume 23 No. 1* (1982)

Kingcome, Brian & Ford Peter, *A Willingness to Die*, London Tempus (1999)

LaGrandeur, Philip, *We Flew, We Fell, We Lived: The Remarkable Reminiscences of Second World War Evaders and Prisoners of War*, Grub Street (2007)

LaGrandeur, Philip, *We Flew, We Fell, We Lived*, Canada Vanwell Publishing (2006)

Lawler, Nancy Ellen, *Soldiers, Airmen, Spies, and Whisperers – The Gold Coast in World War* II, Ohio University Press (2002)

Longmate, Norman, *How We lived Then: A History of Everyday Life During the Second World War*, Arrow Books (1973)

Lowe, Keith, *Savage Continent – Europe in the Aftermath of World War II*, Viking Penguin (2012)

Lynn, Vera, with Cross, Robin & de Grex, Jenny, *We'll Meet Again*, Sidgwick & Jackson (1989, reprinted 2005)

MacDonald, J. F., *The War History of Southern Rhodesia 1939–45: Volume II*, Naval & Military Press (2014)

Mackenzie, K. W., DFC, AFC, *Hurricane Combat*, William Kimber (1987)

Martin, Thomas, *The Anglo-French Divorce over West Africa and the Limitations of Strategic Planning, June–December 1940, Vol. 6.1* Diplomacy and Statecraft (1995)

Martin, Thomas, *The French Empire at War 1940–1945*, Manchester University Press (1998)

Mason, Francis K., *The Hawker Hurricane*, RAF Museum edition (1962)

Mason, Francis K., *The Hawker Typhoon and Tempest*, Aston Publications (1988)

McKinstry, Leo, *Hurricane! Victor of the Battle of Britain*, Hachette (2010)

Milton, Brian, *The Last Witnesses*, André Deutsch (2010)

Monks, Noel, *Fighter Squadrons*, Angus & Robertson, Australia (1941)

Moore, Bob & Fedorowich, Kent (Eds.), *Prisoners of War and their Captors in World War II*, Oxford, Berg 1996

Nell, David, *POW The Diary of a Prisoner of War*, MechAero Publishing (2004–2011)

Neil, Tom, *A Fighter in My Sights*, J&KH Publishing (2001)

Nichol, John & Rennell, Tony, *The Last Escape: The Untold story of Allied Prisoners of War in Germany 1944–1945*, Viking (2002)

Overy, R. J., *The Air War 1939–1945*, Europa (1980), Papermac (1987)

Overy, Richard, *Why the Allies Won*, Random House (1995)

Pearson, Simon, *The Great Escape*, Hodder & Stoughton (2013)

Pottinger, Ron, *A Soldier in the Cockpit – From Rifles to Typhoons in WWII*, Mechanicsburg PA Stackpole Books (2007)

Pottinger, Ron, *A View from the Office (a Typhoon pilot's tale)*, Design Engineering Services UK Ltd (2004)

Rae, J. D., *Kiwi Spitfire Ace: A Gripping World War Two Story of Action, Captivity and Freedom*, Grub Street (2001)

Air Historical Branch (IWM), *The Middle East Campaigns Vol. X: The West Africa Reinforcement Route*

Richards & Saunders, *The Royal Air Force 1939–1945* in 3 volumes, London HMSO (1953)

Roberts, Andrew, *The Storm of War*, Allen Lane (2009)

Rolf, David, *Prisoners of the Reich: Germany's Captives 1939–45*, Pen & Sword Books (1988)

Ryan, Cornelius, *The Longest Day*, Simon & Schuster (1959)

Salt, Beryl, *A Pride of Eagles. A History of the Rhodesian Air Force*, Covoc Books (2000), reprinted Helion & Co (2015)

Saunders, Tim, *Operation Epsom: VII British Corps v 1st SS Panzer Korps*, Leo Cooper (2003)

Scott, Desmond, *Typhoon Pilot*, London Leo Cooper (1982)

Sebald, W. G., *On the Natural History of Destruction*, Hamish Hamilton (2003)

Sekgoma, Gilbert A., 'Second World War and the Sierra Leone Economy: Labour, Employment and Utilisation 1939–45' in Killingray, David & Rathbone, Richard (Eds.), *Africa and the Second World War*, Macmillan (1986)

Schulz, Eugene G., *The Ghost in General Patton's 3rd Army*, XLIBRIS (2012)

Shephard, Ben, *The Long Road Home: The Aftermath of the Second World War*, Bodley Head (2010)

Sherry, Norman, *The Life of Graham Greene: Volume II: 1939–1955*, Jonathan Cape, London (1994)

Shirer, William L., *The Rise and Fall of the Third Reich*, Arrow (1998)

Shuckburgh, *Colonial Civil History Vol 1*, Rhodes Livingstone Library Oxford (1986)

Ray Silver, L., *Last of the Gladiators: A World War II Bomber Navigator's Story*, Airlife Publishing (1995)

Smith, Colin, *England's Last War Against France – Fighting Vichy 1940–1942*, GB Weidenfeld (2009)

Select Bibliography

Sniders, Edward, *Flying In Walking Out: Memories of War and Escape 1939–1945*, Leo Cooper (1999)

Spivey Maj. Gen USAF, *POW Odyssey*, Colonial Lithograph, Inc. (1984)

Stafford, David, *Endgame 1945*, Abacus (2008)

Stargardt, Nicholas, *The German War: a Nation under Arms, 1939–45* Bodley Head (2015)

Sutherland, Jonathan & Caudwell, Diane, *Vichy at War: The French Air Force That Fought the Allies in WWII*, Pen & Sword Aviation (2011)

Sydnor, Charles W., *Soldiers of Destruction: The SS Death's Head Division, 1933–1945*, Princeton University Press (1977)

Tappenden, Michael, *Pegasus to Paradise*, Acorn Independent Press UK (2013)

Terraine, John, *The Right of the Line*, Hodder & Stoughton (1985), new edition Pen & Sword (2010)

Thomas, Hugh, *Spirit of the Blue*, Sutton Publishing (2004)

Thomas, Andrew & Weal, John, *Hurricane Aces 1941–45*, Osprey Aircraft (2013)

Thorold, H. D. Air Commodore, 'Report on Formation and Development of RAF station Takoradi and West Africa reinforcement route July 1940–Sept 1941', Secret Dossier 1942 held in IWM

Thorold, H.D., *British Propaganda in the Gold Coast Journal of African History* Vol. 26, No. 4 (1985)

Toland, John, *The Last 100 Days*, New York, Random House (1965)

Tooze, Adam, T*he Wages of Destruction – the Making and Breaking of the Nazi Economy*, Allen Lane History (2006)

Townsend, Peter *Duel of Eagles* Paris, France (1969), London transl. Weidenfeld (1970)

Townshend Bickers, Richard, *Air War Normandy*, Leo Cooper (1994), Pen & Sword Aviation (2015)

Ullrich, Karl, *Like a Cliff in the Ocean: A History of the 3.SS-Panzer Division Totenkopf,* Fedorowicz (2003)

Wansell, Geoffrey, *Terence Rattigan*, Fourth Estate, London (1995)

Wellum, Geoffrey, *First Flight*, Viking (2002)

Werner, H. A., *Iron Coffins: A U-boat Commander's War 1939–45*, London Cassells (1999)

West, Richard, *Back to Africa – A History of Sierra Leone and Liberia*, Holt, Rinehart & Winston (1970)

Williams, Andrew, *Battle of the Atlantic*, BBC Books (2002)

Wilson, Patrick, *The War behind the Wire*, Leo Cooper/Pen & Sword (2000)

WS Convoy Series June 30–July 10 WS9B, London IWM

Van Drogenbrock, Ben, *The Camera became My Passport Home*, 3 Volumes, private publication (2012) (RAF club library)

Acknowledgements

This book could not have been written without the encouragement of friends and family and the generosity and diligence of those academics and authors whose working lives have been spent in historical research.

If I could, I would thank my father for his courage in breaking silence to put 'on record' events as he saw them. My mother's fictionalised writings and family letters, papers and photographs have also been a valuable source.

Confirmation for their story took me to flying logbooks, squadron records and many archive sources for verification. I am grateful for the open welcome accorded to researchers by The National Archives at Kew, the Imperial War Museum, the RAF Museum and the British Library. The Stalag Luft 3 chapters could not have been completed without the guidance of Marck Lazarz at the Muzeum Obozow Jenieckich in Sagan, Poland. I have done my best to footnote all these sources and all the published works consulted are in the bibliography. Needless to say any omissions are my responsibility. The sheer volume of published works on World War II can be overwhelming.

No Ordinary Pilot might never have reached a publisher without the input of four dear friends. Walter Schwarz (ex-Guardian foreign correspondent) commented on an early draft chapter by chapter, painstakingly applying his journalist's eye to the development of the story. Dorothy Schwarz (teacher and writer) also read an early draft and determinedly pressed me to polish and finish. Christopher and Caroline Yapp (both professionally involved with books) urged me to find a 'good' publisher. Which brought me via another networking contact, Julia Hobsbawn, to Bloomsbury and to Lisa Thomas. Lisa has been an enthusiastic and patient editor guiding this rookie (my last book was published before the age of the internet) through today's publishing process. It was Lisa who suggested finding a serving RAF officer to contribute a foreword. I am enormously grateful to

299

Wing Commander Chris Hoyle, Commander of 1 Squadron for taking up that challenge at a busy time.

As the manuscript grew over two years, my sister Elizabeth read chapter by chapter often with no more comment than 'Great. Keep going'. That was consoling. The person I really have to thank is my husband Simon Campbell-Jones, who bent his considerable experience in documentary filmmaking to commenting on the development of each chapter and applying his impeccable English grammar to my idiosyncratic writing style. He was my companion and driver in search of locations in this country, in France, Germany and Poland. Always a patient listener as fresh leads were found to corroborate Bob's story.

I dedicate this book to Simon and to all the future generations who might read of a World War II fighter pilot's experiences. After all 'what's past is prologue'.

Copyright acknowledgements

Photographs

All photographs © Suzanne Campbell-Jones with the exception of the following plates: p.3 (top) Imperial War Museum; p.5 (below) Getty Images; p.7 Imperial War Museum; p.10 (below) Getty Images; p.11 Getty Images; the images on pp.12, 13 and 14 are illustrations by Flying Officer Terence Entract, from *The Log*, a 'private' publication edited and published by Squadron Leader Bryce Cousens in 1947 and distributed to those with a connection to the prison camp at Stalag Luft 3 (Belaria); p.15 (top) Getty Images.

The author and publisher gratefully acknowledge permission to use short extracts from the following works:

p.12, 18 Wellum, Geoffrey, First Flight, 2002, courtesy of Penguin Books.

p.33, 58 Graham Greene, *The Heart of the Matter*, (Vintage Classics) courtesy of David Higham Associates

p.57 Norman Sherry, *The Life of Graham Greene, Vol. 2 1939–1955*, 1994, (Jonathan Cape) courtesy of David Higham Associates

p.62, 63 Michael Darlow and Gillian Hodson, *Terence Rattigan – The man and his work*, 1979, (Quartet Books) courtesy of Quartet Books.

Acknowledgements

p.64 Terence Rattigan, *Flare Path*, 1953, (Nick Hern Books) courtesy of Nick Hern Books (www.nickhernbooks.co.uk)

p.67 Drake, Billy quote AIR27/933 128 Squadron Intelligence Report 22/8/41-31/8/41, courtesy of The National Archives.

p.69–70 Geoffrey Wansell, *Terence Rattigan*, 1995, (Oberon Books) courtesy of Oberon Books.

p.99 Graham Greene, *Journey Without Maps* (Vintage Classics) courtesy of David Higham Associates.

p.93 Max Hastings, *All Hell let Loose – the world at war 1939–1945*, 2011, (Harper Press) courtesy of HarperCollins Publishers.

p.129 Desmond, Scott, *Typhoon Pilot*, 1982, (Pen & Sword), courtesy of Pen & Sword

p.137 John Terraine, *The Right of the Line*, 1985, (Pen & Sword), courtesy of Pen & Sword

Index

302

Index

303

Index

Index

Index